SECOND EDITION

COMPOSE

Gearing Up for Writing in the 21st Century

Susan Caggiano
Maria Turnmeyer

Credits:

Cover Image: © Can Stock Photo Inc./scanrail

Acknowledgments:

pp. 13–14: Reprinted by arrangement with The Heirs to the Estate of Martin Luther King Jr., c/o Writers House as agent for the proprietor, New York, NY. Copyright © 1963 by Dr. Martin Luther King Jr. Copyright © renewed 1991 by Coretta Scott King.

pp. 15–18: "Pericles' Funeral Oration" As appeared in *Sources of the Western Tradition, Vol. 1: From Ancient Times to the Enlightenment.* Translation by Marvin Perry. Copyright © 2012 by Cengage Learning, Inc. Reprinted by permission of the publisher via the Copyright Clearance Center.

pp. 32–33: As appeared in *Atlantic Monthly* online, April 22, 2012. Copyright © 2012 by Atlantic Monthly. Reprinted by permission of the publisher via the Copyright Clearance Center.

pp. 44–45: As appeared in the *New York Times* online, June 10, 2012. Copyright © 2012 by the New York Times Company. Reprinted by permission of the publisher via the Copyright Clearance Center.

pp. 51–53: As appeared in the *Los Angeles Times* online, August 9, 2009. Copyright © 2009 by the Los Angeles Times Syndicate. Reprinted by permission of the publisher via the Copyright Clearance Center.

pp. 70–72: As appeared in *City Lab* online, March 20, 2013. Copyright © 2013 by Atlantic Monthly. Reprinted by permission of the publisher via the Copyright Clearance Center.

Change the course.

530 Great Road
Acton, MA 01720
800-562-2147

ACKNOWLEDGMENTS

Susan Caggiano and Maria Turnmeyer would like to acknowledge and thank the following colleagues and friends for their inspiration and encouragement and their assistance in reviewing, designing, critiquing, and/or classroom testing the first and current edition of *Compose*: Nicole Warwick, Diane Arieff, Susan Sterr, Molly Nguyen, Derek Tang, Kevin Menton, Kathleen Motoike, Jim Pacchioli, George Davison, Christina Hoppe, Noelle Panczel, Joanne Laurance, and Lisl Spangenberg. We would also like to thank the students who allowed us to share their work, and the editors, Shelly Walia, Natalie Danner, and Sharon Calitri, for their professionalism and guidance throughout the writing of this textbook.

PREFACE FOR INSTRUCTORS

Students come to composition courses with an astonishing variety of skills, attitudes, goals, and experiences. As instructors, we come to our composition courses having applied the best teaching practices to help our students improve what they already know about writing. We wrote this text to serve the needs of students and instructors alike; to help students further develop and hone the skills necessary to communicate effectively in our digital age, and to help instructors facilitate that learning. With those two objectives foremost in our minds, we developed a scaffolded structure of lessons, exercises, and other resources, all designed to facilitate learning and teaching.

We chose to forgo the traditional model of a composition reader for several reasons. Recent research suggests that students learn best when they apply and practice concepts, rather than observe them, even with excellent models and expert guidance. To that end, each chapter focuses on a specific composition skill or concept, and leads student practice toward independent mastery. Also, we wanted to encourage instructors to use the themes, texts, and materials relevant to their specific student learning environments and use this book to help guide how students handle those texts. And lastly, given current technologies of Internet links, access to databases in college libraries, e-books, etc., we instead included a suggested readings list, most with hyperlinks, to guide students to different subject areas, and encourage them to seek other texts relevant to the discussions happening in their classrooms, on campus and elsewhere in their lives.

We also acknowledge that students are expected to understand and employ many different print and electronic genres in twenty-first-century writing situations. *Compose* exposes students to the idea of composition beyond the academic essay, and addresses specifically the inner workings of composition, and the various ways of thinking and organizing ideas that can be applied to most genres.

We direct student attention to the various circumstances all writers encounter, helping them identify the writer's purpose and audience when they read and how to explore (and exploit) their own rhetorical situations when they write. This, in turn, helps them to form substantive ideas, choose appropriate genres, and develop clarity in their communications, whatever genre they find themselves writing in across the disciplines and onward in their careers.

We emphasize how to manage the information coming from ever-expanding varieties of sources and how to evaluate the quality of those sources by first addressing introductory elements of rhetoric. Later, by providing three chapters at appropriate intervals, we guide students through the research paper process: how to choose topics and generate critical positions (see chapter 7), how to research those topics, how to manage and evaluate the researched material (see chapter 8), and lastly, how to weave their ideas and research together in a cohesive academic essay (see chapter 13). This crucial and ubiquitous form of the academic essay is treated in this text as a culminating, or summative assessment activity, allowing students to showcase their understanding of their rhetorical situation, and many of the discrete skills of composition they will have acquired during the course.

To set the groundwork for student understanding of purpose and audience, the early chapters of this text work to expose critical thinking, reading, and writing processes. Yet, a quick perusal of the table of contents (and the 15-week planner) will reveal an unusual structure to this text: we chose to follow a typical semester's track, which can easily be adapted to a quarter system, or perhaps expanded to suit a two-semester course for developing writers. This structure serves two important purposes: one is logistical to provide a framework to allow an instructor to either build a syllabus and schedule from scratch, or to add his or her own material from an existing syllabus. The other, pedagogical purpose is to deliver a scaffolding strategy for student mastery of concepts and skills. Scaffolding builds upon skills learned earlier to help develop new skills as the course progresses. And while the scaffold design determines the shape of the entire text, it also determines the shape of the chapters. With these scaffolds built in, this text acknowledges and supports the separate, yet crucial learning process, while also instructing students in critical thinking, reading, and writing.

We start by offering a 15-week planner, an overview of how the text, and its scaffolded structure can fit into a semester-length course, so instructors can see how to work the content of this text into their course schedule, and students can preview the course and anticipate learning. Then, chapters 1 and 2 focus on developing writing process strategies and thinking process strategies through critical reading and writing activities. Chapters 3 and 4 focus on developing critical responses to texts. Chapters 5 and 6 focus on revising, editing and proofreading to nurture attention toward the audience's needs and expectations. At midterm, chapter 7 addresses the concept of the research question, and how to develop a critical response to that question, while chapter 8 helps students learn research strategy, evaluate and manage their researched sources, and helps students begin a Research Journal Project. This project is designed to help scaffold the research process, providing built-in research assignments to be completed over the remainder of the term. The goal of the project is to teach how to develop and manage such a large and often overwhelming task as a college research paper. Chapter 9 discusses conventions of genre, and technology's influence on writing, while chapter 10 highlights analysis of visual rhetoric. Chapters 11 and 12 address developing logos and ethos, by introducing formal logic and fallacy, and offering practice in counterargument, and concession through a formal debate activity. The last chapter,

13, demonstrates how to weave student research meaningfully into an essay to serve a student's particular rhetorical situation.

Each chapter also presents a scaffolded lesson. The lesson begins by introducing a concept, or a skill. It then provides a model application of the concept with detailed explanations, and then directs student practice of the concept. Such practice is offered in flexible classroom activities, often including collaborative group work. Practice is also offered in writing activities designed as homework. This scaffolded structure, we discovered, exploits some aspects of the "flipped classroom" model. Since the chapters are designed for students to read before class, we found that we spent less class time introducing the material, and more time analyzing the models, practicing the concepts, writing responses, and developing critical ideas. This scaffolded design, along with substantive readings chosen in part by the instructor, and critical ideas generated from student collaboration, research, and written responses, will help students develop deeper understanding of the concepts, having had more time and opportunities to discuss writing as a practical concern, and assist each other in solving specific writing difficulties and problems.

As you begin to read the chapters you may also notice that the voice we chose has a distinct conversational tone. This would not be the first text on writing to use this strategy, but we couldn't find many textbooks with this tone that addressed developing and first year composition students' concerns about academic language. They are frequently uncertain about the nature of academic tone, how to achieve it and why it is necessary. And though reading a textbook, one that focuses on instruction, is by definition a didactic experience, a didactic tone is not often a good learning experience, especially for developing and early college readers and writers.

In order for students to understand the nature of academic writing, they first need to immerse themselves in critical reading, thinking, and writing. A developing academic tone will often become the byproduct of those activities because critical ideas demand specific language. Yet, achieving fluency in that kind of specific language is a learning process, one that can take an entire undergraduate career (and beyond) to complete. Since students take many classes where academic language is modeled for them, certainly this one course, whose purpose is to help students master critical reading and writing in academia and beyond, could be delivered in language less intimidating to engage students in their own thinking and writing, and engender a nascent understanding of academic tone. And with that understanding, develop a conscious awareness of language that can be useful to them wherever they go.

Yet, as we departed from the idea that modeling our expectations of language and tone is how to engender them in our students' writing, we also recognized that we must address academic language and tone directly as a learning goal. In chapter 6, we specifically address reasons to develop style and tone, and offer revising and editing strategies to help them develop it in their own writing. And, where the subject matter required academic language, or subject-specific terminology, we defined our terms using examples and ideas easily accessible to early college students; by connecting their existing knowledge and imagination to the new academic terms, we scaffold the development of academic tone. We also provide a glossary for denotative meaning of the academic terms and the e-book version of this text links the terms electronically from their context to the glossary.

Our intention and hope is that this text will help you expand your students' ideas about writing and thinking. And it is meant to help students learn and practice writing toward purpose and clarity, to help them to build a composition toolbox they can rely on when they must complete any writing task, and perhaps most important, it is meant to help them develop enough confidence in their skills and ideas to join the conversations and processes of decision-making happening all around them.

PREFACE FOR STUDENTS

This book was written for you. Since, as students, you are the primary audience for a textbook, your learning needs influenced our choice of several components for this textbook. These components aim at helping you develop skills for composition in our digital age, no matter what subject you major in, what information you read, or what kinds of writing you will do in your careers and beyond.

This book will help you develop strong college level thinking, reading, and writing skills in a direct, informative, and efficient structure. As you read each chapter, notice the structure designed to help you build your skills: each chapter introduces you to a concept, then shows you how to apply the concept by modeling it, and then the last part of each chapter provides activities for you to practice the concept, either in class, or as homework.

These chapters are also designed to be read before class. When you read, ask questions of the models it provides, try to answer on your own the questions it raises for you, and bring those questions into class with you to focus your group and individual practice. Composition class is no walk in the park for most people, but the benefits you gain from actively practicing and engaging with the concepts outweighs the difficulties in learning them. The more you practice while in a course, the easier it, and your future college courses will be, whether in a chemistry class, a business class, or a language class. Becoming an expert in critical thinking, reading, and writing in your field of choice and beyond is your purpose in taking composition and other academic courses.

Also, in light of the many different types of print and electronic writing you are expected to understand and employ in twenty-first-century writing situations, we wanted to expose to you the idea of composition beyond the academic essay and address the inner workings of composition, the ways of thinking and organizing ideas that can be applied to most types of writing. This, in turn, will help you to form substantive ideas, choose the appropriate type of writing for your needs, and develop clarity in your communications, whatever type of writing you may find yourself using across academic disciplines and onward in your careers.

We also emphasize how to evaluate and manage the vast amount of sources and information available to you. Three different chapters will guide you through the research paper process: how to choose substantive topics and generate critical positions, how to research those topics, how to manage and evaluate the researched material, and lastly, how to weave your ideas and your research together in a cohesive academic essay.

First, take a look at the 15-week planner, in conjunction with your instructor's syllabus, to get an overview of your composition course. By anticipating learning, you can construct an idea of what is expected of you, and how to respond to those expectations, as well as create a time-management calendar for yourself (you can do this with all of your courses in a semester to prepare yourself better for learning). Then notice that chapters 1 and 2 focus on developing writing process strategies and thinking process strategies, in both critical reading and writing activities. Chapters 3 and 4 focus on developing critical responses to texts. Chapters 5 and 6 focus on revising, editing, and proofreading to nurture the attention you give to language, and the needs of your audience. At midterm, chapter 7 addresses the concept of the research question, and how to develop a critical response to that question, while chapter 8 helps you learn research strategy, evaluate and manage your researched sources, and helps you begin a Research Journal Project. This project is designed to help scaffold the research process (working step-by-step), providing built-in research assignments to be completed over the remainder of the term for use in your research paper as assigned by your instructor. The goal of the project is to teach you how to develop and manage such a large and often overwhelming task as a college level–research paper. Chapter 9 discusses conventions of genre, and technology's influence on writing, while chapter 10 highlights analysis of visual rhetoric, such as advertisements and art. Chapters 11 and 12 address developing logos and ethos, introduce formal logic and fallacy, and later, counterargument and concession through a formal debate activity. The last chapter, 13, demonstrates how to weave the research meaningfully into an essay to serve your particular rhetorical situation.

You may also notice as you begin to read the chapters, that the voice we chose has a distinct conversational tone. We chose to address you directly, often using personal pronouns to enhance this conversational tone. This is not meant as a model for your own writing, as developing an academic tone is part of the process of becoming a college level writer. So, where we do introduce academic language, we define our terms, using examples and ideas, and we provide a glossary for you (in the e-book version, the terms are linked electronically to the glossary). Since you take many classes where academic language is modeled for you, we decided that this one course, which is designed to help you understand critical reading and writing in academia and beyond, could be delivered in language less intimidating to help you engage with your own thinking and writing, and with your new understanding of your purpose and audience, you will develop a conscious awareness of language that can be useful to you wherever you go.

We hope this text will help you expand your ideas about writing and thinking: to help you write with purpose and clarity, to help you build a composition toolbox you can rely on when faced with any writing task, and to help you develop confidence in your skills and your ideas, and use them to the join conversations and decision-making processes happening all around you.

15-Week Planner

Week One: Introduction	Week Two: Chapter 1	Week Three: Chapter 2
Read Student Preface.	Rhetorical Situations, Writing Processes and Elements of Rhetoric Engaging the Gears: • Recognizing and Identifying Elements of Rhetoric • A Letter to Your Instructor • Your Writing Process	Approaches to Critical Thinking and Reading Engaging the Gears: • Locating Meaning and Practicing Interpretation • Composing a Reading Response • Reading Inventory
Week Four: Chapter 3	**Week Five: Chapter 4**	**Week Six: Chapter 5**
Critical Writing Engaging the Gears: • Making Inferences • Summary Practice • Synthesis Practice	From Critical Ideas to the Thesis Statement Engaging the Gears: • Practicing the Thesis Statement • Critical Ideas to the Thesis Statement • Developing a Thesis Statement	Revision: Strategies and Approaches to Revising Texts Engaging the Gears: • Critical Reading Practice • Revision Practice • Group Revision Practice
Week Seven: Chapter 6	**Week Eight: Chapter 7**	**Week Nine: Chapter 8**
Editing and Proofreading Style, Voice, and Polish Engaging the Gears: • Sentences, Wordiness, and Word Choice Practice • Peer Editing Practice • Revising for Rhetorical Situation	Research: Finding a Topic and Discovering the Arguments Engaging the Gears: • Practice Narrowing a Topic • Research Activity • Writing the Research Proposal	Research: How to Strategize, Evaluate, and Manage Sources Engaging the Gears: • Practice Navigating Search Engines • Research Strategy Practice • The Research Journal Project
Week Ten: Chapter 9	**Week Eleven: Chapter 10**	**Week Twelve: Chapter 11**
Writing Technologies: Composition and Genre Engaging the Gears: • Composition Toolbox Practice • Choosing a Genre • The Police Report	Images and Visual Rhetoric: Interpretation and Analysis Engaging the Gears: • Analyzing Images • Advertisement Analysis • The Visual Essay	Logical Reasoning and Logical Fallacies Engaging the Gears: • Identify Underlying Assumptions • Creating Syllogisms • Finding Fallacies • Defending a Position
Week Thirteen: Chapter 12	**Week Fourteen: Chapter 13**	**Week Fifteen**
Developing Ethos in Argument and Debate: Counterargument and Concession Engaging the Gears: • The Class Debate	Writing the Research Paper: Do's and Don'ts Engaging the Gears: • Evaluating a Research Paper	Final Week Workshop the Research Paper; Reflect on the Semester/Course

CONTENTS

Rhetorical Situations, Writing Processes, and Elements of Rhetoric

A rhetorical situation is, in simplest terms, the situation for which you write. Specifically, it includes your purpose for writing, your topic, your audience's assumptions and expectations, and your own assumptions and expectations (as the writer). All of these situation-specific factors must be clear in the writer's mind before she or he beings the writing process.

Approaches to Critical Thinking and Reading

Though we look at reading and thinking as distinct skill sets, frequently they not only occur at the same time, but they also rely on each other: thinking requires ideas, ideas (reading) require thinking.

Critical Writing

This chapter furthers the task of forming ideas in response to texts you have read to communicate those ideas with clarity and cohesiveness—to develop them in such a way so that another critic can view your response as well-reasoned and thoughtfully developed.

From Critical Ideas to the Thesis Statement

A thesis, from Greek, meaning "proposition," is a critical idea "proposed." So, a thesis statement is that main critical idea expressed in language to serve a purpose, usually to persuade or analyze, but can also be used to inform, or educate. By expressing a critical idea in a specific form, the thesis statement also aids the reader in a number of important ways.

To revise something is to alter its ideas, to rearrange them, to present them in the best light so that our purpose is achieved, and our audience is satisfied. We look at the areas of our thesis and ideas, our critical thinking and logic, our evidence and examples, and we look at all of that in the context of the given conventions, or the characteristics, of genre and our audience's expectations.

Editing and proofreading are distinct activities, and they are also distinct from revision, in that the focus shifts among the three. If we approach these activities similarly, as most students often do, then none of them are done well, or sometimes even adequately, and at best, our audience is confused, or mistaken in their interpretation of our ideas, and at worst, we may have lost their trust in us, and so our ethos is undermined by the lack of clarity and correctness in our language.

Choosing your own topic, and writing the research paper puts you well on the path toward becoming a person who can self-teach. You will learn how to learn whatever it is you want to learn. And truly, that is one of the goals of higher education: to help you become a lifetime learner by becoming your own teacher! Knowing how to ask the right questions, and to evaluate reasonable and plausible answers that you can successfully argue with reasonable people are marks of an educated person. Research papers, especially those where you must develop your own topic and argument, help to teach you those skills.

Your paper, your thesis—your argument is only as good as the research it rests upon. Hasty research may appear to support the thesis and purpose, but if not carefully qualified and applied, it can be detrimental to your logos and your ethos. Your research is where the support, the very foundation of your argument, rests. If you have a great thesis, and not-so-great research, all was for naught.

Technology allows us the ability to integrate other mediums of information that make our compositions come to life, where, along with our written words (text), we can include sounds, moving and static images. Composition also offers you a variety of genres to choose from to suit your rhetorical situation.

CHAPTER ONE

Rhetorical Situations, Writing Processes, and Elements of Rhetoric

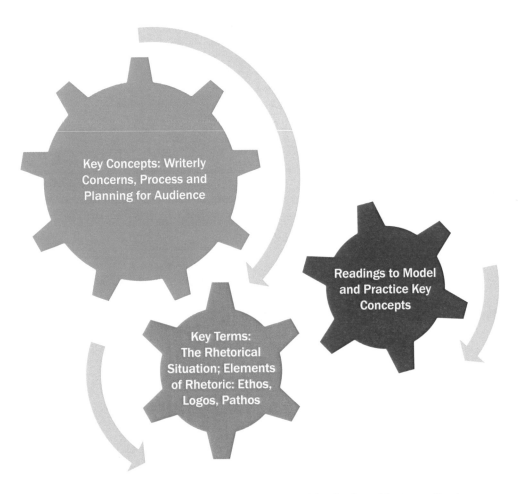

Key Concepts: Writerly Concerns, Process and Planning for Audience

Readings to Model and Practice Key Concepts

Key Terms: The Rhetorical Situation; Elements of Rhetoric: Ethos, Logos, Pathos

. . . but every person who does serious time with a keyboard is attempting to translate his version of the world into words so that he might be understood.

—Betsy Lerner, *The Forest for the Trees*

Capture your reader, let him not depart, from dull beginnings that refuse to start.

—Horace

> **Rhetoric:** language used to please or persuade audiens'
>
>   – the situation for which you write
>
>   – includes:
>   ↳ Purpose
>   ↳ topic
>   ↳ audiencdepersection
>   ↳ writers persecption

...nts, is "we write to complete an assign... know" and these answers wouldn't be ...ntext in which students are most often

...s asked to write?" or "why is writing so ...d the answers we come up with might be ...ntially ask us to imagine, again, why we

...e write for a number of reasons, and we ...a variety of topics. Mindful consideration ...rs," as John Trimble calls them. When we ...our *rhetorical situation*.

Rhetoric is the language we use to effectively please our audience, or persuade them—and it is also the study of the techniques and rules for using language effectively to persuade. A rhetorical situation is, in simplest terms, the situation for which you write. Specifically, it includes your purpose for writing, your topic, your audience's assumptions and expectations, and your own assumptions and expectations (as the writer). All of these situation-specific factors must be clear in the writer's mind for good writing to occur.

Think about it: If we don't consider all of these factors, miscommunication is more likely to occur. And you know this already, even if subconsciously, because you make these kinds of considerations every time you engage in a conversation with another person. As a writer you need to develop more conscious awareness of these factors. Here is an example of what we mean:

It's your grandmother's birthday, and you send her an e-mail to wish her happy birthday since she lives so far away. You just bang out that e-mail, because an e-mail is just an e-mail, right?

```
Hey Grandma! Wanted 2 say hi 2 you on ur bday. Hope
u r kickin' it! Cant wait 2 c u @ xmas this yr!

<3 Sally
```

Now, how might your grandmother (or most grandmothers) respond to such an e-mail? Could she even read it (does she even use e-mail)? And if she could, what might she think of your effort? Or your education? What might you have failed to consider when writing to your grandmother? What are your grandmother's (**audience**) expectations? Did you meet them? If you didn't meet them, were you still able to communicate (**purpose**) your happy birthday wishes (**topic**) in writing? How did you think about the differences between you and your audience, or the similarities, and use language to connect to your audience?

In addition to considering topic, purpose, audience, and yourself, you must also see the broader context in which you write, and the culture in which you write, as these can also affect how you approach your topic, purpose and audience. For example, look at the following hypothetical rhetorical situation and ask yourself, "How might each factor change or affect the way I write?"

► Your topic is "declining biodiversity due to climate change"
► You are a high school student
► Your audience is a third-grade class (as part of a presentation project in your environmental science class)
► Your purpose is to inform, educate and call to action
► You will give this presentation in a local park
► You live in a large modern city in America

If you consider all of these factors, you will discover a new "wrinkle" in the way you approach your writing task (or in this case, your presentation task). It will affect what you talk about, how you talk about it, what examples you might or might not use, what style of language you might choose, or even where you might even *begin*, since your third-grade audience might not be aware of either "biodiversity" and its importance, or climate change and its importance.

Now, let's take a look at how we can use these factors to improve our writing.

Understanding You, the Writer

First, let's take a look at you, one of two or more communicators in the proposed written message, blog, e-mail, essay, article, memo, poster, presentation, etc. What about you, the writer, is important to consider? The answer is: basically everything that can affect how you think about yourself, others and the larger issues or circumstances people find themselves in:

► Your age
► Your education
► Your experiences
► Your gender or social class
► Your culture or subculture
► Your political or religious beliefs

Your age affects much about your writerly become more knowledgeable about the top limited. Or your age may affect your languag loquial, or if you are from an older generatio age by a large degree, then you will have to k

[handwritten note: Things that factor into your writing ↳ Possibly a way of showing personal bias]

Refer to the specific rhetorical situation we outlined above: if you, the writer, are in high school, and your topic is biodiversity and climate change, and your audience is in third grade, how might these age differences change how you write?

Your education can change the way you see a problem, or a solution, or interpret ideas. Any differences between you and your audience's education will alter what you talk about and how you might talk about it. In the situation presented above, your considerable advantage in this regard over the third graders must be neutralized so they might be able to understand you. Providing more background about the science, and using more age-appropriate vocabulary would be a good place to start. On the other hand, if you are in high school, and your audience is climate scientists, you have a lot of preparation ahead of you as a writer, or presenter.

Your experiences matter as well. If you have extensive experience, or no experience with the topic you are writing about, the surety of your ideas will be different. In the first, your writing may be anecdotal, where you share your experiences, your acquired expertise. However, in the latter, your writing may be more researched and formal. Or you might use a combination of both to please your audience and satisfy their needs and expectations.

Your gender certainly will affect how you write, simply because different genders in most cultures have very different experiences in life, and as a result may have very different viewpoints. Consideration of this is very important. As an example of this, think about how different genders might view reproductive rights, health care or family law?

Your culture influences you in ways that you might not recognize. But to become a skilled writer, you must learn to see how your culture can affect your ideas about everything from fashion, sports and entertainment to morality, philosophy and religion. Your perspective might not be shared by your audience, but if you walk into your rhetorical situation thinking your assumptions about the world are fact, or commonplace, you could step in it.

And like culture, **your political beliefs** and leanings are usually influenced by every other factor we mentioned here. Be aware, be sensitive, and don't assume your beliefs are fact, or shared by your audience. In some cases they might be, but frequently, you would be amazed at how those kinds of assumptions can get you into trouble.

And this by no means is a complete list, but it is a good start. If you consider these factors about yourself carefully, you will likely find yourself succeeding in your purpose.

Understanding Audience

Now, let's take a look at the other "communicator" in this rhetorical situation: the audience. You can consider nearly all the factors that might be important about yourself. But, since you are the messenger, you have certain responsibilities to serve the needs of the audience, so let's also add an important factor to consider about your audience.

Review the list below, and note how it is nearly the same as the list for you, the writer, except at the last point.

- ► Age
- ► Education
- ► Experiences or lack of experience
- ► Gender or social class
- ► Culture or sub-culture
- ► Political or religious beliefs
- ► *Expectations of writing style and topic*

Audiences don't always need to be entertained, but they do have certain expectations that must be met for you to communicate effectively. Those expectations are often shaped by all the factors listed above about the writer, and by the topic, and purpose, and these factors then interact with and influence each other.

Consider Grandma again. In writing to her, does she expect you to treat her like one of your friends, or does she expect you to treat her with more respect, or deference? Maybe she wants you to demonstrate the education she helped pay for, or maybe she prefers sentimental cards. Maybe she doesn't want to hear about that experience you may have had in the dance club? Or maybe she does! Whatever it is, in order to communicate effectively with your Grandma, you must consider her expectations, and those are shaped by her age, education, culture, political and religious beliefs, experiences, and her vision of you (grandchild and writer).

Understanding Purpose

Let's looks at the reasons why you, the writer, might write, your purpose in communicating with your audience. In order to write effectively, it is imperative that you understand your purpose. If you are trying to persuade your audience that your ideas are worth consideration, you will need some combination of the above list. But if you mistake your purpose, and only write to inform, you will have likely failed to persuade. Often, you need to inform in order to pers~~uade, since a consideration of your audience~~ might reveal they need to know more abo~~ut~~ choice. How could readers be persuaded t~~o~~ with what they already know?

Here are the most common purposes we h~~ave when~~

- ► To persuade
- ► To inform
- ► To educate
- ► To entertain
- ► To call to action

[Handwritten note:] There are many common purposes in writing
↳ these have to tie with the things that factor into your writing

ype of purpose:

npting to change the audience's mind, usu-
do this effectively, you must ascertain your
ut the topic. You must determine what they
factually correct, and how they might per-
argument accordingly. For example, in your
ersuade third graders to be more aware of
change. You will first have to inform them
affects biodiversity and how their behavior
e that you might have then persuaded them

When you write **to inform**, you are providing the audience with only the *information* about a topic. This might have been your main purpose in a high school research paper. You find out what information is available on your topic, cite your sources, and explain the relevant information in a logical, often linear way. In the end, the audience now knows more than they did about a particular topic.

When you write **to educate**, you are combining knowledge (writing to inform) with a set of critical criteria used to help process that information in a particular context. For example, one might inform an audience about the loss of biodiversity over the last five decades. Writing to educate might also include evidence to suggest the meaning behind those facts, or the implications regarding the health of our ecosystems.

When you write **to entertain**, you write with the expectations of the audience fore-most in your mind, as what entertains each audience may differ. Shakespeare knew this strategy very well when he wrote his plays and sonnets. He had two general audiences to please: the commoners, who made him popular, and his patrons, the aristocracy in most cases, who funded his writing career and life. Their needs and expectations of what constituted entertainment varied greatly, so Shakespeare became expert at the double entendre, words or phrases that may have two meanings in context, in order to effectively please both audiences. Think about your third graders again. If your topic, biodiversity and climate change, is to keep your audience of eight-year-olds focused, you will have to entertain them. How might you do that while discussing such a serious topic?

When you write to **call to action**, you are both persuading people to think differently, and to behave differently. This type of persuasion is mostly seen in advertising, where these writers are trying to get you to buy the product in the advertisement. Here they must persuade you to believe their product will serve your needs, and they must per-suade you to go out and part with your money (we will discuss persuasive advertising in greater detail in chapter 10). Calls to action also include other types of persuasive writ-ing, such as public service announcement (PSAs), political speeches, propaganda, etc. The main components in calling people to action is an appeal to their logic (thought) and emotions (which then alter behavior). In the case of your third graders, you might discover that a little of all of these purposes will result in action from the third grad-ers. First, you *inform* them of the facts, then *educate* them about the reason these facts occurred and how they can help, then entertain them with a cartoon character of one of the species at risk (especially one that might be "cute," or "fun" in the eyes of eight-year-olds), then give them a shocking image, or statistic about the loss of that specific species, and voilà! You have a classroom full of third graders willing to shut the lights out or recycle more, or buy less.

Understanding Genre and Purpose

When considering purpose, you should also consider the form of the writing, or what we call the *genre*. For the most part, genre can be viewed as the style or type of writing you might choose given your rhetorical situation. If you are writing a birthday note to Grandma, you probably wouldn't choose an editorial, or a persuasive essay, but if you were writing for an academic audience on the importance of changing climate, you might use either of those styles. Some genres include:

- ► Persuasive essay (most common college essay format)
- ► Report (often the choice of science writing)
- ► Literary genres of fiction, drama or poetry
- ► Narratives
- ► Biography (or autobiography)
- ► News article
- ► Reviews
- ► Editorials
- ► Rhetorical analysis
- ► Literary or social critique

Again, this is not meant to be a complete list, but gives you the general idea. And some-times you might even combine genres. A persuasive essay may include brief narratives, or anecdotes, to help illustrate a main point. In the case of your third graders, a short story (narrative) would help them develop empathy for the living things on the planet in a specific way, and then they are more likely to be persuaded to act on behalf of conservation. For more details about choosing the right genre for your purpose, see chapter 9.

A correct assessment of your writing situation always results in better writing. It aids you in your approach and can make the process of writing less harrowing and more satisfying. It makes a false start in the process less likely, and the development of ideas more smooth, since it asks you to ask specific questions about what you write, why you write it and for whom you write it.

The Writing Process

Writing. Many of us love to do it—most of us, though, see it as a burdensome and sometimes overwhelming task to complete for a variety of purposes and situations. Even if we are lucky enough to be clear about what it is we write about, why we need to write, and to whom we write (our rhetorical situation), we still see it as chore, an effort whose outcome is uncertain at best, and ineffective at worst. Yet, that is no way to view any human activity—especially one so important to successful navigation of our complex modern world! But even Mary Oliver, a Pulitzer Prize and National Book Award winner, once said, "Have some lines come to you, a few times, nearly perfect, as easily as a dream arranges itself during sleep? That's luck. That's grace. But this is the usual way: hard work, hard work, hard work. This is the way it's done." So even an accomplished writer such as she acknowledges that writing doesn't come to anyone easily.

How can we unravel this mystery so that writing feels as natural to us as breathing? We first need to understand what writing is. Is it a natural process like breathing? Or is it something we must learn to do? The answer to these questions feels a bit murky, and that is why we writers can feel so lost. Because we associate writing with speaking and listening, which are so natural to humans, we think that everyone should be able to do it as well and as naturally as speaking and listening. But we also know that we have spent countless years in school trying to learn how to write well. So which is it: a natural process, or a thing we must learn?

To be clear: Writing is a technology. Unlike speaking and listening, which are natural and instinctual language skills, writing is a tool invented by humankind to augment, or improve, social and economic activity. We invented it, the same way we invented the wheel, the axe, the ship, the car, or the computer. So we must, all of us, learn to use this tool we call writing. We begin learning to use it quite young, first as readers, when we read with our parents or in a scholastic program for preschoolers. Then, when we enter school we learn how to use writing by learning to shape letters, sentences, and paragraphs, and finally essays, reports, etc.

But like all tools, making use of writing so that it becomes as natural to us as breathing means lots of practice. Think about people who became great at other skills: Albert Einstein, Kobe Bryant, Martin Luther King, Bill Gates, and this list goes on and on. How did they become great at using the tools of their trade? Practice. And lots of it. But not just blind practice, stabbing in the dark for some measure of success. They had a plan, a process, a means of achieving higher skills, and higher success.

All products that are made, whether it is a top-ten basketball record, or a legacy of scientific invention, or a chair, are made using a process, a step-by-step approach to accomplish that goal.

Writing is like that too. The writing process (see chart below) is a way to begin your focused practice in the art of writing well. Even if you have no plans to become the next Kobe Bryant of writing, you can still use and practice this process to make writing less burdensome, more certain and more effective.

Everything below here is writing we do for ourselves. Here, we write to learn what we know, to learn what we think, and to learn why we think it.

PREWRITING IS: Researching a topic, generating main idea, generating supporting ideas, and organizing ideas:

Research: Sources: magazines, newspapers, periodicals, literature, media—radio, TV, Internet, film—movies and documentaries, music. Conduct an interview based on your topic, visual art—observing or creating personal experiences discussion and brainstorming, role playing, personal interest inventories, class interest inventory.

Idea generation: free writing, journaling, lists, visualization, brainstorming—individually or as a group webbing/mapping/clustering graphic organizers, topic or word chart.

Idea organization: thesis statement, outline, list.

WRITING/DRAFTING IS: Writing what you know in sentences and paragraphs:

WRITE! WRITE! WRITE! Don't stop once you start writing. Revising and editing come later. Just let the words flow. Follow your outline or list to keep your ideas focused. Don't count words, ask your teacher how long it should be or when it is done. When **YOU** feel that you have completed your ideas, you are ready to go to the next stage.

HOLD IT! Before going to the next stage, make sure you have enough content to work with. If you feel that you are lacking content, go back to your prewriting for more ideas and details, and add them.

Everything below here is writing we do for our audience. We write to improve understanding, clarity, and aid our purpose in communicating with readers.

REVISING IS: Making decisions about how you want to improve your writing for your reader, looking at your writing from a reader's point of view, picking places to make your writing more informative, explanatory and more convincing to your reader:

A.R.R.R. Method of Revision:

Adding: What else does the reader need to know to understand your ideas?

Rearranging: Is the information in the most logical and most effective order?

Removing: What extra details or unnecessary bits of information are in this piece of writing?

Replacing: What words or details could be replaced by clearer or stronger expressions?

EDITING IS: Picking places where your writing could be clearer, and more interesting to your reader:

Sentence structure, variety, subject/verb agreement, consistent verb tense, precise word choice (diction), spelling, capitalization, punctuation, and grammar. Ask questions to aid your editing: Can you read it out loud without stumbling? Does every word and sentence, paragraph have a specific purpose? Are vivid and descriptive words used to describe characters and/or events? Do you use a variety of verbs throughout the piece? Are all sentences complete or are there sentence fragments?

PROOFREADING IS: The final polishing steps before you declare your paper a finished product!

It is double-checking for careless errors in: spelling, capitalization, punctuation, and grammar. And also checking for correct format and correct citations.

Tip

Be selective in the ideas that you include. You don't have to include *every idea* you generated! Pick your best ideas. Make sure they relate to your topic, your thesis statement, and to each other.

Remember to use the factors that apply to your rhetorical situation in order to plan your essay effectively!

Following the process step-by-step improves writing precisely because is it done with full attention to each step. Most student writers fail to see these steps, or fail to realize how important they are to good writing. Most students do some form of prewriting, and drafting. But then the process gets jammed up, literally. Beginning writers often conflate (jam together) the part of the process that focuses on the reader's needs. They proofread for mistakes, sure, but often do not think about *re-vision*, seeing the writing from new eyes: the reader's eyes. The same goes for editing. Failure to focus attention on these important areas can cause the whole thing to unravel. If your readers are not attended to, they simply will not attend to your writing (except of course, your instructor, who cannot walk away, but must grade that hot mess!).

When a writer establishes for themselves the rhetorical situation, prewrites, and drafts in discrete steps, then revising, editing and proofreading, the parts of the writing process designed exclusively to please the reader, become more fluid, less work, and develop clarity and coherence, which are the marks of good writing in any genre.

The Elements of Rhetoric

Once we discover our rhetorical situation, and we begin our writing process, and first draft, later, when we begin to revise and edit, we need to consider the elements of rhetoric that will best suit our purpose. There are many elements to consider, but in this chapter we will look only at three of them: logos, pathos, and ethos. They are primarily focused on the audience and their needs, or what will appeal to them in order for your writing to communicate (and persuade, inform, call to action, etc.) more effectively.

Logos comes from the Greek word for logic. Appeals to logos are appeals to the intellect. They use facts, data, and statistics; in short evidence, or proof for your claim is an appeal to logos. But appeals to logos can also include such details as tone of language (developed almost entirely by diction) that would be neutral, or objective, or without bias, and how the ideas are organized. This is a powerful tool in your toolbox to create the clarity needed to communicate effectively. Yet, over-relying on logos can drive your reader to boredom, so a balance of the other elements is necessary, even in academic rhetorical situations.

Pathos too, comes from Greek and it refers to emotions. Other words we know that use this root word are sympathy, empathy, apathy, etc. In a rhetorical situation, though, it means language or ideas used to appeal to your audience's emotions. These appeals include diction that is emotionally loaded, or biased toward (or on rare occasions, against) your audience's expectations, vivid description, and narrative, since stories always make us feel something. For example, if you were to tell a story about a particular child in an informative essay about world hunger, this would make the sometimes abstract notion of world hunger concrete by making it personal, and more real to an audience who may not experience hunger on a regular basis. These appeals are powerful. They can take an audience from "who cares?" to "where can I sign up?" quickly. However, pathetic appeals should be used with caution, as overuse can turn off some audiences, especially academic audiences who rely on evidence-based arguments and claims. For example, there is an advertisement for the humane society, where a famous pop singer, Sarah McLachlan, is singing her hit song "Angels" while the camera focuses on some mildly graphic images of many abused animals, some with one eye, or a missing leg, or burn marks. The idea is that we will feel so terrible about the fate of these helpless creatures that we will donate money to help prevent that abuse. But many people cite the manipulative nature of the ad (too many animals, the sad melody, etc.) as overkill, and some were turned off by the ad so much that they changed the channel.

Ethos also comes from the Greek word for "moral character, nature, disposition, habit, custom" (etymonline.com), and in the case of the elements of rhetoric, ethos applies to the writer's ability to demonstrate the qualities of credibility, honesty, and trustworthiness. It only makes sense. If a reader is to be persuaded, it follows that he or she would expect the writer to be fair, honest and worthy of that trust. Ethos refers to the writer's good habits as a writer, and persuader. You develop these qualities by balanced and fairminded approaches to the topic, correct and appropriate language for your audience, careful and accurate research, etc. For example, if your research came from dubious or untrustworthy sources, or you made many grammar errors, or you only speak about your topic from one point of view using language that is highly biased, it is likely that readers might think you in-credible, not believable, and therefore not worthy of their trust. As an unfortunate result, you will have failed to persuade them of your ideas.

The list below lays out the ways to appeal to each element, and describes a corresponding effect on the language and/or reader when a writer uses those appeals:

Appeals to logic (logos) use:

- ► Theoretical, abstract language
- ► Definitions and denotative meanings
- ► Literal and historical analogies
- ► Factual data and statistics
- ► Quotations, citations or examples from experts and authorities; informed opinions

Logical appeals evoke a cognitive, rational response from the reader.

Appeals to emotion (pathos) use:

- ▶ Vivid, concrete language
- ▶ Vivid descriptions
- ▶ Emotionally loaded language
- ▶ Figurative language, or images
- ▶ Connotative meanings
- ▶ Emotional examples and/or emotional tone
- ▶ Narratives of emotional events (anecdotes)

Pathetic (emotional) appeals create an emotional tone, and draw the reader's attention away from logical appeals; they inspire action in response to passion

Appeals to character (ethos) use:

- ▶ Language that is appropriate to your audience
- ▶ An effective balance of logos and pathos
- ▶ Appropriate level of vocabulary
- ▶ Correct grammar, mechanics and usage

Character (ethos) appeals demonstrate the author's reliability, competence, and respect for the audience's ideas and values through reliable and appropriate use of support and general accuracy (all of which are frequently determined by the specific audience you identified when examining your rhetorical situation).

Read the following examples that demonstrate an almost exclusive use of each element:

Logos:

> It is difficult to define pleasure in its highest sense; the definition involving a number of apparent paradoxes. For, from an inexplicable defect of harmony in the constitution of human nature, the pain of the inferior is frequently connected with the pleasures of the superior portions of our being. Sorrow, terror, anguish, despair itself are often the chosen expressions of an approximation to the highest good. Our sympathy in tragic fiction depends upon this principle; tragedy delights by affording a shadow of the pleasure which exists in pain. This is the source also of the melancholy which is inseparable from the sweetest melody. The pleasure that is in sorrow is sweeter than the pleasure of pleasure itself. And hence the saying, "It is better to go to the house of mourning than to the house of mirth" (Ecclesiastes 7.2). Not that this highest species of pleasure is necessarily linked with pain. The delight of love and friendship, the ecstasy of the admiration of nature, the joy of the perception and still more of the creation of poetry is often wholly unalloyed.
>
> —Percy Bysshe Shelley, from "A Defence of Poetry"

As you can plainly see, this famous poet, of all people, left us behind in a dusty cloud of abstract ideas, and some appeals to philosophy and religion. Without pathos, we are left numbed by the language, unable to penetrate it without a close and careful reading. Now, for his chosen audience (other literary professionals), this strict appeal to logos works. However, for the majority of us (students or a general audience), an appeal to pathos would improve our understanding of this piece. Imagine if he had told a story that showed how it is "better to go to a house of mourning, rather than a house of mirth." Would we not be able to make better sense of what at first appears to be counterintuitive? How can pleasure be more pleasurable when in pain? Had he demonstrated this, with an anecdotal story, or used some vivid descriptions of this peculiar idea, or even the entire original passage from Ecclesiastes as the example, we might better understand his message.

Pathos:

Next, note a passage from Martin Luther King's famous speech, "I Have Dream," which appeals directly to pathos, with some appeals to logos and ethos:

> But one hundred years later, we must face the tragic fact that the Negro is still not free. One hundred years later, the life of the Negro is still sadly crippled by the manacles of segregation and the chains of discrimination. One hundred years later, the Negro lives on a lonely island of poverty in the midst of a vast ocean of material prosperity. One hundred years later, the Negro is still languishing in the corners of American society and finds himself an exile in his own land. So we have come here today to dramatize an appalling condition.
>
> —Martin Luther King, Jr. "I Have A Dream"

Note the use of figurative language and language with strong connotative meanings: "manacles," "chains," "lonely island of poverty and vast ocean of prosperity," "lingering," "appalling." Also note the repetition of the line "one hundred years later."

The effect of this appeal to pathos is to create an emotional response in the reader, emotion and empathy. We can almost feel those "manacles and chains" repressing opportunity and freedom, or the "loneliness" of segregation. We can pity the "lingering," and become "appalled" by that state of existence. But this strong emotional appeal works because it is also balanced by logos. When King combines the figurative and concrete language of "manacles" and "chains" with the abstract language of "segregation" and "discrimination" he makes the abstract appear concrete. His audience, many of whom may not see or experience these ideas, can now feel, through this language, their presence, causing them to doubt the morality of such conditions for African-Americans.

Ethos:

Lastly, note the appeal to ethos in an edited excerpt of Martin Luther King Jr.'s "Letter from a Birmingham Jail." In this essay, Dr. King is responding to an editorial written by local pastors and ministers criticizing him and his coalition for coming to Birmingham to "cause trouble."

> My Dear Fellow Clergymen:
>
> While confined here in Birmingham city jail, I came across your recent statement calling my present activities "unwise and untimely." . . . But since I feel that you are men of genuine good will and that your criticisms are sincerely set forth, I want to try to answer your statement in what I hope will be patient and reasonable in terms.
>
> I think I should indicate why I am here in Birmingham, since you have been influenced by the view which argues against "outsiders coming in." . . . I, along with several members of my staff, am here because I was invited here. I am here because I have organizational ties here.
>
> But more basically, I am in Birmingham because injustice is here. Just as the prophets of the eighth century B.C. left their villages and carried their "thus saith the Lord" far beyond the boundaries of their home towns, and just as the Apostle Paul left his village of Tarsus and carried the gospel of Jesus Christ to the far corners of the Greco-Roman world, so am I compelled to carry the gospel of freedom beyond my own home town. Like Paul, I must constantly respond to the Macedonian call for aid.
>
> Moreover, I am cognizant of the interrelatedness of all communities and states. I cannot sit idly by in Atlanta and not be concerned about Birmingham. Injustice anywhere is a threat to justice everywhere. . . . Never again can we afford to live with the narrow, provincial idea of the "outside agitator" idea. Anyone who lives in the United States can never be considered an outsider anywhere within it bounds.
>
> —Martin Luther King Jr. "Letter from Birmingham Jail"

King appeals to ethos in several ways here. He first addresses the ministers who criticized him as "fellow clergymen," establishing his position as equal to their own. It puts him on the same level, but also it makes him one of them, spiritually and intellectually. If they can't trust that, they can't trust themselves. Then he describes the clergy as "men of genuine good will" whose "criticisms are sincerely set forth," an appeal to ethos that establishes the writer's (King's) respect for his critics. Then he directs their attention to logic, in the form of the reasons why he comes to Birmingham, alludes to the Bible, a direct appeal to ethos for clergymen, and continues with more discussion of the logic of "outsiders." He uses firm language, but which is also simultaneously respectful and confident. The clergymen must succumb to his credibility as a clergyman/writer even if they remain unconvinced after reading the entire essay (which is much longer than the excerpt provided) precisely because he pays such careful attention to his audience's need for trust.

Engaging the Gears: Activity for Practice

Classroom Activity

Read the following excerpt from Pericles' "Funeral Oration," by Thucydides.

Use the concepts and guides from this chapter to identify the rhetorical situation (writer, topic, purpose, and audience) and the elements of rhetoric (ethos, logos, and pathos).

With a partner or small group, answer the questions that follow the reading.

The Funeral Oration of Pericles

Thucydides

The central figure in Athenian political life for much of the period after the Persian Wars was Pericles (c. 495–429 B.C.E.), a gifted statesman and military commander. In the opening stage of the Peloponnesian War between Athens and Sparta (431–404 B.C.E.), Pericles delivered an oration in honor of the Athenian war dead. In this speech, as reconstructed by the historian Thucydides, Pericles brilliantly described Athenian greatness.

Pericles contrasted Sparta's narrow conception of excellence with the Athenian ideal of the self-sufficiency of the human spirit. The Spartans subordinated all personal goals and interests to the demands of the Spartan state. As such, Sparta—a totally militarized society—was as close as the ancient Greeks came to a modern totalitarian society. The Athenians, said Pericles, did not require grinding military discipline in order to fight bravely for their city. Their cultivation of the mind and love of beauty did not make them less courageous.

To be sure, Pericles' "Funeral Oration," intended to bolster the morale of a people locked in a brutal war, idealized Athenian society. Athenians did not always behave in accordance with Pericles' high principles. Nevertheless, as both Pericles and Thucydides knew, Athenian democracy was an extraordinary achievement.

'Let me say that our system of government does not copy the institutions of our neighbors. It is more the case of our being a model to others, than of our imitating anyone else. Our constitution is called a democracy because power is in the hands not of a minority but of the whole people. When it is a question of settling private disputes, everyone is equal before the law; when it is a question of putting one person before another in positions of public responsibility, what counts is not membership of a particular class, but the actual ability which the man possess. No one, so long as he has it in him to be of service to the state, is kept in political obscurity because of poverty. And, just as our political life is free and open, so is our day-to-day life in our relations with each other. We do not get into a state with our next-door neighbour if he enjoys himself in his own way, nor do we give him the kind of black looks which, though they do no real harm, still do hurt people's feelings. We are free and tolerant in our private lives; but in public affairs we keep the law. This is because it commands our deep respect.

'We give our obedience to those whom we put in positions of authority, and we obey the laws themselves, especially those which are for the protection of the oppressed, and those unwritten laws which it is an acknowledged shame to break.

'And here is another point. When our work is over, we are in a position to enjoy all kinds of recreation for our spirits. There are various kinds of contests and sacrifices regularly throughout the year; in our own homes we find a beauty and a good taste which delight us every day and which drive away our cares. Then the greatness of our city brings it about that all the good things from all over the world flow in to us, so that to us it seems just as natural to enjoy foreign goods as our own local products.

'Then there is a great difference between us and our opponents, in our attitude towards military security. Here are some examples: Our city is open to the world, and we have no periodical deportations in order to prevent people observing or finding out secrets which might be of military advantage to the enemy. This is because we rely, not on secret weapons, but on our own real courage and loyalty. There is a difference, too, in our educational systems. The Spartans, from their earliest boyhood, are submitted to the most laborious training in courage; we pass our lives without all these restrictions, and yet are just as ready to face the same dangers as they are. Here is a proof of this: When the Spartans invade our land, they do not come by themselves, but bring all their allies with them; whereas we, when we launch an attack abroad, do the job by ourselves, and, though fighting on foreign soil, do not often fail to defeat opponents who are fighting for their own hearths and homes. As a matter of fact none of our enemies has ever yet been confronted with our total strength, because we have to divide our attention between our navy and the many missions on which our troops are sent on land. Yet, if our enemies engage a detachment of our forces and defeat it, they give themselves credit for having thrown back our entire army; or, if they lose, 'they claim that they were beaten by us in full strength. There are certain advantages, I think, in our way of meeting danger voluntarily, with an easy mind, instead of with a laborious training, with natural rather than with state-induced courage. We do not have to spend our time practising to meet sufferings which are still in the future; and when they are actually upon us we show ourselves just as brave as these others who are always in strict training. This is one point in which, I think, our city deserves to be admired. There are also others:

'Our love of what is beautiful does not lead to extravagance; our love of the things of the mind does not make us soft. We regard wealth as something to be properly used, rather than as something to boast about. As for poverty, no one need be ashamed to admit it: the real shame is in not taking practical measures to escape from it. Here each individual in interested not only in his own affairs but in the affairs of the state as well: even those who are mostly occupied with their own business are extremely well-informed on general politics—this is a peculiarity of ours: we do not say that a man who takes no interest in politics is a man who minds his own business; we say that he has no business here at all. We Athenians, in our own persons, take our decisions on policy or submit them to proper discussions: for we do not think that there is an incompatibility between words and deeds; the worst thing is to rush into action before the consequences have been properly debated. And this is another point where we differ from other people. We are capable at the same time of taking risks and of estimating them beforehand. Others are brave out of ignorance; and, when they stop to think, they begin to fear. But the man who can most truly be accounted brave is he who best knows the meaning of what is sweet in life and of what is terrible, and then goes out undeterred to meet what is to come.

'Again, in questions of general good feeling there is great contrast between us and most other people. We make friends by doing good to others, not by receiving good from them. This makes our friendship all the more reliable, since we want to keep alive the gratitude of those who are in our debt by showing continued goodwill to them: whereas the feelings of one who owes us something lack the same enthusiasm, since he knows that, when he repays our kindness, it will be more like paying back a debt than giving something spontaneously. We are unique in this. When we do kindnesses to others, we do not do them out of any calculations of profit or loss: we do them without afterthought, relying on our free liberality.

'Taking everything together then, I declare that our city is an education to Greece, and I declare that in my opinion each single one of our citizens, in all the manifold aspects of life, is able to show himself the rightful lord and owner of his own person, and do this, moreover, with exceptional grace and exceptional versatility. And to show that this is no empty boasting for the present occasion, but real tangible fact, you have only to consider the power which our city possesses and which has been won by 'those very qualities which I have mentioned. Athens, alone of the states we know, comes to her testing time in a greatness that surpasses what was imagined of her. In her case, and in her case alone, no invading enemy is ashamed at being defeated, and no subject can complain of being governed by people unfit for their responsibilities. Mighty indeed are the marks and monuments of our empire which we have left. Future ages will wonder at us, as the present age wonders at us now.'

Questions for Practice

1) Identify Pericles' Rhetorical Situation:

Topic:

Purpose:

Audience:

2) Using Pericles' purpose and audience as a guide, choose one example of each element of rhetoric you discovered, reproduce it below and discuss why you think this is a good example of that element:

Ethos:

Pathos:

Logos:

Using the analysis you've just completed, what conclusion can you come to about Pericles' use of these elements? Which element did he rely on most? Why did he rely upon it or them? Remember, these elements serve a purpose.

Write the answer in one (or two sentences):

First Writing Activity

A Letter to Your Instructor

> Compose a 250–300 word letter to your instructor. In this letter you should briefly introduce yourself as a student in your instructor's class, briefly describe your expectations of the class (what would you like to learn), your learning style (how do you learn—lectures, group work, individual work, visuals, creative assignments?), and your concerns or excitement about writing or this course in general. You may want to include what you believe are your personal and academic strengths.

> Remember that you are writing a letter to your instructor, an instructor that is new to you and who does not know you. Remember what you are writing and sharing and how that information might be used to make your class experiences less stressful and more enjoyable. Remember that how we use ethos, pathos, and logos can determine how our audience (the instructor) understands and interprets the message you will be sending.

> Do all of this as part of your prewriting process. Then begin to draft your letter, revise carefully, edit for language and effective use of the elements of rhetoric, and proofread.

Second Writing Activity

Your Writing Process

> The goal of this assignment is to enable you to gain awareness of the process you use to write papers that are assigned in classes. Such awareness will help you consider how you may want to modify or change your writing process.

> Here are some ideas to consider before writing:

> Think about a paper you have written recently for a class. Describe the assignment and the class for which it was intended. How did you feel about the assignment? Were you interested in it immediately? Did you find it difficult or confusing? Think about what steps you took to complete that assignment. List as many activities associated with that assignment as you can recall. Some questions to contemplate:

What was the first action you performed in order to complete the writing task?

What actions followed?

- ▶ Did you think about writing when you were involved in other activities (driving a car, for example)?
- ▶ Did you talk with anyone about the topic or assignment?
- ▶ How did you draft the paper?
- ▶ What sort of revision did you do?
- ▶ Was the process you used for this assignment typical of your usual writing behavior?
- ▶ Do you feel your writing process is effective? Why or why not?
- ▶ Do you use a different process when you are working on something that you have decided to write, rather than an assignment? If so, how is it different?

Writing Task

Compose a 250–500 word (1–2 pages) essay/blog that responds to the following prompt:

Is your writing process effective?

If yes, explain why it works for you. If no, determine what changes would make it more effective. In either case, you must explain your process in detail as supportive evidence for your opinion. To help you get started you could examine the process you used to write a recent paper in another class. Again, review your rhetorical situation and which element(s) of rhetoric will serve it best.

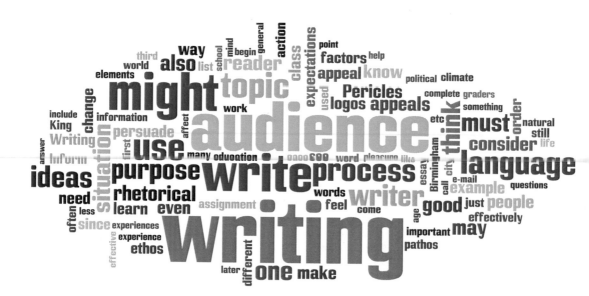

CHAPTER TWO

Approaches to Critical Thinking and Reading

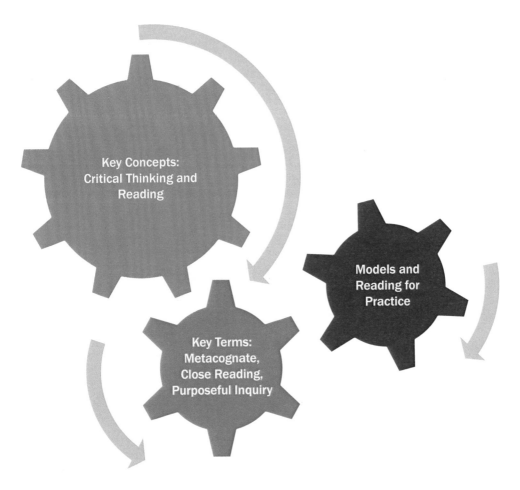

Key Concepts: Critical Thinking and Reading

Models and Reading for Practice

Key Terms: Metacognate, Close Reading, Purposeful Inquiry

The essence of the independent mind lies not in what it thinks, but in how it thinks.

—Christopher Hitchens, *Letters to a Young Contrarian*

Critical thinking is thinking about your thinking while you're thinking in order to make your thinking better.

—Richard Paul

Critical Thinking and Critical Reading

Instructors often tell students they should become critical readers and critical thinkers. It is a fundamental skill instructors wish to impart when teaching any subject. Instructors often ask students to *"think between the lines," "think outside of the box,"* or simply, *"think more,"* and students often feel they understand what it means to "think critically." Yet, when they are asked to explain or describe their particular *thinking processes,* they can be at a loss for words. This is not a deficiency, but it may be a result of too few discussions regarding what critical thinking actually looks like, what processes, or steps it requires.

Generally, when instructors tell students to read and think critically they are also asking students to think about how thinking occurs, and often how it occurs when engaged in active, critical reading. So, how does one become a critical thinker and reader?

Let us begin responding to this question with the understanding that though we look at reading and thinking as distinct skill sets, frequently they not only occur at the same time, but they also rely on one another: thinking requires ideas, ideas (reading) require thinking and so on.

Critical Thinking

What Is Thinking?

> Thinking is often referred to as an art, with its own purposes, standards, principles, rules, strategies and precautions. And it is an art well worth learning, for every important thing we do is affected by our habits of mind.
>
> —Vincent Ryan Ruggerio, Professor Emeritus, SUNY Delhi College
> *The Art of Thinking: A Guide to Critical and Creative Thought*

Thinking takes many forms, but when we are engaged in thinking, we usually do not *think* much about how we think. Yet, when we do think about HOW we think, we *meta-cognate,* we think critically. It is important to learn to think about thinking, and to do it well, because it allows us to know which type of thinking is necessary in particular situations, and it also teaches us how we come to the beliefs we hold, the conclusions we have drawn, and most important, it allows us to re-examine those beliefs and ideas to be sure they hold true over time, and circumstances.

Let's look at the different ways of thinking for a minute to see how critical thinking might work:

Let's say you are thinking about your future. You dream of one day becoming a member of the medical field: a nurse, a doctor, or a technician. You aren't sure. But you want to help people. You imagine that it will provide you with a good living; you picture your-self in a specific position, or in a hospital, or care center. Or you dream of becoming a teacher, or an economist, or one day simply graduating college with marketable skills. You feel that this direction is a good one and your hopes are strong that you will achieve one of these goals.

This is **imaginative thinking**, a kind of investigation of potential, a "poke your head up" kind of thinking. It mostly wanders, with some aim, around ideas, tests them for appeal or possibility. No conclusion is drawn, but often we feel as though we *did some thinking,* because our thinking maintained a topic, and kept our imaginations active for a while; it was thinking that went beyond a daydream, or being "lost in thought," but it wasn't focused, informed, or goal oriented, other than the loose goal of "exploring" ideas or feelings.

Now, let's say you are thinking about your future again. This time, you weigh the cost of education and the time and commitment it will take against the benefits of increased knowledge and skills, which often translates into better opportunity and decision making. You look into details about your ideas for programs. You research schools, tuition, and expenses, and finally conclude, as most who are reading this text have, to attend college.

This kind of thinking is **critical thinking** because we focused our thinking using a set of parameters: we looked at specific details (cost and benefits) that govern the topic of choosing an education. Then we looked at details of those costs (tuition, books, expenses, distance from home, etc.) and details of the benefits: career, and vocation. We may have compared and contrasted the detailed information regarding specific school and pro-gram costs and benefits, and our goal was to narrow down, or choose a path forward.

Professor Ruggerio tells us that thinking is a "purposeful mental activity over which we exercise some form of control" and that "control is the key word." Critical thinking is conscious and focused control over the paths our thoughts take, the information that will be included, and how that information will or should relate. In other words, it is attentive, focused and goal oriented. It is purposeful inquiry and analysis.

This type of thinking is the most difficult precisely because it takes much work. First you must be trained to think this way. We all can think imaginatively, using our impres-sions, feelings and experiences, and knowledge to guide and direct our thoughts. But to focus on specific details "with . . . purpose, standards, principles, rules, strategies and precautions" (Ruggerio) is to work at a problem, unravel its mysteries, to be an active, aware and omniscient being in our own minds.

A course in composition requires you to engage in purposeful inquiry and analysis. Inquiry means that as we read and think, we must ask important questions (who, what, where, when, why, and how) and we must analyze (compare and contrast, debate, engage in civil arguments, examine cause and effect). As students read, listen, discuss—thinking occurs naturally. Purposeful inquiry and analysis occurs when we are aware of what we are reading, what we are hearing, and what we are thinking while we are reading.

Critical Reading

If critical thinking is being conscious and purposeful in our thoughts, then critical reading is being conscious and purposeful in our reading, to employ a focused strategy that helps us think about what we are reading, how it connects to prior knowledge, and how it relates to other ideas.

We read for many purposes and each type of reading engages slightly different strategies for understanding and critical thinking.

What We Are Reading, How We Are Reading

What is a Text? Types of Reading Sources

While some people continue to read newspapers, magazines, journals in print ("traditional" texts)—the Internet and technology has changed what we read, the quality of what we read, and the amount and speed at which we receive "information." However, despite the mode of delivery of reading materials, we read according to *purpose.* In the twenty-first century much of our reading occurs on a computer or digital screen. These innovations allow readers to surf information on a global level and in monstrous amounts. We can download entire novels and read them on a tablet or other reading device. Video clips are embedded in much of what we read on the Internet, allowing us to see and hear, augmenting what we read. Students locate and read research materials on the Internet and must decide, using critical reading and thinking skills, which material can be deemed accurate and reliable. While our choices and formats may have increased, critical reading still requires the acts of processing and thinking.

When we read via the Internet we often access social media, perusing the postings of friends and family members. It is a way to *communicate,* when speaking is not always possible. Such "posts" are usually abbreviated and provide direct information. Some users post and "share" photographs, factoids, news, and articles of interest to other participants who might be interested. Social media also provides for "groups" with common hobbies or interests. At the beginning of the twenty-first century everyone from all walks of life and professions found creative and effective ways to share.

Whether we like to read texts in a traditional manner (printed materials) or whether we enjoy the ease and speed of technology-enhanced texts, it is often necessary to combine the two. Instructors in specific disciplines may require students to read printed materials in textbooks and other printed sources. While schools integrate the use of technology-as-text (websites, blogs, PowerPoint, video feed, forums, chat), much of school still requires students to read texts written by people who are professionals in the field or area you are studying. Much of this reading (in the sciences, mathematics, arts, and humanities) is new to you—the structures are new, the vocabulary is challenging, the tone and voice can appear foreign and incomprehensible. But, there are critical reading strategies that you can adopt to help you develop critical responses to all types of writing.

Reading for Personal Enrichment, Interest, and Entertainment

Generally, we read materials that *interest* and *engage* us. We might read *Sports Illustrated* if our interests are in athletics. We might read novels like *The Hunger Games* or *The Hobbit* because they appeal to our sense of imagination. We might even read books written by our life-heroes. This type of reading is motivated by personal desire to know more about people, places, and subjects that inspire and interest us and we approach this type of reading willingly and with glad anticipation. However, as we read for entertainment, we also engage in learning.

All reading allows us to learn more about the world we live in. It allows us to think about our values and how those values relate to our own lives. For example, an article in *Sports Illustrated* may give us information about how athletes become better at their sport. As we read this article we may learn about discipline, commitment, and motivation. When we read a novel such as *The Hunger Games* or *The Hobbit* we may begin to analyze our definition of good and evil, or wrong and right actions.

Reading for Personal Responsibility

To ensure our lives function efficiently we must often read texts or materials that directly impact our well-being or the well-being of our families. Take, for instance, reading a cell phone bill. How is such reading approached? First, we might read how much are we are being charged for services. Then we might read what types of services we are receiving. Then what types of service fees and taxes we are paying. We may then confirm that the information on the bill is accurate. If we hastily read, or do not carefully consider these kinds of questions while reading important documents such as bills, contracts, payments, and loans, we could make costly errors that may lead to financial difficulties or misunderstandings.

In our daily lives we often read a wide variety of texts to make decisions. When shopping for groceries we might read the labels on food packages in order to make purchasing decisions. Are packages labeled "healthy" really healthy? Are foods labeled "fresh" really fresh? Maybe we have to pick up medication from the pharmacy—what does the label on the medication tell us about dosage, side effects, and other drug interactions? Such reading provides us with information we need for good health and safety. We approach this type of reading with seriousness as our reading has outcomes that impact our daily lives.

When we read documents we use basic reading skills; we read the words and numbers on the page. As we read the words and numbers on the page we read to identify specific types of information. This is different from how (and why) we read *Sports Illustrated* or *The Hunger Games*. We often do not think about the different ways we read because we have learned to decide how to read automatically. A critical reader is aware of what type of reading he or she uses in any given situation, she pays attention to the detail that might signal to her that she must read more carefully, or to the signal that indicates she has learned and analyzed enough information to conclude, or decide what action to take.

Reading in the Professions or for Work

The type and amount of reading we do at work depends upon the type of work we do. Your composition or writing instructor engages in many different forms of reading. She is required to review textbooks and must decide upon which textbook best suits the requirements of her course and the needs of her students. She will read hundreds of articles related to teaching rhetoric and writing. She will read novels, student produced writing such as essays, reports, analysis papers, and research papers. If you become a lawyer, you will read legal documents. A police officer will read reports and statistics, narratives and legal documents. A mechanic, or engineer? She will read diagrams and measurements and legal documents. Each task requires a specific approach because each task has a different purpose.

Regardless of profession, as employees, we are often required to read employee policy manuals, e-mails that include changes in work procedures or policies, and materials that keep us up-to-date on our specific field of work. We often engage in this type of reading with the understanding that what we are reading is literal, instructive, and direct. For example, our employee policy manual may specifically instruct us about dress codes, or the amount of time we can take for breaks and meals. How we read in our professions or for work determines how we work and the quality of the work we deliver.

Reading for Education

As college students, you are often asked to read a wide variety of texts selected by educators to fulfill specific learning goals. An American history instructor may ask you to read a textbook full of names, dates, and events that provide students with a chronological understanding of what has happened and why. The instructor may also assign students to read *The Autobiography of Benjamin Franklin* and the writings of Martin Luther King Jr. to provide students with different perspectives and experiences in American history. Comparing the texts by Franklin and King Jr. provides a space for critical reading and critical thinking.

College students are faced with understanding how to approach a variety of reading tasks for a variety of classes. How should you approach reading a mathematics book, a textbook for a health class, an article written by a psychiatrist for a psychology class? To answer this question you must understand that reading such texts requires similar strategies you often already use on a daily basis. How is approaching the reading of a mathematics textbook much like reading and understanding a bill or the nutrition label on a box of cereal? How is reading a chapter in a health book like reading a use and drug interaction label on pharmaceutical medication? At the same time, those disciplines also have specific types of information that you should look for. So, to be a critical reader, you must become aware of what you are reading, what you are thinking when you read, and how this information relates to prior knowledge and outside texts, or ideas.

Reading Steps—the Close Reading Process

The careful reading of a text is like peeling away the layers of an onion. This method of reading requires us to see through many layers of a text. We first take off the skin of the onion (what is on the exterior—or—what does the text appear to be about). We next work our way to the next layer, noticing our reactions, and asking, what are we feeling, or understanding as we read? Finally we get to the core, the center, the interior that is not visible from the "outside" and the implications or relations these ideas have. This is what some might call *a close reading* of a text.

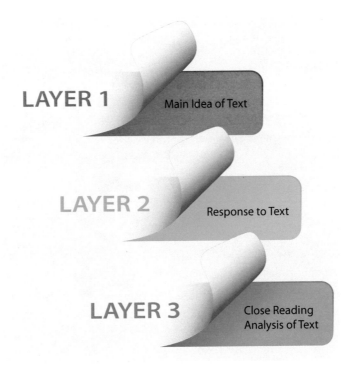

LAYER 1 — Main Idea of Text

LAYER 2 — Response to Text

LAYER 3 — Close Reading Analysis of Text

To read closely and critically, you must read for content, meaning, interpretation, and analysis. While all this may sound complicated, with practice, these skills and strategies can become instinctual and our use of these skills, organic to our study strategies.

Pre-Reading	Understanding	Interpreting	Reflecting
What can we predict or expect from this text?	What are you thinking about while you are reading?	How does this information relate to prior knowledge and outside texts, or ideas?	What are the effects of these strategies?
Scan text for clues about the message or purpose of the text.	Annotations: what do the sections or paragraphs tell us?	Apply: Inference/Analysis/Synthesis	What meaning is present? Do I agree? Why? Why not?
What genre does the text belong to?	Who is the author or source? What do you know about the author or the source?	Rhetorical Strategies: What parts of the text appeal to the elements of ethos, logos, and pathos?	Does it contrast with other knowledge? What was left out? Why?
Try to predict what information you will get from the text.	Ask yourself what might be the purpose and audience.	Interpretation: What effect does this text have on the audience?	What questions do I still have?

Understanding the Background of the Writer, and the Historical and Cultural Context

General research on a writer serves three purposes. First it gives us an understanding of the background of the author. It also allows a reader to locate similarities and differences. How is the author like me? How is the author different? Second, it allows a reader to assess the reliability and *authority* of the author. Finally, it is important to regard the *intended audience,* or who the writer is writing for and why. Also realize that this may not include you: think of Thucydides, from chapter 1. His "Funeral Oration" was written for a very specific audience (Athenians) and for a very specific reason.

Before reading it is always good practice to think about the historical time period (era, century, year) in which the writing was produced. When a text is written determines how and why it is written. Sometimes students feel "disconnected" or "bored" with a reading not because the writing is terrible, but because there is a minor misunderstanding sometimes called a "generation reading gap." For example, an instructor may require students to read *To Kill a Mockingbird* by Harper Lee. This novel was published in 1960. With a superficial reading, it may seem to students born in 1990, or 2000 that this novel is not relevant to them. Yet, students who read this book and who also might note that when the book was published the Civil Rights Movement was just getting underway, might now find it relevant to their lives today in many ways, as our perception of what a civil right is evolves over time. Actively reading, and asking critical questions about historical contexts can prevent the "generation reading gap" that often leads to reading boredom.

Cultural context is important to notice and respond to not only because the audience has cultural expectations relevant to the rhetorical situation, but also so you can examine the assumptions that you, the reader, bring to the table, or that the writer set up with his or her own cultural assumptions.

Concrete Reading Strategies

Planning

Planning for reading is beneficial. How much time will you need for an assigned text (be generous in this determination)? How much time will you need to read, think, and annotate a reading assignment? When do you read at your "best" (in the morning, afternoon, evening)? Where do you do your best reading (at the library, a coffee shop, your own room)? Consider becoming a habitual reader—one who forms reading habits. Many of us have routines . . . some of us shower in the evening to save time in the morning. Some of us shower in the morning because it "wakes" us. We all brush our teeth, pack our materials, and find our way to school. The order in which we establish our routines differs. A reading routine works the same way. How do you prepare to read? What do you do while you read? After you read?

Scanning

Scanning a reading assignment begins with the title. What does the title suggest about the content? Go on to scan the first sentences of each paragraph—what do the topic sentences suggest about the direction of the text? If the reading assignment is lengthy, scanning may occur frequently. For example, you may read the first three pages of a longer work, then scan ahead a few pages before returning to where you left off.

Never Confuse Scanning with Reading!

Often, when pressed for time, we are tempted to scan a reading assignment. Some students may go online to read summaries of lengthy texts. Such an approach to reading never succeeds. There are no shortcuts to critical reading. Scanning allows a reader to become familiar with the content that will be presented. Scanning allows readers to become acquainted with an author's style and voice. Scanning allow readers to prepare to receive the content of a text. Scanning is preparing. Scanning is the opposite of close reading, and fails to provide you with enough details to form new ideas and support them.

Annotating

Annotating is active reading that requires physical participation. Your eyes will follow the text, your mind will react to the text, your wrist and hand will write your reactions as you read. Because it requires you to notate as you read, it is helping you achieve awareness of what you are thinking while you read or think about ideas. Annotation provides you with quick and brief margin summaries that will help you recall and process (think about) a text because you will annotate for content, strategy, meaning, interpretation and analysis.

When you annotate you should:

- ▶ Annotate areas that interest you or confuse you
- ▶ Annotate questions you form for class discussions
- ▶ Annotate areas you agree or disagree with
- ▶ Annotate ideas you come up with for writing assignments

Be specific. Don't just mark the main idea. Mark the main idea, why you think it is the main idea, what you think about it (opinion), what questions arise.

Post-Reading/Reflecting

Post-reading asks you to reflect and connect both the subject matter of a reading and the possible meaning/implications.

- ▶ What new information did you "get"?
- ▶ What information can you "add"?
- ▶ How does what you read connect to your experiences or understanding?
- ▶ Has the reading changed your way of thinking? How? Or why?
- ▶ What else have you read (or watched, or experienced) to connect to the reading?

Engaging the Gears: Activity for Practice

Classroom Activity

Reading with others is an effective strategy in understanding how meaning develops and how interpretation occurs. Each reader has a unique response to texts and sharing those responses is a reasonable method to understanding a text in a variety of ways.

Reading with Others

With another reader, read the following short essay, "East Coast Cities at Risk in Future Tsunamis." It is possible that as a reader, you have never witnessed a tsunami. Perhaps you live in a geographical region that will never experience a tsunami. It is also possible you have heard or read about tsunamis like the recent catastrophic tsunamis in Indonesia, Japan, and the Philippines. Before reading, you might ask yourself—what do tsunamis have to do with me? Engage in critical thinking and reading by focusing your reading, and annotating for the following ideas:

1. What is the *purpose* of Metcalfe's text?
2. What might this article *mean*?
3. What *questions* arise once its purpose and meaning are clear?
4. How does *analyzing* the message add to your understanding?

After reading, discuss your ideas and annotations. Be sure to make note of the discussion on a sheet of paper—these notes will allow you to see how meaning develops and interpretation occurs. Your instructor may facilitate a discussion after this activity is completed.

East Coast Cities at Risk in Future Tsunamis
John Metcalfe
(The Atlantic)

If a major tsunami were to occur off the Atlantic coast, cities from New England to New Jersey could be hardest hit by the incoming walls of speeding water.

John Ebel, an earth-sciences professor at Boston College, put his hometown and its coastal kin on the danger map during a presentation on Friday at the Seismological Society of America's annual meeting. Ebel was inspired to take up the question of East Coast tsunami damage after a "swarm" of 15 earthquakes struck about 170 miles east of Boston in April 2012, with the largest being of 4.0 magnitude. The same year, several other tremors occurred off the coasts of Newfoundland and Cape Cod along the Atlantic continental shelf.

It's clear the Atlantic can rumble. Although the ocean doesn't experience the number of tsunamis that the Pacific gets—a consequence of volcanic explosions and more shifting tectonic plates—there have been a few big ones, like the 1755 earthquake and tsunami that destroyed much of Lisbon and 1929's huge waves that crashed into Grand Banks, Newfoundland, causing surreal scenes like these . . .

Photos courtesy of the Centre for Newfoundland Studies.

Ebel believes that the upper East Coast is most at risk because the recent seismic activity in the Atlantic is similar to what preceded the 7.2 magnitude Grand Banks quake. That temblor triggered an underseas landslide that swamped Newfoundland with towering waves, crushing homes and killing 29 people. Ebel says:

> The setting for these earthquakes, at the edge of the continental shelf, is similar to that of the 1929 M7.3 Grand Banks earthquake, which triggered a 10-meter tsunami along southern Newfoundland and left tens of thousands of residents homeless.

Ebel's preliminary findings suggest the possibility than an earthquake-triggered tsunami could affect the northeast coast of the U.S. The evidence he cites is the similarity in tectonic settings of the U.S. offshore earthquakes and the major Canadian earthquake in 1929. More research is necessary, says Ebel, to develop a more refined hazard assessment of the probability of a strong offshore earthquake along the northeastern U.S. coast.

Of course, our monitoring systems are much better today than in the 1920s, so we'd have a real-time warning of any incoming tsunamis. And many cities on the East Coast have sea walls or harbors that protect them. So it's not something to freak out about, just maybe worth a ponder—perhaps the next time you're out swimming in the ocean, alone, and notice a distant wave on the horizon.

What post-reading thinking and discussion questions did each person pose? Try to answer these questions as a group. Share your ideas and responses with the class.

First Writing Activity

This activity will allow you to practice reading, critical thinking, and analysis skills. Conduct a careful reading of an essay assigned by your instructor, or one listed in the Suggested Readings section at the end of this book. After you have read the essay, compose a thoughtful, reasoned, critical, and analytical response to that essay. Below are some suggestions and guides to complete this activity.

Composing the Reading Response

To write a thoughtful, well-reasoned and well-analyzed response/reaction to the text assigned, you should refer directly to the text (direct quotation/reference) whenever possible. You should avoid over-summarizing (don't retell or rewrite the text) only include the details of importance to you.

Remember what to look for:

► Who is the author?
► What is the author's general background?
► What is the publication date/year of the assigned text?
► What is the history surrounding the text?
► What is the author's purpose/message?
► Who is the audience for the text?
► How does the author appeal to ethos, pathos, and logos to deliver the purpose/message?
► What rhetorical devices does the author use to stylize the text?
► Is the author's purpose/message convincing?

- ► Where do I agree? Disagree?
- ► What does the author omit from the subject of the text?
- ► What conversation/discussion would you "add" to the text?

Using a chart may be helpful

Author's main points	Direct quotes of passages that interest me, or support main points	My ideas about the author's points	What questions do I have?

Second Writing Activity

Chapter 1 introduced us to the rhetorical situation and how who we are can shape the ways in which we communicate. To begin thinking about how we read and how we learn it is a good idea to reflect on our age, education, unique life experiences, and values. Below are excerpts from a writing assignment that began with a simple prompt:

How Do You Read?

The activity that follows will allow you to reflect on your reading experiences and processes.

Priscilla Alfaro on Reading: Reading Confessions

I have always enjoyed reading when allowed to choose my own novels; romantic, comedy, and some biographies have been the genres I have generally explored through reading throughout the years. Assigned readings that are given in my educational venture have always been more of a struggle; assigned reading quickly bores me if I find no interest in them. Sometimes I fall asleep while reading school assigned readings. Recently, over the summer of 2013, I developed more of an open minded strategy about assigned readings and tried to find some connection between what I was reading and my life. Sometimes a difficulty that arises as I read is comprehending the text itself. If I am not familiar with a particular organization or structure the paragraphs or pages of the book or article have to be read over several times. Also, where I read can affect my reading concentration. For instance, if I read at night I become sleepy and my concentration fails. On the other hand, if I read during the day I have more energy and motivation to get through the reading. Overall reading is a skill that takes time and dedication to perfect.

Paula Tellez on Reading: How I Read

I am the type of person that will read a book if I have to read it, but would not engage in analyzing details of the reading. I read for "fun and fulfillment" but only if the book catches my interests. Books that interest me are ones that explain and describe people and events and makes me understand why something happened. The books that bore me are usually ones that have complicated language, like Old English. Complicated language or "old" language is hard for me to understand and can get confusing, so I guess I sometimes try to find the easy way out and do not bother to read them. I am a slow reader and if I am trying to analyze at the same time, I need to give myself more time to read. If I want to analyze a book, it takes time to make the connections. I do not read often, and I only read if it is required to do so. This is something I have to change because reading and analyzing is something I will often have to do in and out of my college classes. Analyzing is important because if I can begin to analyze a text or a book then I am able to explore and think deeply to find the new meaning in everything. I want to analyze better so I can make connections between a book or other text to my life. Once I begin to analyze a book, I will begin to analyze everything that surrounds me, and I will learn more.

Priscilla and Paula enjoy different types of reading. Priscilla focuses on her need to increase her vocabulary and concentration. Paula states that she is a slow reader. What they both share in common is their understanding that college reading requires them to connect to what they read in some way. Finding those connections is a skill that all college students need in order to understand, process, and apply what they read.

Take a moment to write an informal reflection on how you read. Write out a "reading inventory" of texts you have read for personal gain, academic gain, or professional/work development. Assess your reading and writing skills by reflecting on your strengths. Which areas would you like to improve? What steps will you need to take and what skills will you need to practice and develop to reach your personal, academic, or professional goals?

Here are some questions to guide your reflection:

- ▶ What types of text do you most commonly read and why?
- ▶ What types of technologies are involved in your common reading practices?
- ▶ What do you "look" for when you read?
- ▶ How do you determine the "value" of what you read?
- ▶ What do you "bring with you" (prior knowledge and experiences) when you are reading?
- ▶ What is "interesting" reading? How do you define the adjective "interesting"?

► How does genre and academic discipline shape your attitude before you begin reading?

► If we find ourselves struggling with a reading assignment, how do we overcome it?

Share and compare your reflection and assessment with others. Discuss strategies (traditional and new), and if possible, speak to peers who may have insights and suggestions. Offer your own insights, suggestions, and experiences with your peers.

CHAPTER THREE

Critical Writing

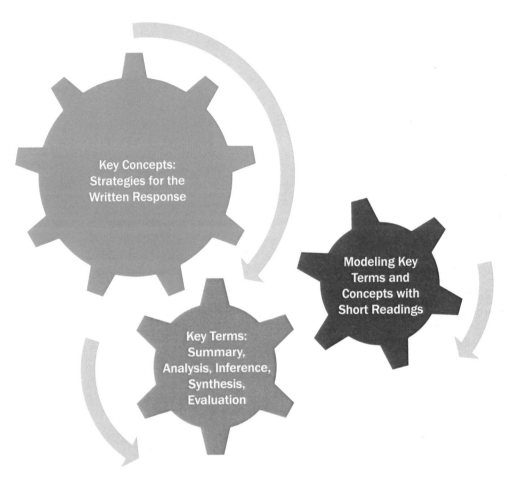

If people cannot write well, they cannot think well, and if they cannot think well, others will do their thinking for them.

—George Orwell

If you have an apple and I have an apple and we exchange these apples then you and I will still each have one apple. But if you have an idea and I have an idea and we exchange these ideas, then each of us will have two ideas.

—George Bernard Shaw

This chapter furthers the task of forming ideas in response to texts you have read to communicate those ideas with clarity and cohesiveness—to develop them in such a way so that another critic can view your response as well-reasoned and thoughtfully developed. Though there are many ways to perceive and communicate ideas, developing these five basic skills will aid this work: Summary, Analysis, Inference, Synthesis, Evaluation. To demonstrate the differences and importance of these skills, we will use a short essay so we can model each of these skills, and then ask you to work independently toward a well-reasoned and thoughtful response to different and longer readings.

Let's define our terms first.

Summary

Summary is a brief outline of the main ideas presented by a writer. It is a "list" of the important aspects of that reading's main purpose. Only the ideas present and important should be included. The culling of these main ideas or important details relies on the careful and close reading you do, and the clarity and focus of the annotations you made while doing that careful critical reading. It also depends on the purpose for the summary. If you are summarizing for argument, that is using the summary as evidence or example for your own argument, then you choose the important items in the text that support your argument. But, if you are writing the summary to inform, you include most of the key concepts or ideas in the text. If you summarize to compare or contrast with another text (sometimes as work toward synthesis—see below), then you might include key points of compare/contrast of both texts. In any case, a summary is a brief summation of the key concepts and ideas you need for your purpose.

Below is a list of what a summary is NOT:

- ► Your opinions should NOT be included.
- ► Direct quotes should NOT be included, or should be limited.
- ► Your criticism or evaluation should NOT be included.
- ► Your analysis should NOT be included.
- ► Your interpretation should NOT be included.

Summaries are not written for only one purpose. They, too, are written for specific purposes, and those purposes might alter what information you choose to include. For instance, if the summary is for a police report, it would highlight only the facts pertaining to the incident. If it was a murder scene, information about the weather might not be relevant, whereas if it were an accident report, weather is often a factor. Additionally, if you are writing a summary to inform an audience you might keep your summary to the general ideas included, whereas if you were writing a summary to persuade, or argue, you might include the details/evidence that do that work. Since, in college writing, you will most often be asked to persuade or argue a position, in this chapter, and beyond, the focus will be on summary for argument.

Some Examples of Summary

A **reading summary** is a statement of the general thesis and/or main points of a text.

Here is a sample summary composed by a student, Tonny. For a class assignment, he read *Seedfolks* by Paul Fleishman, a novel written for children between the ages of eight and eleven. This is Tonny's summary of the text. See if you can understand the general outline and idea of what Tonny read.

> *Seedfolks* is a children's novel by author Paul Fleischman. It was first published in 1997. The novel takes place in a rough neighborhood in Cleveland, Ohio. The setting is an empty lot filled with garbage and overrun by rats. A young Vietnamese American girl named Kim and twelve neighbors transform the empty lot into a community garden. The garden becomes a symbol of diversity and friendship, for each person plants a vegetable that is personally and culturally meaningful. The once "unfriendly neighbors" become a real community filled with color and culture. The story is told by thirteen different voices and becomes a single story of unity, peace, and honoring diversity.

Another example of a summary, one that may be more familiar to you is the movie summary. Movie producers provide a summary of an upcoming film for the purpose of audience preview. The preview presents an audience with the main idea and main action of the film. However, note that the rhetorical situation of the preview is to entice people to see the film. In this case the summary serves as a persuasive device.

Here is a summary of the movie *Iron Man*:

> With the world now aware of his dual life as the armored superhero Iron Man, billionaire inventor Tony Stark faces pressure from the government, the press, and the public to share his technology with the military. Unwilling to let go of his invention, Stark, along with Pepper Potts, and James "Rhodey" Rhodes at his side, must forge new alliances—and confront powerful enemies.
>
> Anonymous from IMDB

Note that the summary above does not "give away" the ending of the film. The summary above is a plot summary—or a summary of the main action line in the film. Also note that this summary does not provide opinions or critiques about the quality of the film.

It is worth repeating that academic summaries avoid analysis, persuasion, or critique. An academic summary is direct and the length of the summary is determined by the length and depth of the reading or viewing assignment. An example of an academic summary is provided after the reading, "Mind Over Mass Media," by Steven Pinker on page 44.

Analysis

A quick definition and explanation of the process of analysis, simply put, means to take apart a whole and examine the parts. Yet what parts? That is an important question, and the answer, in part, is largely dependent on the specific text you are analyzing. However, for a general idea of what analysis "looks" like, you can:

▶ Examine each idea as an independent piece of information.

▶ Evaluate the connection of the part to the whole: the paragraphs (ideas) to the thesis statement or main idea, and how those ideas relate to one another.

▶ Examine how the parts are organized (structured) and understand how the structure helps to produce meaning.

▶ Understand patterns of reasoning within the entire text (are there places where ideas support or contradict? What transitions are used to indicate patterns of thought?).

▶ Determine purpose.

To understand how a car works, an auto technician examines the engine, the electrical components, the computer systems, the steering system, the weight, the design of the body. In this way, a technician or engineer can begin to assess the overall effectiveness of the car. Analysis begins in this way, by taking apart a whole and examining individual parts or pieces.

Once an object or idea has been taken apart—the parts must be examined. The process of examination requires us to learn how each part works in the system of the whole. When consumers ask for better gas mileage, engineers must examine what parts of the car affect how far a car will go on a gallon of gas. How much does the car weigh? What parts are the heaviest and what types of materials are those heavy parts made of? Is it safe to use lighter materials to improve gas mileage? What about the tires? How does tire design, pressure and placement affect how far a car can go on a gallon of gas? Examination of parts allows a closer analysis of how something works, or how someone thinks.

If you return to the critical questions to ask when reading, you will see that largely analysis and critical reading share much in common. Analyzing a reading assignment, tearing it apart, is much like the process of analyzing an object. What are the parts of writing? Words make up sentences. A string of sentences create paragraphs. A string of paragraphs create a whole text (an essay, a story, an article, a research paper, a letter to a friend). How do the words, sentences, and paragraphs form meaning for a reader?

The Main "Parts" of a Text

Whole Text	Paragraphs	Sentences	Words
The whole of a reading includes a main idea (thesis)—an idea, proposal, argument, or experience an author would like to share with the reader/audience.	The paragraphs, units or blocks of writing are designed to offer a single idea in support of the main idea (thesis).	Sentences are individual units of writing that collectively support the main idea of the paragraph. Sometimes, it takes only one sentence to construct a paragraph.	Words, carefully selected, become sentences that directly link and connect to the ideas in other sentences in the same paragraph.

Analysis is necessary in all reading, thinking, and writing and will be discussed again in this textbook.

Inference

Inference is a conclusion we make about what is not known by examining what is known, or what is factual. That may sound a bit confusing, but this is something you already know how to do! You do this every day to help navigate the world, though it does get harder when the known elements being examined are many, or if they are highly complex.

For example, if you walked into someone's home, and looked into the dining room, you would see a table, chairs, and all the other items that you would expect to see in a dining room. But, on the table, you see notes, books, a laptop, highlighter pens, and pencils. From this scene, you can infer that the dining room in this house doubles as a study area, and from that inference, you might also infer that a student of some age lives in the house, or is at least present at the time. To be confident in your inferences you must ask: Are you likely to be correct? Or are there other equally plausible inferences to make? If so, then you would need more facts to make a strong inference.

Yet, in this case, it is likely that the inference about how the dining room is used is correct, since there were so many facts to point to "studying." So the reliability of inference often requires careful examination of all the known facts, and a careful examination of the quality of those facts, before a strong inference can be made. But you might also look at what facts that should be there to support your inference are missing. Is the student there? Or is the occupant of the house merely doing research of a personal nature rather than academic? What is absent is also important. Weak inferences can undermine your ethos, so be sure you can make a strong inference before arguing the point, or using it as evidence to support another point.

Inference is often a complex task, and one that requires a close reading so that all of the facts that are present, or absent, in the text become "known" to you, and then you can more accurately infer what else may be happening in the text.

Inferences are conclusions drawn by combining known information to discuss the unknown. If multiple explanations can be derived by a same set of facts, then the inference is weak. The fewer the possibilities that explain a set of facts, then the stronger the inference becomes. A good critical thinker will keep asking, "What else might explain this?" And then search for more facts to narrow the possibilities to find a strong inference.

Synthesis

Synthesis is the combining of ideas to form new ideas, usually through a thorough analysis of the text/idea(s) separately, finding similarity or dissimilarity, and examining the underlying assumptions that each idea relies on. Then, when you, the writer, apply synthesis, you combine that information/data to form a new, related idea.

For example, in chemistry, synthesis can be observed when molecules combine. If you take a carbon molecule and combine it with two oxygen molecules, you arrive at completely new compound called CO2, or carbon dioxide.

In your day-to-day life, you also use synthesis to determine the best course for you. For example, when you choose your major course of study, you examine many factors or ideas such as interest, long-term goals regarding work you might do, time it might take to complete and financial cost and availability of funds. Then you weigh all of these facts together to determine the best major to choose. You synthesize: you combine separate ideas to determine a specific new idea, in this case, the choice of a major course of study.

In reading, and writing, the goal is to derive a new idea from the combination of known ideas. This helps us to realize original ideas, or expand/enhance an existing one. When you read texts with themes or main ideas that rally around a certain topic, or genre, such as articles in fashion magazines, or images, like advertisements, or you read articles that discuss a similar topic, but whose subjects are different, you can begin to synthesize.

For example, you see an environment or health text with an article about water conservation tips, a public service announcement about water test results from the local beach authority, and an advertisement for your local farmer's market, you can do the following:

Summarize main points of each text; note the argument, or the evidence they present, the writer's purpose, and underlying assumptions they might have made.

Analyze the text: taking each idea within one text apart, looking at the details that support or influence the main idea.

Identify the relationships between each text's main idea(s), evidence, purpose and assumptions.

Compare them against what you already know about the subject, using the knowledge you have gained from this activity.

When you do this, new ideas do begin to form as this is a process of idea generation. It is your brain at work. It will form ideas when you use this process, and be the most efficient way to think toward synthesis: summarize, analyze, synthesize (making insightful connections) toward a compelling thesis of your own.

Evaluation

The word evaluate comes from Latin through the French language. It means "to find the value of," and when we evaluate a text, we compare that text to the values we already hold either about texts themselves, or about the content, or topic.

When we read an article about the "bad" behavior of a celebrity, we evaluate the evidence of the "badness" of his behavior against a set of rules governing the behavior we value. When we decided that a particular restaurant serves "good" food, we are weighing the food against criteria chosen in advance for what "good" food is.

When we read a text, like the one below, called "Mind Over Mass Media," we will weigh the ideas Steven Pinker has about the mass media, against the way we value that media, and how we use it.

Sometimes you can choose to evaluate from a variety of positions. If you looked at that article as a journalist, how would you respond? If you were Steven Pinker, what values lead you to the same argument? What might an opponent of this idea be? A psychiatrist? A writer? A musician? A businessman? A politician? A mother? From how many different perspectives and values can a particular text be evaluated? The list is long, but as a reader, you can choose which is best for your own purposes.

Once you do that, it is time to write a response.

Now let's model these skills with a short article written for the *New York Times*, by Steven Pinker, a professor of psychology at Harvard, regarding the discussions going on about the effects of technology on language and the brain. Below is an annotated version and a sample summary.

Mind Over Mass Media

Steven Pinker

Topic introduces a common argument made by many
"Is media damaging important areas of human society?"

NEW forms of media have always caused moral panics: the printing press, newspapers, paperbacks and television were all once denounced as threats to their consumers' brainpower and moral fiber.

Pinker begins argument against this idea.

So too with electronic technologies. PowerPoint, we're told, is reducing discourse to bullet points. Search engines lower our intelligence, encouraging us to skim on the surface of knowledge rather than dive to its depths. Twitter is shrinking our attention spans.

But such panics often fail basic reality checks. When comic books were accused of turning juveniles into delinquents in the 1950s, crime was falling to record lows, just as the denunciations of video games in the 1990s coincided with the great American crime decline. The decades of television, transistor radios and rock videos were also decades in which I.Q. scores rose continuously.

Here he provides historical examp of other notior about media causing social intellectual dam from pop cultu

Pinker provides current examples from science, philosophy, and culture that debunk the notion of "damage by pointing out the success and increasing knowledge in these fields.

For a reality check today, take the state of science, which demands high levels of brainwork and is measured by clear benchmarks of discovery. These days scientists are never far from their e-mail, rarely touch paper and cannot lecture without PowerPoint. If electronic media were hazardous to intelligence, the quality of science would be plummeting. Yet discoveries are multiplying like fruit flies, and progress is dizzying. Other activities in the life of the mind, like philosophy, history and cultural criticism, are likewise flourishing, as anyone who has lost a morning of work to the Web site Arts & Letters Daily can attest.

In the first of these three paragraphs, Pinker introduces the science that the naysayers rely on to claim the damage is occurring, but in the 2nd and 3rd paragraphs he clarifies the oversimplified understanding of that science, and then explains it in detail; experience does not affect "basic information processing" capacities.

Critics of new media sometimes use science itself to press their case, citing research that shows how "experience can change the brain." But cognitive neuroscientists roll their eyes at such talk. Yes, every time we learn a fact or skill the wiring of the brain changes; it's not as if the information is stored in the pancreas. But the existence of neural plasticity does not mean the brain is a blob of clay pounded into shape by experience.

Experience does not revamp the basic information-processing capacities of the brain. Speed-reading programs have long claimed to do just that, but the verdict was rendered by Woody Allen after he read "War and Peace" in one sitting: "It was about Russia." Genuine multitasking, too, has been exposed as a myth, not just by laboratory studies but by the familiar sight of an S.U.V. undulating between lanes as the driver cuts deals on his cellphone.

Moreover, as the psychologists Christopher Chabris and Daniel Simons show in their new book "The Invisible Gorilla: And Other Ways Our Intuitions Deceive Us," the effects of experience are highly specific to the experiences themselves. If you train people to do one thing (recognize shapes, solve math puzzles, find hidden words), they get better at doing that thing, but almost nothing else. Music doesn't make you better at math, conjugating Latin doesn't make you more logical, brain-training games don't make you smarter. Accomplished people don't bulk up their brains with intellectual calisthenics; they immerse themselves in their fields. Novelists read lots of novels, scientists read lots of science.

This sentence makes the connection between the evidence and his argument more clear, and leads us with more detail to his thesis (found at the end of the article).

The effects of consuming electronic media are also likely to be far more limited than the panic implies. Media critics write as if the brain takes on the qualities of whatever it consumes, the informational equivalent of "you are what you eat." As with primitive peoples who believe that eating fierce animals will make them fierce, they assume that watching quick cuts in rock videos turns your mental life into quick cuts or that reading bullet points and Twitter postings turns your thoughts into bullet points and Twitter postings.

Here he acknowledges the problems of distraction, while noting it is not a new problem, arising from new media, but an old one that suggests we deal with it like adults have always dealt with distraction: discipline yourself to realize your situation and behave according to that situation's needs.

Yes, the constant arrival of information packets can be distracting or addictive, especially to people with attention deficit disorder. But distraction is not a new phenomenon. The solution is not to bemoan technology but to develop strategies of self-control, as we do with every other temptation in life. Turn off e-mail or Twitter when you work, put away your Blackberry at dinner time, ask your spouse to call you to bed at a designated hour.

* Thesis statement

And to encourage intellectual depth, don't rail at PowerPoint or Google. It's not as if habits of deep reflection, thorough research and rigorous reasoning ever came naturally to people. They must be acquired in special institutions, which we call universities, and maintained with constant upkeep, which we call analysis, criticism and debate. They are not granted by propping a heavy encyclopedia on your lap, nor are they taken away by efficient access to information on the Internet.

Here Pinker stresses the point that intellectual depth is a thing that has always been taught, and not simply arrived by nature, in institutions such as universities.

The new media have caught on for a reason. Knowledge is increasing exponentially; human brainpower and waking hours are not. Fortunately, the Internet and information technologies are helping us manage, search and retrieve our collective intellectual output at different scales, from Twitter and previews to e-books and online encyclopedias. Far from making us stupid, these technologies are the only things that will keep us smart.   *Thesis and rationale is reiterated in the whole concluding paragraph.*

Steven Pinker, a professor of psychology at Harvard, is the author of The Stuff of Thought.

Now, let's take a look at how the annotations can help us to achieve a summary. Here is a condensed list of the annotations we made:

- ▶ Topic introduces a common argument made by many, "Is media damaging important areas of human society?"
- ▶ Pinker begins argument against this idea (paragraph 3)
- ▶ Here (paragraph 3) he provides historical examples of other notions about technology, such as the printing press, causing social or intellectual damage
- ▶ Here (paragraph 4) Pinker provides current examples from science, philosophy and culture that debunk the notion of "damage by pointing out the success and increasing knowledge in these fields"
- ▶ In the first of these three paragraphs, (paragraphs 5–7) Pinker introduces the science that the naysayers rely on to claim the damage is occurring, but in the second and third paragraphs he clarifies the oversimplified understanding of that science, and then explains it in detail; experience does not affect "basic information-processing" capacities
- ▶ This sentence, "The effects of consuming electronic media are also likely to be far more limited than the panic implies," makes the connection between the evidence and his argument more clear, and leads us with more detail to his thesis (found at the end of the article)
- ▶ Here (paragraph 9) he acknowledges the problems of distraction, while also noting it is not a new problem, and suggests we deal with it like adults have always dealt with distraction: discipline yourself to realize your situation and behave according to that situation's needs
- ▶ Here (paragraph 10) Pinker stresses the point that intellectual depth is a thing that has always been taught, and not simply arrived by nature, in institutions such as universities
- ▶ The last sentence of the article, "Far from making us stupid, these technologies are the only things that will keep us smart" embodies his thesis: his rationale is the whole of the concluding paragraph (the "wrap up")

Or perhaps, you might prefer to use a visual aid, so, using a chart may be helpful:

In the following chart, you could also quote the specific language that provides the evidence in order to include those details in your summary if the purpose of the summary requires it; or, as modeled in chapter 2, you can add a column to ask your questions, or list your agreement or disagreement and examples or ideas you have in response. Simply add more fields to increase the size of the chart.

Author's Main Points	Author's Evidence/Support
Media does not damage our brains or society.	Introduces the common fallacy that media does hurt us; provides examples of earlier technology that has been criticized in the same manner that we now know is harmless.
Arguments that support the idea that media does damage our brains and society rely on poor evidence.	Demonstrates using current science why the naysayers are wrong.
Distraction has always been a problem for human society; discipline of the mind and education support ways to fend off distractions.	Explains that human societies must learn to adapt to the changing tools, and use time-honored strategies that accomplish this.

Now, below is a summary, written for argument, using the above annotations and chart:

Steven Pinker, a Harvard psychology professor, argues in "Mind Over Mass Media," that new media is just *new* media, and that other times of technological change often caused "moral panic" about how these innovations might affect the future of human society, and how they may affect our individual brains. He cites the cry over the invention of the printing press as similar to complaints we hear about "PowerPoint" and "Twitter posts." He argues that as in the past, today, we oversimplify the problem, and panic about its implications. He provides a brief explanation of the science that tells us that our experiences using this technology do not alter the way we think as much as the panic implies. While acknowledging the distractions that new media create, he argues that distractions themselves are not new, and we should deal with new media distractions as any other: with discipline of the "mind over mass media" and educated thinking. He argues that we come to see the new media not as a negative influence, but a tool that will only aid our progress in knowledge and intellect.

The summary above includes the facts most relevant to an argument regarding this topic, more specifically, it included information that supported Pinker's position.

A summary then simply takes our careful annotations of key concepts, ideas and examples, and merges them into a coherent paragraph of summary, while leaving out our own perspectives, values, ideas, and much of the supporting details that Pinker provided. Instead we summarized them, characterizing them into a certain type of detail. In fact, if you look at WHAT was actually annotated, it was a summary of each paragraph, giving main idea, and to some degree a description of that paragraph's purpose in the article. The written summary then, in a way, is a summary of our annotations, if we focused our annotations purposefully, and in this case to highlight the areas that directly related to our own purpose: to argue the influences of new media.

Since this was a summary we might include as part of our own argument (as in an academic essay, or other critical response), we summarize the part that supports or directly refutes our own ideas as in counterargument, a concept we will discuss in detail in chapters 12 and 13.

For example, if, in an essay, you are arguing that media is a damaging force, you might only include in your summary Pinker's ideas as an opposing idea: that discipline and education solve for problems the Internet created. But afterward you must refute Pinker's conclusion. You would argue a counterpoint to Pinker's: not all users of this technology develop disciplined thinking, even when they attend college and universities, and so, as a social influence, the damage can still be done. You would need to provide adequate evidence of this lack of discipline in college graduates, along with other considerations, but in doing all of this, you would build a stronger argument.

Using summary in this way helps to avoid over-quotation in a critical writing assignment. As a rule, only approximately 10 percent of your own text should be direct quotation, and included only because the quote really just says better, or more clearly, what you might paraphrase (See chapter 13) or summarize.

Engaging the Gears: Activity for Practice

Classroom Activity: Making Inferences

Suppose you read an article about a car accident in the newspaper. In that report, you learn facts such as the direction and speed of the vehicles before the crash, the time of the crash, the type of vehicles, and the ages of the victims. Though there is no mention of the drivers' whereabouts prior to the crash, given the facts, or evidentiary information below, what might you infer about the crash or what the drivers were doing right before the crash? Let's try it:

Fact 1	Cars A and B both were traveling north on a two-lane road away from downtown area
Fact 2	Car A is a Honda Civic, blue, with white racing stripes and high performance tires
Fact 3	Car B is a BMW black, with chrome rims and an air spoiler on the back
Fact 4	Estimated Speed of Car A on impact: 100 mph
Fact 5	Estimated speed of Car B on impact: 70 mph
Fact 6	Speed limit for that road: 35 mph
Fact 7	Long tire marks on road leading to Car B
Fact 8	No tire marks leading to Car A
Fact 9	Car B is a little south of Car A, but tracks indicate a swerve away from Car A
Fact 10	Time of Crash: 2 am
Fact 11	Drivers of Cars A and B are minors
Fact 12	Empty alcohol bottles found in trunk of Car A

Classroom Discussion Guide

What logical inference might we make with all of these facts presented in the article? What facts are missing that would help us infer more accurately?

Write down the inference, and indicate the choice of facts you used to make this inference. Share with your classmates, or groupmates.

And, once we infer, is that inference a fact? No, but it does imply what may have happened to cause the crash, what the drivers may have been doing just prior to the crash, and even which car crashed first. The police investigating this scene could use these inferences to guide their questioning of the witnesses. The victims themselves would have to corroborate, or in the event they could not, or would not, more facts would be needed to determine the truth. Inference is not fact, since facts are information that can be verified. Inferences that rely on too little, or poor quality of evidence, should be avoided.

First Writing Activity

Summary Practice

Select a film or television show you have recently viewed. Write a summary of the film or television show. Critically think (metacognate) about the strategy you used to focus on summary and avoid critique or opinion.

A variation on this activity would be to locate a classmate who has viewed the same movie or television show you have viewed. Separately, compose individual summaries. Compare the summaries and discuss the differences and similarities.

Your instructor may ask you to complete a short reading and compose an academic summary. Or, you may be asked to practice both!

Second Writing Activity

Synthesis Practice

Both the following article, by David Ulin, and a TED conference presentation by James McWhorter, (http://www.ted.com/talks/john_mcwhorter_txtng_is_killing_language_jk.html) discuss the same topic that Steven Pinker discusses in the article we just summarized above.

- a. Critically read the article, annotating carefully from a close reading.
- b. View McWhorter's "Ted Talk."
- c. Write your own summary of each author, including Steven Pinker's article "Mind over Mass Media."
- d. Now using these three summaries as your sources, synthesize their ideas about how technology affects people in order to create your own idea about the ways that new media is shaping our world, our sense of ourselves and our minds.
- e. Write that idea in one or two sentences.

Your assignment should then include three summary paragraphs followed by one or two sentences explaining your idea about technology's effects on individuals or society.

Additional reading: "Is Google Making Us Stupid? What the Internet is doing to our brains," http://www.theatlantic.com/magazine/archive/2008/07/is-googlemaking-us-stupid/306868/.

The Lost Art of Reading

David L. Ulin

The relentless cacophony that is life in the twenty-first century can make settling in with a book difficult even for lifelong readers and those who are paid to do it.

August 9, 2009

Sometime late last year—I don't remember when, exactly—I noticed I was having trouble sitting down to read. That's a problem if you do what I do, but it's an even bigger problem if you're the kind of person I am. Since I discovered reading, I've always been surrounded by stacks of books. I read my way through camp, school, nights, weekends; when my girlfriend and I backpacked through Europe after college graduation, I had to buy a suitcase to accommodate the books I picked up along the way. For her, the highlight of the trip was the man in Florence who offered a tour of the Uffizi. For me, it was the serendipity of stumbling across a London bookstall that had once been owned by the Scottish writer Alexander Trocchi, whose work, then as now, I adored. After we got married four years later, we spent part of our honeymoon in Dollarton, outside Vancouver, British Columbia, visiting the beach where "Under the Volcano" author Malcolm Lowry had lived for more than a decade with his wife Marjorie in a squatter's shack.

In his 1967 memoir, *Stop-Time*, Frank Conroy describes his initiation into literature as an adolescent on Manhattan's Upper East Side. "I'd lie in bed . . .," he writes, "and read one paperback after another until two or three in the morning. . . . The real world dissolved and I was free to drift in fantasy, living a thousand lives, each one more powerful, more accessible,and more real than my own." I know that boy: Growing up in the same neighborhood, I *was* that boy. And I have always read like that, although these days, I find myself driven by the idea that in their intimacy, the one-to-one attention they require, books are not tools to retreat from but rather to understand and interact with the world.

So what happened? It isn't a failure of desire so much as one of will. Or not will, exactly, but focus: the ability to still my mind long enough to inhabit someone else's world, and to let that someone else inhabit mine. Reading is an act of contemplation, perhaps the only act in which we allow ourselves to merge with the consciousness of another human being. We possess the books we read, animating the waiting stillness of their language, but they possess us also, filling us with thoughts and observations, asking us to make them part of ourselves. This is what Conroy was hinting at in his account of adolescence, the way books enlarge us by giving direct access to experiences not our own. In order for this to work, however, we need a certain type of silence, an ability to filter out the noise.

Such a state is increasingly elusive in our over-networked culture, in which every rumor and mundanity is blogged and tweeted. Today, it seems it is not contemplation we seek but an odd sort of distraction masquerading as being in the know. Why? Because of the illusion that illumination is based on speed, that it is more important to react than to think, that we live in a culture in which something is attached to every bit of time.

Here we have my reading problem in a nutshell, for books insist we take the opposite position, that we immerse, slow down. "After September 11," Mona Simpson wrote as part of a 2001 *LA Weekly* round-table on reading during wartime, "I didn't read books for the news. Books, by their nature, are never new enough." By this, Simpson doesn't mean she stopped reading; instead, at a moment when it felt as if time was on fast forward, she relied on books to pull back from the onslaught, to distance herself from the present as a way of reconnecting with a more elemental sense of who we are. merits my attention, when in fact it's mostly just a series of disconnected riffs and fragments that add up to the anxiety of the age.

Of course, the source of my distraction is somewhat different: not an event of great significance but the usual ongoing trivialities. I am too susceptible, it turns out, to the tumult of the culture, the sound and fury signifying nothing. For many years, I have read, like E. I. Lonoff in Philip Roth's "The Ghost Writer," primarily at night—a few hours every evening once my wife and kids have gone to bed. These days, however, after spending hours reading e-mail and fielding phone calls in the office, tracking stories across countless websites, I find it difficult to quiet down. I pick up a book and read a paragraph; then my mind wanders and I check my e-mail, drift onto the Internet, pace the house before returning to the page. Or I want to do these things but don't. I force myself to remain still, to follow whatever I'm reading until the inevitable moment I give myself over to the flow. Eventually I get there, but some nights it takes 20 pages to settle down. What I'm struggling with is the encroachment of the buzz, the sense that there is something out there that merits my attention, when in fact it's mostly just a series of disconnected riffs and fragments that add up to the anxiety of the age.

Yet there is time, if we want it. Contemplation is not only possible but necessary, especially in light of all the overload. In her recent essay collection "The Winter Sun" (Graywolf: 196 pp, $15 paper), Fanny Howe quotes Simone Weil: "One must believe in the reality of time. Otherwise one is just dreaming." That's the point precisely, for without time we lose a sense of narrative, that most essential connection to who we are. We live in time; we understand ourselves in relation to it, but in our culture, time collapses into an ever-present now. How do we pause when we must know everything instantly? How do we ruminate when we are constantly expected to respond? How do we immerse in something (an idea, an emotion, a decision) when we are no longer willing to give ourselves the space to reflect?

This is where real reading comes in—because it demands that space, because by drawing us back from the present, it restores time to us in a fundamental way. There is the present-tense experience of reading, but also the chronology of the narrative, as well as of the characters and author, all of whom bear their own relationships to time. There is the fixity of the text, which doesn't change whether written yesterday or a thousand years ago. St. Augustine composed his "Confessions" in AD 397, but when he details his spiritual upheaval, his attempts to find meaning in the face of transient existence, the immediacy of his longing obliterates the temporal divide. "I cannot seem to feel alive unless I am alert," Charles Bowden writes in his recent book, "Some of the Dead Are Still Breathing" (Houghton Mifflin Harcourt: 244 pp., $24), "and I cannot feel alert unless I push past the point where I have control." That is what reading has to offer: a way to eclipse the boundaries, which is a form of giving up control.

Here we have the paradox, since in giving up control we somehow gain it, by being brought in contact with ourselves. "My experience," William James once observed, "is what I agree to attend to"—a line Winifred Gallagher uses as the epigraph of "Rapt: Attention and the Focused Life" (Penguin Press: 244 pp., $25.95). In Gallagher's analysis, attention is a lens through which to consider not just identity but desire. Who do we want to be, she asks, and how do we go about that process of becoming in a world of endless options, distractions, possibilities?

These are elementary questions, and for me, they cycle back to reading, to the focus it requires. When I was a kid, maybe 12 or 13, my grandmother used to get mad at me for attending family functions with a book. Back then, if I'd had the language for it, I might have argued that the world within the pages was more compelling than the world without; I was reading both to escape and to be engaged. All these years later, I find myself in a not-dissimilar position, in which reading has become an act of meditation, with all of meditation's attendant difficulty and grace. I sit down. I try to make a place for silence. It's harder than it used to be, but still, I read.

Ulin is book editor of the *Los Angeles Times*.

CHAPTER FOUR

From Critical Ideas to the Thesis Statement

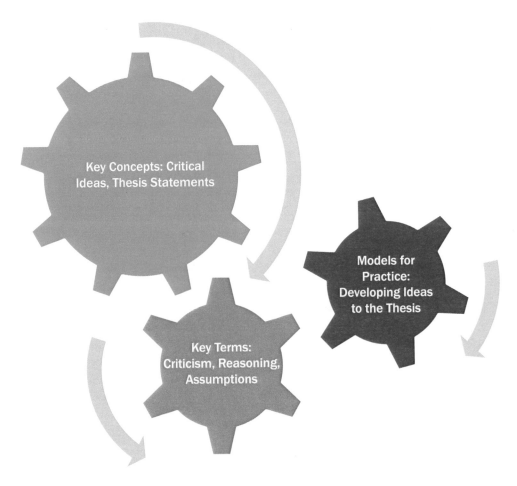

Nearly every man who develops an idea works it up to the point where it looks impossible, and then he gets discouraged. That's not the place to become discouraged.

—Thomas Edison

There is only one way to avoid criticism; do nothing, say nothing, and be nothing.

—Aristotle

What Are Critical Ideas?

Chapter 3 presented a brief overview of the definition and purpose of analysis. Critical ideas and critical thinking often emerge from analysis. Analysis includes careful observations, engaged and active reading of various quality source materials, reasoned and reasonable responses to reading materials, and careful consideration of various perspectives.

As we embark on forming critical ideas about a subject or subject area, we must ask ourselves a few questions:

1. What makes up our "satellite knowledge" or the knowledge we bring with us?
   a. What is our existing knowledge or understanding regarding the subject?
   b. What are our assumptions—or—what do we think we know?

2. What new knowledge have we acquired through reading and discussion?
   a. Does the new knowledge conflict with prior knowledge?
   b. How does this new knowledge affect our prior understanding of the subject matter?
   c. How can we integrate the new knowledge with the prior knowledge?

3. What new ideas, understandings, or solutions emerge?

Once we begin to form answers in response to these questions, we can begin to develop our critical ideas. But what do we do with our answers? What if the new knowledge conflicts with old knowledge? Must we solve that problem first? Sometimes, the answer is yes, and sometimes our answers tell us that we must engage in discussions, debates, or an honest evaluation of the sources for both new and old knowledge to develop a cohesive set of facts. Sometimes, the work of developing a solution to this kind of conflict is done by continuing the process of developing ideas until a solution emerges. It often depends on the conflict itself, and of course how strongly it interferes with our ideas. Yet, having these answers, or partial answers, makes it easier to shape the critical idea.

Criticism Is Necessary

The word criticism can stir our emotions, and some of our emotional responses can feel negative. While the word criticism may put us on the defensive, it is important to understand that there are different forms of criticism. In our everyday lives, the use of the word *criticism* usually implies a negative judgment about us or something we care about. And judging is exactly what it is. But, as readers and writers, we can view criticism as critique, or a thoughtfully reasoned judgment. To critique, or to engage in (or receive) criticism is to evaluate a text using specific criteria.

If we looked at the keyword here, *criticism*, we know, that to be a critic, or to critique, or apply criteria is to look at the value or merits of an object, person, place, action or idea, and measure that against some type of "norm," or expected value. Notice *criticism*, *critique*, and *criteria* all share the same Latin root: *crit*, which means: to separate, or choose. How we make that choice depends on the field we study, or topic we are critiquing. Our choices would look very different when applied to the topics or texts of medicine or history or sports. But the questions, what we seek, are often similar:

What is valuable?

What is reliable?

What is included?

What is left out?

Why was it left out?

What questions remain after reading a text?

For example, given the topic of *good meals*, let's ask ourselves, "What makes up a good meal?" First we would have to define "good." Do we mean nutritious? Tasty? Filling? Inexpensive? Or a combination of all or some of these criteria.

Perhaps we decide that the criteria of a *good meal* is one that is nutritious, tasty, and affordable.

Imagine then that we are offered this $5.00 meal:

As we critique this meal, keep in mind our criteria: nutritious, tasty, and inexpensive.

► Is this hamburger meal nutritious? (How can our prior knowledge help us decide?)

► Is this type of meal (a hamburger) tasty? (How does our prior experience help us answer this question?)

► Is this hamburger meal inexpensive? (How can our prior knowledge and experience help us decide?)

Imagine then that we are offered a salad meal for $7.00 from the same restaurant that offers the hamburger meal.

► Is this salad meal nutritious? (How can our prior knowledge help us decide?)

► Is this type of meal tasty? (How does our prior experience help us answer this question?)

► Is this salad meal inexpensive? (How can our prior knowledge and experience help us decide?)

► How does the hamburger meal compare to the salad meal?

► What standards and guidelines will you use to begin the critique?

As we analyze the nutrition, taste, and affordability values of the hamburger meal and the salad meal, we may find that we discover **new ideas**. For example, we may research what doctors, nutritionists, and food professionals have discovered about how beef and vegetables affect our health.

The process of analysis and criticism (combined) can add to an existing conversation about the subject of how we make our food choices. Who chooses the hamburger meal? Who chooses the salad meal? How are their decisions based? What additional information do you obtain in listening to how others make a choice?

What problems arise as we discuss this question of the hamburger versus the salad? Some may select the hamburger meal because it meets the criteria of "inexpensive," though it may fail the nutrition qualification. The cost of the meal may be a higher priority for them, since they may not be able to afford the salad. Are there possible solutions to this?

Take some time to think about or discuss with peers or family the "hamburger versus salad" example above. Determine how many different critical ideas emerge from the discussion. Keep in mind that while a debate may occur, the focal point should be to track how many critical ideas emerge from the critique of the situation.

What Is the Difference Between an Opinion and a Critical Idea?

Avoiding Bias in Critical Thinking

We can be biased in favor or against an idea, a group, or an individual. Bias is often "created" when we are exposed to a single view or understanding. For example, Morgan Spurlock, the director and "star" of the 2004 documentary, *Super Size Me*, presents himself as a human "lab rat" by overindulging in fast food (mostly hamburgers) to prove the negative impact fast food has on our health. Clearly, Spurlock's main goal is to persuade his audience to reduce (if not eliminate) the consumption of fast food hamburgers. However, in the same documentary Spurlock introduces us to Don Gorske. Don Gorske, author of 22,477 *Big Macs* boasts eating over 20,000 Big Mac hamburgers with no negative health impact. Why would Spurlock include Gorske's life-long "experiment" if it would be detrimental to his argument? To avoid bias, Spurlock points out that Gorske eats only one Big Mac at a sitting—he does not indulge in french fries or other side bites.

The critical idea that emerges from the seeming contradiction is that fast food hamburgers are not the only contributing factor to the negative health impact of fast food—but rather—that it is a combination of menu items as well as portion size. By avoiding bias, Spurlock offers a more complex analysis of the problem of fast food consumption.

A critical analysis based on critical thinking can lead us to several new ideas and several new conclusions. Perhaps, we conclude that while the salad lunch is $2.00 more than the hamburger lunch, in the long run maintaining good health is valuable.

Or perhaps, after analyzing this particular situation, the critical conclusion is to buy a hamburger, exclude the purchase of french fries, and exchange the soda for ice water. A hamburger and ice water lunch comes to $3.00. What has happened is that through forming a critical idea we create more options, or in this case, come to realize that there are a variety of choices than what is superficially apparent.

Why Are Critical Ideas Important?

We all have varied opinions and ideas of a large number of critical (and popular) issues that impact our daily lives. When we must face a situation and act, we must ask questions that will lead us to the appropriate action. We ask: Why does this matter? How do we determine the value this situation, event, or text for that matter? If someone else is doing all the thinking/writing—and such authors are engaging in the development of critical ideas—why should we engage in the conversation (beyond reading)? The answer, of course, is that we, too, are a part of the world, often asked to vote, contribute, or otherwise examine and respond to the numerous issues we face in a complex world.

To do this effectively, we must learn to respond critically, yet also efficiently so that our engagement with the world and the contributions we might make feel both necessary and possible.

Let us examine a different situation: Should we change the freeway speed limits? Higher or lower? Why?

While individually, we might believe that the speed limit should not be raised, others may have differing ideas. Our opinions regarding maintaining the current speed limit on freeways at sixty-five miles per hour may be shaped by recent reports on increased accidents in our geographic location. Other drivers may argue that automobiles have been engineered to be safer in accidents, thus increasing the speed limit is no longer as dangerous as in the past. Of course, there are many valid arguments regarding this issue. Engaging in a few thinking activities can help to raise important critical ideas.

DIALOGUE
ASSUMPTIONS
GENERALIZATIONS

Dialogue: Taking your ideas to others and discussing them can help to refine your ideas and improve the quality of your ideas.

Here is a hypothetical dialogue regarding this topic to help you see how a train of thought regarding highway speed limits develops into critical ideas:

> Jane's initial opinion: Increasing the speed limit should not be a problem. Cars are safer. All cars have standard air bags; they are engineered to handle better in all types of weather. Many cars are designed to safely handle high impact crashes. I can't tell you how many times I have seen a car accident on the freeway where both cars are badly damaged, but, the drivers and passengers are standing outside the cars, unhurt.

While Jane's idea regarding increasing the speed limit appears valid (there is some general support and general observations provided as evidence), what further critical ideas can we develop that might make an essay or article on the issue a bit more complex and sophisticated?

We might mention, in responding to Jane, that safer cars do not always account for safer drivers. A car may be built well, but the point is to avoid accidents as much as possible. Increasing the speed limit means drivers will have to be skilled enough to drive at higher speeds.

This brief dialogue already has Jane considering alternative critical ideas: driver errors are an important factor in considering changes to the speed limit.

Perhaps she also has the opportunity to discuss the topic with someone who is older than she is:

> Grandfather: "I recently watched a news report that a new problem is distracted driving. Drivers are making phone calls, texting, even watching movies while driving. Technology has improved communication, but it does not prevent people from trying to multitask while driving."

Perhaps Jane takes her grandfather's opinion into perspective. Since she is looking at the way cars have become safer, she, who supports increasing the speed limit, might reply to her grandfather's statement by adding that car companies are doing their best to integrate communication devices safely. Some cars have hands-free communication technologies designed to keep drivers from being distracted.

Here communicating with peers, instructors or others helps us to both expand and refine our original opinion, and sometimes change it altogether!

Assumptions: We often read or take in new information with a set of assumptions on a subject. We assume some things to be true, and we don't question them, but use them to form new opinions. Dialogue and discussion can either reinforce or challenge the assumptions we make. If our assumptions are challenged we are forced to think differently than what we might expect.

Jane's original opinion that higher speeds should be allowed was formed in part with the assumption that driving faster is a more efficient way to arrive at a destination. We can see this assumption by examining her opinion and asking, "Why would someone want higher speed limits? Or why would someone want to drive faster? Then we see her assumption: traveling at faster speeds gets us to our destinations faster. Her conclusion: higher speeds limits are more efficient.

Now we examine, or question, her assumption and see that it might be correct if there were no obstacles in the way, such as traffic lights and other drivers or pedestrians. Then, we see that her assumption is incorrect because it failed to consider obstacles that, if not noticed at higher speeds, might cause accidents, and we can determine that her opinion is faulty because it was formed by a faulty assumption (for more discussion regarding assumptions, see chapter 11 on logic and reasoning.)

It is important that we practice understanding what assumptions we bring to our opinions, and question them in order to form solid critical ideas.

Generalizations: We also often form our ideas from a base set of generalizations. Generalizations are formed by taking specific examples, or experiences, and applying that to a general statement. Generalizations are common ways people form ideas. We take a specific set of examples and then apply that to a whole class of ideas. For example, Jane might have based her assumption about higher speeds being more efficient by generalizing the few times she got to work or school earlier when she drove faster. But we must be careful not to make hasty generalizations, or to rely on them too much because it only takes one instance contrary to the generalization, to make it faulty (see logical fallacies in chapter 11).

After examining her ideas, reasoning her way toward a solid critical idea, Jane might begin to change her position. This phenomenon is quite common when we begin to think critically, since our "gut" feelings or assumptions about topics are often not enough to develop good critical ideas. Critical reading and thinking does that.

So, now Jane might argue that freeway speed limits should not be increased. While her initial "gut" feeling about speed and car safety might still be correct, when examining it against the realities of driving conditions and driver skills, her feelings about increasing the speed limits becomes less persuasive. This is especially true if she also examines her own initial ideas that relied on the assumption that speed equals arriving more "quickly" as a false or problematic idea.

So, Jane concludes that since we do not live in a world with no obstacles, driving faster might not be the most efficient, and can be more dangerous. She also concludes that though automobiles have been made safer (in the event of an accident), such engineering does not take into consideration the possibility for human error: faster automobiles require advanced driving skills, and drivers become distracted by communication technologies. Taken altogether, these ideas point to Jane the critical idea that drivers need time to respond to conditions on the road, and faster speeds diminish the time drivers might have to respond.

Gathering different viewpoints can direct us to better research and a more focused main point. Once we have made every effort to study all aspects of an issue or concept, we can move forward to developing a purpose that is directed toward the needs of our readers.

Jane is now ready to improve her revised critical ideas by making them much more specific and focused. After taking a position that an increase in speed limits might result in unsafe road conditions, she can select the evidence to support her ideas by doing research about who shares her idea, why or why not, etc. Then she can organize her critical ideas around a thesis statement and present her evidence in ways that suit her audience's needs.

Addressing the Expectations and Needs of the Reader

In chapter 1, we discussed the importance of considering how to present critical ideas to an audience. Our audience can be a peer group, an instructor (or in some cases, several instructors), our community, family, and friends, and sometimes complete strangers. While shaping our ideas to serve a purpose, we must also actively engage our reader in that purpose. Once we determine who our audience is we can begin carefully selecting supporting ideas and evidence that will keep our audience engaged and informed. We can use the guide from chapter 1 on audience to decide who our audience might be:

Age
Education
Experience or a lack of experience
Gender or social class
Culture or sub-culture
Political or religious beliefs
Expectations of writing style and topic

Now, Jane has her topic (speed limits) critically examined (should not be increased) and her purpose (to *persuade* her audience that a proposal that increases speed limits is a bad idea.) And she knows her audience: readers of her campus newspaper. Because she is lending her opinion about a current proposal, rather than reporting facts about the proposal, she must choose the editorial genre, rather than an informative news article.

After establishing the rhetorical situation above, the next step for Jane is to examine how best to formulate her writing using the information she gathered, and the position Jane arrived at, to meet the expectations and needs of her audience. Since her audience is an academic audience with varying age groups, yet a base age of adulthood, and a base education of high school, etc., and her purpose is to persuade in a newspaper editorial, her audience will likely expect her to present a thesis statement, and evidence to support her thesis. To develop her thesis statement and support for it, she should begin with these questions:

1. What does her audience need to know (providing background and foundation)?

   They don't know that the proposal to increase the speed limits is under review.

   Most of her audience probably drives to school, but they may not know of the criteria used to determine speed limits.

   The may not know the statistics about driver error, accident rates in high speed limit zones, etc.

2. What might her audience already know (predicting general understanding to avoid repetition)?

   They know there are speed limits to protect drivers and passengers.

   They may also feel that speed limits are arbitrary, or out of date.

   They may also assume, falsely, as she did, that driving faster gets you to your destination more quickly.

3. What would she like her audience to understand (developing purpose)?

   That speed limits, as they are, protect and create efficient travel, and increasing them could cause more accidents and fatalities.

4. How can her audience use her critical ideas (creating a connection with the audience)?

   To slow down their own speeds, or to be more tolerant of slower drivers.

   To actively participate in the proposal review and argue against increased speed limits.

5. Who benefits from her critical ideas?

   All who drive, insurance companies, and their customers: general public safety benefits.

6. How can she apply the elements ethos, pathos, and logos to support her critical ideas and appeal to the needs of the audience (or appeal to the values of the audience)?

   Since her audience is in a busy city, most drivers are impatient to go faster, and therefore get where they are going more quickly, and her audience is an also a general academic one, expecting a fair and balanced approach to ethos, logos and pathos (see chapter 1). The logic she came up with (driver skill, distractions and the lack of evidence that speed increases arrival times) is most appealing to an academic audience, but to really change their minds, some appeals to pathos in the form of examples of accidents caused by higher speed limits, distracted drivers, etc., might be used too.

Now, having properly applied the writing process step of prewriting (gathering ideas, formulating a critical response to those ideas, taking a position and considering her rhetorical situation and rhetorical elements), Jane is ready to write her thesis statement, organize her ideas and then draft her newspaper article.

But . . . wait! How does a writer go about writing the thesis statement? What is a thesis statement?

Writing the Thesis Statement

What Is a Thesis Statement?

A thesis, from Greek, meaning "proposition," is a critical idea "proposed." So, a thesis *statement* is that main critical idea expressed in language to serve a purpose, usually to persuade or analyze, but can also be used to inform, or educate. By expressing a critical idea in a specific form, the thesis statement also aids the reader in a number of important ways:

► Establishes the trajectory of the essay (or other text/material being composed) to provide the reader with "fair warning" about the subject and attitude, or position that is presented before them.

► Allows the reader to understand the approach of the material (establishing genre). Will this be an argument? A comparative and informative essay?

► Provides a map or outline for the reader to follow. While keeping your main idea in mind using the thesis statement's propositions, the reader can predict what evidence or ideas you will examine to support your ideas, thereby keeping them focused on your main idea.

► Allows readers to evaluate your evidence and examples against your main idea to better understand your critical thinking and the conclusion, or critical idea you arrived at.

► Makes the writer's purpose clear, and provides the reader a sense of understanding of why the essay is important and what the author hopes to establish. It demonstrates a reasonable, debatable position on a specific topic.

So the elements of a thesis statement must address all of these important tasks. There are three elements of a thesis statement that will do this:

► the topic
► your position/opinion
► your reasons, or rationale, for your position

Obviously, a topic is needed. Just as in your rhetorical situation, if you don't have a topic, you have, literally, nothing yet to say!

Additionally, a position, or opinion on the topic is needed. The position, or opinion you hold, can take a couple of forms: argument and persuasion.

▶ An argument thesis presents multiple sides of a debatable topic, yet the thesis statement indicates which argument the author proposes is the best argument, by placing the author on a particular "side" of the debate, or promoting a particular aspect of the debate.

▶ A persuasive thesis asks the reader to change a belief, perspective, or, behavior, as it can serve as a "call to action."

These terms are often used interchangeably: a persuasive thesis argues for a change in thinking or behavior, while an argument thesis *persuades* the reader that a particular side of a debate is more valuable or "correct" than another.

It is also important to recognize that an argument is not necessarily, or merely, a "pro" or "con" debate. Such positions are often oversimplified and can prove reductive or contrary to the formation of critical ideas by presenting only two sides to the argument. Think back on the discussion of the fast food hamburger meal versus a fast food salad meal. Why only the two choices? A pro/con debate would have left out the other option discovered: choosing a hamburger without the fries and soda might be as equally nutritious and less expensive than the original options presented.

A reasoned opinion is also a requirement when stating your position. All opinions are not created equally, nor are of the same quality. The opinions found in a strong and sound thesis statement are reasonable, and can be reasonably argued against. Opinions that rest without supportable reasoning, such as food preferences, or other "likes and dislikes" are not positions for debate. Your opinion on an issue can only be argued if sufficient reasoning supports those ideas, and only if arguing the opposing position isn't ridiculously impossible.

For example, one cannot argue that child abuse is wrong and should be stopped. Although on the surface, this seems to be the only argument one could make about child abuse, this is not a reasonable thesis because it is not something one could argue against since you can't reasonably say that child abuse is good and should be encouraged. That idea is not a reasonable position from anyone's perspective. But might you argue that current measures taken to prevent child abuse are inadequate and propose changes that might improve the lives of children? Yes, that we can argue about, since there may be many ways to prevent abuse and improve children's lives.

The final element, or component, is to reveal the reasoning, or critical thinking you used to develop your position, so that readers can see how you arrived at your position, and use it to evaluate the effectiveness of your argument and its support.

Constructing a Thesis Statement

Let's return to Jane's critical ideas about a proposal to increase the speed limits. Here is a recap:

▶ Jane concluded that increasing speed limits is a bad idea. Her reasoning (evidence) suggests that while cars are safer, driver skills, distractions and impatience are still dangerous factors at higher speeds.

So, if we look carefully at her critical ideas we see a thesis emerging. Now which aspects of her critical ideas fit the elements of thesis statement?

▶ Her topic: increasing speed limits proposal

▶ Her position: speed limits should not be increased

▶ Her reasoning: better driver skills are needed at those speeds, drivers are increasingly distracted, and faster speeds do not get you to your destination more quickly

Now how do we get this into a single statement? One of the easier ways to do this is to recognize that we can use cause and effect language to get started. Since the elements of a thesis statement ask you to indicate the *reasons* why you have that opinion, we can say "I believe this (position) about (topic) **because** *of these reasons* (reasoning)."

This sentence, however, written out in this way would be terribly simplistic, and possibly too wordy to be a polished thesis statement, but it helps to get started that way to be sure you have a solid, working thesis statement. Then you can proceed to drafting your text. Later, once you have completed drafting your text, you can revise and edit to improve all of the language, including the wordiness or simplicity of your thesis statement.

Let's try it and provide Jane with a good workable thesis:

(I believe) The proposal to increase speed limits should not be implemented because drivers do not have the skills they need to drive safely at higher speeds, drivers are becoming increasingly distracted, and an increase in speed limits does not make travel time more efficient.

This thesis statement has all of the elements of a thesis statement, a topic, position and a rationale, or the reasoning used to arrive at the position Jane took.

But, is it a sophisticated thesis? Can it be improved?

These are questions you can ask later in the editing stage of the writing process. For now, it provides the map needed to plan the organization of the essay you are writing, or the presentation you are giving, or the succinct opener needed for a public hearing at the town hall you might be attending.

Note that there is no standard "length" for a well-constructed thesis statement. The length of the thesis statement, and the complexity of the thesis statement depends upon the subject matter and the depth of the exploration of the subject matter, your purpose and your audience: what rhetorical situation is present.

Also, note that there is no standard "location" of a thesis statement. A thesis statement can appear somewhere in the first two or three paragraphs. A thesis statement can be restated within the body of the essay in several parts. A thesis statement can occur in the final paragraphs of an essay. As we develop as writers we learn how the genre, audience expectations and the purpose of an essay can determine where our thesis statement will be best placed.

Academic essays often require the thesis in the opening (or second or third, depending on length of paper) paragraph because academics have a specific expectation: to be informed of the before argument that resulted from the thinking. They want to evaluate the evidence you present while you present it (as they read), not at the end, after all of the evidence is presented. But if you read essays or articles written for general audiences, or other non-academic audiences, the thesis statement can be placed elsewhere, and be written in different form.

Non-academic thesis statements often omit the reasoning element, and instead choose a thesis that implies the reasoning. We can infer the reasoning from the evidence itself (since this is where your positions come from), where in academic writing, it should be explicitly claimed. If we made Jane's thesis statement above an implicit or implied thesis, it may read,

> The proposal to increase speed limits won't accomplish what it claims and may put motorists at risk.

This thesis would likely come at the end of a set of evidence (often body paragraphs in an essay) that explains its position explicitly, and in detail. It also may come at the end of an introduction that lays out the evidence generally (later discussed in detail in the body of the argument), so that restating it in the thesis would make it seem redundant.

Yet in all cases, the thesis remains as a reasonable critical idea formed through the process of critical thinking—analysis, inference, synthesis, and evaluation—and as the main idea of your text.

Engaging the Gears: Activities for Practice

Classroom Activity: Practicing the Thesis Statement

Below is a prompt and a student response. Examine the critical ideas this student developed, and use them to help her or him write a thesis statement.

Prompt: Compose a 200-word response to the question, "What are the advantages and disadvantages of mandatory school uniforms?"

In some Los Angeles public schools wearing a uniform is optional for students. Most students prefer to wear their own clothes. Other students wear the uniform because they (or their parents) do not want to spend time thinking about what to wear for school everyday. Another reason is that some people are on a limited budget and they do not want to spend excessively on clothing for school. Most schools have rules about dressing appropriately. Boys should not wear baggy clothing. Girls should dress modestly. If wearing uniforms becomes mandatory in schools students will be required to wear a uniform everyday. They will not be able to wear other kinds of clothing.

Making uniforms mandatory will limit clothing choices. But uniforms do not allow students to judge other students by clothing. Most students do not realize they can be friends without judging each other by what they wear. Sometimes, students who wear more expensive or brand name clothing become the popular clique.

Parents can save money with the uniform only rule. They still have to buy the uniforms but they will save money over time. Parents do not have to feel bad if they cannot afford to buy their children expensive, trendy clothing.

First Writing Activity

Critical Ideas to the Thesis Statement Practice

This assignment is designed to give you some practice at developing critical ideas and then communicating those ideas in a thesis statement. Read, annotate, and summarize the article below. Then use the questions and guidelines that follow to develop critical ideas and a thesis statement.

Why the Rich Don't Give to Charity

The wealthiest Americans donate 1.3 percent of their income; the poorest, 3.2 percent. What's up with that?

Ken Stern

When Mort Zuckerman, the New York City real-estate and media mogul, lavished $200 million on Columbia University in December to endow the Mortimer B. Zuckerman Mind Brain Behavior Institute, he did so with fanfare suitable to the occasion: the press conference was attended by two Nobel laureates, the president of the university, the mayor, and journalists from some of New York's major media outlets. Many of the 12 other individual charitable gifts that topped $100 million in the U.S. last year were showered with similar attention: $150 million from Carl Icahn to the Mount Sinai School of Medicine, $125 million from Phil Knight to the Oregon Health & Science University, and $300 million from Paul Allen to the Allen Institute for Brain Science in Seattle, among them. If you scanned the press releases, or drove past the many university buildings, symphony halls, institutes, and stadiums named for their benefactors, or for that matter read the histories of grand giving by the Rockefellers, Carnegies, Stanfords, and Dukes, you would be forgiven for thinking that the story of charity in this country is a story of epic generosity on the part of the American rich.

It is not. One of the most surprising, and perhaps confounding, facts of charity in America is that the people who can least afford to give are the ones who donate the greatest percentage of their income. In 2011, the wealthiest Americans—those with earnings in the top 20 percent—contributed on average 1.3 percent of their income to charity. By comparison, Americans at the base of the income pyramid—those in the bottom 20 percent—donated 3.2 percent of their income. The relative generosity of lower-income Americans is accentuated by the fact that, unlike middle-class and wealthy donors, most of them cannot take advantage of the charitable tax deduction, because they do not itemize deductions on their income-tax returns.

But why? Lower-income Americans are presumably no more intrinsically generous (or "prosocial," as the sociologists say) than anyone else. However, some experts have speculated that the wealthy may be less generous—that the personal drive to accumulate wealth may be inconsistent with the idea of communal support. Last year, Paul Piff, a psychologist at UC Berkeley, published research that correlated wealth with an increase in unethical behavior: "While having money doesn't necessarily make anybody anything," Piff later told New York magazine, "the rich are way more likely to prioritize their own self-interests above the interests of other people." They are, he continued, "more likely to exhibit characteristics that we would stereotypically associate with, say, assholes." Colorful statements aside, Piff's research on the giving habits of different social classes—while not directly refuting the asshole theory—suggests that other, more complex factors are at work. In a series of controlled experiments, lower-income people and people who identified themselves as being on a relatively low social rung were consistently more generous with limited goods than upper-class participants were. Notably, though, when both groups were exposed to a sympathy-eliciting video on child poverty, the compassion of the wealthier group began to rise, and the groups' willingness to help others became almost identical.

If Piff's research suggests that exposure to need drives generous behavior, could it be that the isolation of wealthy Americans from those in need is a cause of their relative stinginess? Patrick Rooney, the associate dean at the Indiana University School of Philanthropy, told me that greater exposure to and identification with the challenges of meeting basic needs may create "higher empathy" among lower-income donors. His view is supported by a recent study by *The Chronicle of Philanthropy,* in which researchers analyzed giving habits across all American ZIP codes. Consistent with previous studies, they found that less affluent ZIP codes gave relatively more. Around Washington, D.C., for instance, middle- and lower-income neighborhoods, such as Suitland and Capitol Heights in Prince George's County, Maryland, gave proportionally more than the tony neighborhoods of Bethesda, Maryland, and McLean, Virginia. But the researchers also found something else: differences in behavior among wealthy households, depending on the type of neighborhood they lived in. Wealthy people who lived in homogeneously affluent areas—areas where more than 40 percent of households earned at least $200,000 a year—were less generous than comparably wealthy people who lived in more socioeconomically diverse surroundings. It seems that insulation from people in need may dampen the charitable impulse.

Wealth affects not only how much money is given but to whom it is given. The poor tend to give to religious organizations and social-service charities, while the wealthy prefer to support colleges and universities, arts organizations, and museums. Of the 50 largest individual gifts to public charities in 2012, 34 went to educational institutions, the vast majority of them colleges and universities, like Harvard, Columbia, and Berkeley, that cater to the nation's and the world's elite. Museums and arts organizations such as the Metropolitan Museum of Art received nine of these major gifts, with the remaining donations spread among medical facilities and fashionable charities like the Central Park Conservancy. Not a single one of them went to a social-service organization or to a charity that principally serves the poor and the dispossessed. More gifts in this group went to elite prep schools (one, to the Hackley School in Tarrytown, New York) than to any of our nation's largest social-service organizations, including United Way, the Salvation Army, and Feeding America (which got, among them, zero).

Underlying our charity system—and our tax code—is the premise that individuals will make better decisions regarding social investments than will our representative government. Other developed countries have a very different arrangement, with significantly higher individual tax rates and stronger social safety nets, and significantly lower charitable-contribution rates. We have always made a virtue of individual philanthropy, and Americans tend to see our large, independent charitable sector as crucial to our country's public spirit. There is much to admire in our approach to charity, such as the social capital that is built by individual participation and volunteerism. But our charity system is also fundamentally regressive, and works in favor of the institutions of the elite. The pity is, most people still likely believe that, as Michael Bloomberg once said, "there's a connection between being generous and being successful." There is a connection, but probably not the one we have supposed.

Developing Critical Ideas and the Thesis

1. After reading the article above ask yourself a few basic questions. If you closely read and annotated using the guidelines from chapter 2, this should not be too difficult a task:

   a. What is the subject or **topic** of the text?

   b. Who is the intended **audience**?

   c. What is the author's **purpose/thesis**?

   d. Is there an **explicit** thesis statement? Or is the thesis implied by the main idea?

   e. What is the author's **conclusion**?

   f. What general background **information (or data)** is provided to readers?

   Let's apply these questions to Stern's article:

   a. The subject/topic of the essay is charity.

   b. The intended audience is a political/social interest readership.

    c. Stern compares and contrasts charitable contributions by social class.

    d. Stern's thesis is that being wealthy has little correlation to "giving" and then Stern further concludes that charity more frequently favors the institutions of the wealthy.

    e. The author provides researched data such as statistics about wealthy and poor people's incomes, percentage of charity, etc.

2. Once we understand the basic ideas presented to us in a text we can move to **step two**—making connections between our existing knowledge and new knowledge:

    a. As you read the text, what did you find yourself thinking about?

    b. Did the text provide you with new information?

    c. Did the text affirm knowledge you already knew?

3. Step three requires you to actively interact with the text and create a thesis statement:

    a. Select (highlight/underline) three passages from the text that you feel strongly about.

    b. Think about why you had that response to these passages (what knowledge do you have that helps to generate your feelings or ideas?).

    c. Write at least three statements detailing and explaining your response to the reading.

    d. Look at them for similarity in ideas, or response, or both. What might be different?

4. Formulate a specific idea that all three ideas can connect to:

    a. Begin to form a specific thesis regarding the topic, using the specific idea you formulated using the elements of the thesis.

Share your thesis statement with your classmates or peers either in your classroom blog, website, or social media page, or in class; ask them to evaluate it with the key concepts of this chapter in mind (critical idea and thesis statements), and for the elements of a thesis statement.

Second Writing Activity

Developing a Thesis Statement

Below you will find a list of scenarios. By definition, a scenario is an outline of a movie or other performance production. In this activity the scenarios are outlines of hypothetical rhetorical situations. Also remember that earlier we learned that a thesis is a "proposition"—or a proposal of a critical idea.

Carefully read the "scenarios" and compose a thesis statement (proposition) that responds to the scenarios.

Scenario One

Rhetorical Situation—Speaking to Your City Council

There are three family restaurants in your neighborhood. All three are within a two-block area of where you live. You have received a letter indicating that an auto body paint shop would like to open up in the same neighborhood, a block away from you. As a neighbor, you decide to attend the city council community meeting to discuss this matter because you are concerned about an industrial business so close to where families in your neighborhood dine. You will be presenting your thesis at the next city council meeting.

Scenario Two

Rhetorical Situation—Motivating College Athletes

You are the assistant peer coach for your college tennis team. The head coach is ill and cannot attend the final match of the season. The team has lost eight of ten competitive matches. The head coach has asked you to inspire the team by offering three reasons why this final match is important despite the losing season. Write a thesis that outlines the importance of this final match.

Scenario Three

Rhetorical Situation—Designing a Scholarship

The scholarship committee is charged with developing the criteria for a $3000 scholarship to be given each year to a student of exceptional promise. Write a thesis statement that outlines and briefly explains the criteria a student must meet for this scholarship award.

CHAPTER FIVE

Revision: Strategies and Approaches to Revising Texts

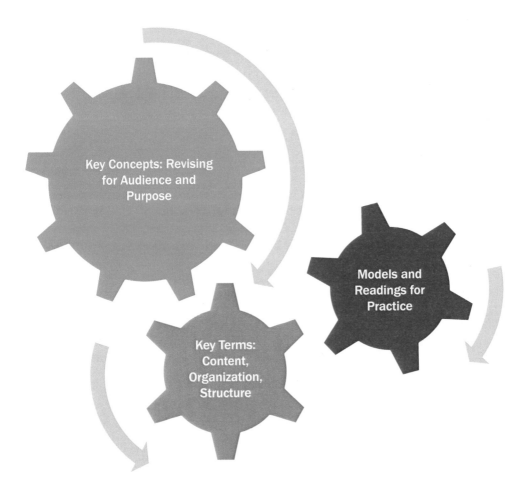

The best advice I can give on this is, once it's done, to put it away until you can read it with new eyes. . . . put it in a drawer and . . . When you're ready, pick it up and read it, as if you've never read it before. If there are things you aren't satisfied with as a reader, go in and fix them as a writer: that's revision.

—Neil Gaiman

I have never thought of myself as a good writer. But I'm one of the world's great rewriters.

—James A. Michener

To *REVISE*: Google's "define" search function tells us that to revise is to "reconsider and alter (something) in the light of further evidence." When composing our thoughts in writing, we may also add that to revise our writing is to re-vision what we have done, re-see it, tweak it; redesign it, alter it in light of the needs of our audience and our purpose. To revise something is to alter its ideas, to rearrange them, to present them in the best light so that our purpose is achieved, and our audience is satisfied. We look at the areas of our thesis and ideas, our critical thinking and logic, our evidence and examples, and we look at all of that in the context of the given conventions, or the characteristics, of our genre choice and our audience's expectations.

What, specifically, then, do we consider when revising? You already know that whenever you write you must consider the rhetorical situation, and develop the purpose using elements of rhetoric. But we have talked about these as only a prewriting or drafting strategy. Now, they are the focus of revision (as you can probably guess by now, they should be on a writer's mind through the whole writing process).

Revision and Rhetorical Situations

If you are writing a persuasive academic essay, the conventions of that type of essay include an introduction with a thesis statement, body paragraphs with topic sentences that support the argument or main idea, use of appropriate vocabulary and a formal tone, evidence in the form of facts, and primarily rely upon the rhetorical elements of ethos and logos, with zero, or only infrequent appeals to pathos (again depending on needs of audience: science writing differs greatly from the writing done in the humanities.)

But, if you are writing an e-mail, with the same purpose—to persuade—those conventions are quite different. A thesis statement might not be necessary, though a main idea would be. Your whole text's, or your paragraph's organization could be loosely organized, since it is less formal, but your purpose will still demand clarity and focus.

Think about an invitation, or a "tweet," or blog, what makes them different from each other? If you are writing in a genre, does your text meet those criteria consistently, or do you stray from those conventions? Apply the rules of convention, and then evaluate your text for its success in purpose, and audience expectation.

Since the rhetorical situation and topic is already well-established by this point in your writing process, it is *your ideas* about the topic you will reconsider, *then* reconsider your purpose and audience, by asking these questions of your composition several times of *each* draft before considering any draft a final draft (whether it is an essay, e-mail, tweet, or Facebook post):

► Does this draft fulfill its purpose?

► Will my audience be satisfied?

Author Judy Blume writes, "I hate first drafts, and it never gets easier. People always wonder what kind of superhero power they'd like to have. I wanted the ability for someone to just open up my brain and take out the entire first draft and lay it down in front of me so I can just focus on the second, third and fourth drafts."

Blume is among thousands of writers who would agree that writing happens when we are reviewing, when we take the first drafts of our own thoughts and turn our attention toward *communicating* those thoughts. The "second, third, and fourth drafts" are where you write for your audience, for a specific purpose, and where communication unfolds. In the first draft, we are merely writing for ourselves, to frame what we think on a specific topic and to understand how and why we think it. The act of revision is to re-vision, re-see our thoughts through the eyes of our readers and our purpose in writing for them. So, to answer these two important questions above you must know your purpose and then you must become your audience. You must walk in the shoes of your readers, you must "re-see" through their eyes. You must stop being the writer, and start thinking like your audience.

This idea seems impossible, but it really only requires you to be aware of your audience. You become your audience by imagining the critical questions they might ask, imagining what arguments, or counterarguments they might have, and imagining what might concern them about your ideas. Then you can become a writer again and address these questions, counterpoints, and concerns in your text.

Part of understanding your audience requires you to understand their expectations, and we also need to understand our genre and its conventions (to read more about genre and conventions, see chapter 9). Focus on how the conventions of an essay or an e-mail, or other genre, will shape the expectations of your audience. Then, putting on your "reader's hat," examine those areas for clarity and purpose. Generally, though, all texts focus on similar criteria, so to evaluate through your readers' eyes, you should look at the conventions of genre first, and then content, organization and structure.

Content

Thesis or Thesis Statement (if the genre, or purpose, requires it)	Your ideas should be expressed clearly, with a focus on the ideas you plan to include in your text. If you find your draft went astray, how can you revise your thesis to reflect that change in your thinking?
Ideas (main ideas that suit your purpose and genre, or sub-topics that support your thesis)	Are the ideas all related to your main idea, can you add more ideas to help, or delete weak ideas that confuse, or contradict?
Evidence/Support/Examples/Research (all of these are dependent on the genre's conventions)	Will your reader understand your ideas better with more, or less examples? Or with different, or more clear examples? Is there enough evidence to support your ideas?

Organization

Order of Ideas (of a paragraph, or an entire text)	Which order puts the best light on to serve your purpose and your audience's expectations? How are your paragraphs arranged according to your argument? Is it the most advantageous way to fulfill your purpose? If not, rearrange until it does.
Logical	Logical organization is one that follows a pre-determined set of criteria: smallest to largest, least important to most important, strongest to weakest, etc. You might use this in writing that evaluates and/or compares one issue to another, or where you might be persuading your audience to act.
Spatial	Spatial organization is one that offers a perspective on the relationship of the topic to the space it resides in. So, if you were to describe a room, applying spatial organization to your ideas you might start with the walls, and floors, doors and windows, and then the objects within, and that would be an outer-inner spatial arrangement. You could also choose upper and lower, or inside and outside, or first eye-catcher to last, etc. You might use this organization when describing a place, or giving directions to a location.
Chronological	Chronos means "time" in Greek. So chronological order is how the events or ideas exist in relationship to time: first, second, third . . . last, or past, present, future, etc. You might use this pattern when retelling an event that occurred, or when describing how to complete a process.

Structure

Paragraphs	Do the ideas remain focused on the topic sentence? If not, break up the ideas, and add detail to each to fill in the gaps.
Topic Sentences	Are your topic sentences related by concept to your main idea/thesis statement? If not, why? How might that paragraph continue to be useful to your purpose/genre/audience? If not, delete it, or add it to the paragraph that could use those details.
Concluding Sentences	Do they serve that purpose? Or does the sentence introduce a new idea? If so, is it a transition to the next paragraph's ideas, or an addition to the current paragraph that needs commentary before the paragraph can conclude?
Transitions	Does your reader need a helping hand to the next idea? Would it make your writing easier to follow? Does the transition link previous or "known" ideas in your essay to the next or "unknown" ideas in your essay? Without enough of them, your essay can feel disorganized, since the absence forces readers to "jump" from one idea to the next. Examples of transitions: Additionally, . . . Also, . . . Consequently, . . . More important, . . . Surprisingly, . . . Therefore, . . . (see addendum, "Transitions," for more examples)

After reviewing your text for its content, organization, and structure, you must also revise for originality. Make sure that you are not applying stereotypes, clichéd phrases, or ideas, repeating your own ideas, or simply regurgitating the ideas found in texts that you might discuss or reference, and check for accidental plagiarism of other's words or ideas.

This is an important step since you are writing to discuss your ideas; you want to write in original phrases, not clichéd or plagiarized ideas. Originality is important in the development of ethos, logos, and pathos in your own writing. If you are writing about a topic that many have written about, make sure that you are writing from your perspective, clearly, and in your own words. Yet, if you are writing a paper on a topic that many people have discussed, you can include the ideas of others. But be sure to demonstrate how those ideas, combined with your own led you to a new, or different idea, or thesis.

Now that we know what revision is, how do we go about doing it? Where do we start? Once we have put our "reader's" cap on, what do we do next? There are many ways to do this, and you can experiment with these to see which work for you best, or works best for the particular task you are writing for.

> ► Have peers in your class, or other people (who are examples of your target audience) read your text and comment on how it addressed their concerns, or present you with ideas that you had not considered before. At this stage, tell them to

ignore grammar and spelling and other editing issues. They can read it again later (see chapter 6) for those types of problems.

▸ "Reverse" outline your text to test for logical organization, or topics that stray from the main idea. This involves looking at your main idea, and writing down what idea each paragraph expresses and how each paragraph helps to support your main idea. This can help you get a "bird's eye view" of your organization and structure without the details confusing you. Then, if you find two paragraphs (or more) that are about a similar idea, but are not near each other, you can delete, rearrange, or combine those paragraphs to reflect that connection.

▸ After reverse outlining, use those notes to further your ideas by playing "devil's advocate." By this we mean you should try to find a way to disagree with your own writing, and if that disagreement is strong, and makes you rethink your ideas, then rethink them and rewrite them. This is particularly important if you did not do a lot of prewriting for the clarity and strength of your ideas.

▸ Of course, the questions we started this chapter with should be asked continuously: *Does this draft fulfill its purpose?* and *Will my audience be satisfied?*

Student Sample—The Writing Process and Revision

Let's take a look at a student sample of revision. The first is a prewriting draft, and after followed by revisions that lead her to the peer workshop draft, which you will find a much better draft than the first, yet still in need of improvement. she used the guidelines discussed in this chapter, the peer workshop draft is a much better version, yet still in need of improvement.

The student is responding to and developing critical ideas about an advertisement:

Link to Adobe Photoshop® image: http://s745.photobucket.com/user/giopetsgraphi-cart/media/adv-madonna-1.jpg.html.

Prewriting Draft—An Annotated List

In this early draft the student describes, lists, and comments on the areas of the composition of the photograph/advertisement. This is not a draft, but a prewriting activity. In draft two, she chooses her strongest points and begins the drafting work in earnest.

Content

The image is a satirical advertisement for a face cream called Photoshop. The celebrity spokesperson is Madonna herself. Her face is split down her nose to her chin, one side shows the before, one shows the after.

Framing

The image only frames her head it is a close up of her face. You can see some of her hair at the top and sides of the frame. The cream is put on the bottom right corner.

Composition

Because her face is split in half the audience can see her flawless side right next to her real side. The person who made this also quoted Madonna by saying that her secret to her success with the Photoshop day cream.

Focus

The center of focus first takes me to her bluest eye on the left. Then I look at her right eye that isn't as blue. Next, I compare the two faces and see the differences. Finally, I am down to her quote "what's the secret to my success its Adobe Photoshop day cream." Then I read the label on the cream.

Lighting

Obviously the flawless side of her face is lighter and brighter than the right side, which is darker.

Angle

The angle is as if you were standing face to face with Madonna.

Significance

This image was purposely satirical to show how American women buy all of these perfecting products for themselves. It is an obsession for us to look like celebrities such as Madonna.

Draft Two—Selecting and Developing Main Ideas

In draft two the student has made specific choices about the points she would like to develop. She does not use all the points from draft one. In this draft the student works on providing background information important to the analysis. Note how the student is forming a thesis statement. What is the argument the student is introducing to the audience?

Madonna will always be remembered as the music icon. She holds on to that legacy very well. The advertisement demonstrate satire in a way that it makes the queen of the 19 eighties look like she has had not aged at all. The truth is she has and that is OK. It is only natural to grill wrinkles and grow a few gray hairs. Unfortunately for many celebrities image is everything.

The ad shows two halves of Madonna's face. One is her normal untouched face. The other one shows a younger, later, more sexy Madonna. Obviously that's the one that is trying to promote the Photoshop day cream. Photoshop is an image editing software manufactured by Adobe Systems Incorporated. The software allows editors to manipulate an image in many ways. In this case it is used to make Madonna look younger and even whiter.

When certain franchises sign a celebrity to endorse their product they often use their words to convince consumers to buy their product. In this scenario madonna says what's the secret to my success? It is Adobe Photoshop day cream. That statement ridicules past statements by other celebrities. Many people might not even know who the person maybe as long as he or she looks good.

This image was purposely and satirically made to show how American women spend billions on these perfecting products. The images and negative side effects makes teenage girls hate themselves, thus resulting in all of these eating disorders and plastic surgery.

Draft Three—Revisiting and Revising the Thesis Statement— Content Revision

Draft three begins with a title that has been designed to reflect the thesis of the essay. Note how the student uses humor in the title to parallel the "humor" in the image she has selected.

Maybe it's Maybelline, Maybe it's Photoshop

The American playwright and activist Eve Ensler once said "there is tyranny that's not accidental which makes women feel compelled to look like someone there not. The idea of beauty in America goes far beyond the same beauty lies in the eye of the beholder. Because our perception of beauty is so distorted we tend to strive for self image perfection." The advertisement of Madonna's Photoshop day cream is a satire that manifests how beauty products corporations manipulator ads in order to get more sales. But little do they realize that those ads are causing more self esteem issues than ever.

In the paragraph above, the student opens with a quote that supports her thesis and argument. The student selects a quote and opinion from a source (Eve Ensler) that is both reliable and verifiable. Revision requires student to research sources that will support the thesis. When students revise writing, they are also revising "ideas." Attention to "logos" is important in revision work. The audience must be offered evidence that is trustworthy.

To begin with the satire in the image is promoting Photoshop day cream. The celebrities spokes woman for this fake product is the queen of the 80's herself, Madonna. The picture splits her face down the middle for an obvious before and after affect.

The paragraph above is brief. The student has a critical idea, but is yet not sure how to develop or support the idea. This does not dissuade the student from including the idea in her paper. Oftentimes ideas need to be temporarily "abandoned" in order to think through how the idea will be supported. At this point in the revision work, the student has decided to work on different paragraphs or main ideas and return to this point at another time.

The advertisement shows a close up of Madonna space. The pop sensation of the 80's has thousands of fans who admire her looks as well as her talents. The left side represents the end results and the right side shows the before face. Immediately the focus lives on her left eye. This baby blue. The focus then shifts to the other eye. The right eye, for real I, it is not as blue. The right eye is a darker more greenish color. Automatically after that, the viewers attention compared the two sides to find that they look like two different people.

At this point in the revision work, the student realizes that she must research her critical ideas. The writer realizes that much of her draft work is based on opinion and personal perspectives. In order to begin her next draft, the student embarks on the process of research. Research is vital to developing critical ideas and must be properly placed and cited. The student must be careful to credit research properly. At this point the student contacts the instructor for a conference and also speaks with her peers about her ideas. In the next draft (below), we are able to see how the student integrates pertinent and properly cited research to support her analysis.

Peer Workshop Draft—Revising Paragraphs, Transitions, Sentences, and Word Choice

Maybe it's Maybelline, Maybe it's Photoshop

Mayra Torres

The American playwright and activist Eve Ensler once said, "There's this tyranny that's not accidental . . . [which makes] women feel compelled to look like somebody they're not." Ensler is referring to the mainstream advertisements seen in the media. Many TV shows, websites and magazines use satire to convey an overall weakness in society. For instance, the advertisement of Madonna's Photoshop Day Cream satirically manifests how beauty product companies manipulate their ads in order to increase sales. We have created an unattainable image of perfection that is widely accepted as the standard for beauty. Due to our distorted misperception of beauty, we advertise photo shopped images resulting in more self-esteem issues than ever.

The satirical image is promoting Photoshop Day Cream. Photoshop is a photo editing software widely used in advertising. The software can literally take ten years off of a woman with just a few clicks. The celebrity spokeswoman for this product is Madonna. The Queen of the eighties, and asks the reader, "What's the secret to my success? It's Adobe Photoshop Day Cream." This product promises to work wonders. This includes the "removal of wrinkles and all skin imperfections." The ad's ending statement reads, "To always look young and glamorous" (www.dangerousminds.net).

The advertisement shows a close up of her face, which is split down the middle for a classic "before and after" effect. The left side represents the flawless side, and the right side shows the untouched "before" side. Next, the focus immediately goes to her left eye. This eye is bright baby blue. The focus then shifts to the other eye. The right eye, her real eye, it is not as blue. The right eye is a darker more greenish color. Automatically after that, the viewer's attention compares the two sides to find that they look like two different people; on younger than the other. The lighting on the right side is darker than the "flawless" side. Also, Madonna's hair is purposely combed to the left side instead of the right, exemplifying the "beautiful" side versus the "ugly" side.

Since the advertisement is satirical, it raises a concern of how American women react to these images. Most compare themselves to these women which lowers their self-esteem. What they do not realize is that most ads have been altered to look "flawless". The writer of the documentary *America the Beautiful*, Darryl Roberts was also fascinated with America's obsession with beauty. He realized that "women have a love/hate relationship with beauty magazines." He also found that "70% of all women that spend three minutes reading a fashion magazine feel shameful, fat or guilty" (Roberts). By living in the United States, one is bombarded by ads everywhere they go. The filmmaker, Jean Killbourne recently came to the conclusion that "the average American is exposed to 3000 advertisements everyday" (Killbourne).

Self-esteem can sometimes represent a root to bigger problems like eating disorders. Eating disorders are any of a range of psychological disorders characterized by abnormal or disturbed eating habits. Many women run around trying to achieve the impossible resulting in a loss of control. Oftentimes we forget that a lot of these eating disorders deal with control, which we do not obtain. In his documentary, Darryl Roberts mentions "catching the media red-handed". He discovered a sociologist from Harvard, Dr. Anne Becker who did a study about exposing television to Fiji. After three years the experiment showed that eating disorders had shockingly increased from 0% to 11%. "Before 1995's TV incident, they thought the bigger bodies were beautiful. Thousands of years of tradition had been undone" (Roberts).

The line in the middle of Madonna's face represents the line that the media creates for women as well. Women either fall into the "beautiful" side or they fall into the "ugly" side. The "beautiful" side never ages while the "ugly" side has wrinkles. Women have such an immense fear of aging it is ridiculous. It's as if only the young model can thrive on adventure while the elder women are stereotyped as being weak and useless. Jean Killbourne the writer of *Killing Us Softly* states that "many women are now turning to plastic surgery. She found that "91% of cosmetic surgery is primarily performed on women" (Killbourne).

Moreover, the left side of Madonna's face is evidently lighter than the right side. The change of color indicates that even though many disagree, racism still exists in modern day society. Madonna is a Caucasian woman who is apparently is not Caucasian enough. Comparing both of her faces, one could easily see that the left side portrays the characteristics of the ideal all-American woman: Blonde hair, blue eyes with very fair skin. There is a discrimination against darker skinned models and celebrities. Jean Killbourne mentions that "women of color are only seen beautiful only if they resemble Caucasian features" (Killbourne). This is evident in another advertisement, only this time the celebrity is Kim Kardashian. Besides her obvious photo shopped thighs, if only pays close attention, one can see that the photo shopped version of Kim is lighter than her real skin color (http://www.good.is).

After 40 plus years of working on this argument, someone asked Jean Killbourne if she still had hope, to which she responded, "yes." She says, "the first step is to become aware." One possible solution to this media epidemic is to inform the public about the photo enhancements. All it takes is a small label next to fake Kim Kardashian saying "Disclaimer: this photo has been photo shopped, she does not really look like that" or even, "Warning, the image above has been digitally modified to lower your self-esteem." If the public is aware of all those enhancements, his/her self-esteem is not as affected. European countries like France and England have already taken matter into the situation with similar approaches (www.good.is).

In the year 2007, Dove launched their Real Beauty campaign promoting natural true beauty. They released a video commercial called *Dove Evolution*. In this commercial the audience is exposed to what really happens to a model before the final billboard photograph is published. The video exhibits the various stages of making this Plain-Jane looking model into a flawless Goddess. The process goes from the doing of the model's makeup, to her hair, to more make-up, then to extensive photo editing, until it finally gets plastered on the billboard (www.youtube.com).

In conclusion, by becoming informed, many can stop this vicious psychological cycle of advertising traps. As consumers we need to remember at all times that "beauty" presented to us by the media is merely constructed and unnatural. Remembering that if we let the idea of perfection reach unattainable levels, we are risking our health. Ultimately, if you obtains self-appreciation you will not let these advertisements overcome the beautiful, real you.

Works Cited

Adobe Photoshop Day Cream: Advertisement. Madonna Shills Adobe Photoshop Day Cream. One Long House, 21 May 2010. Web. 7 July 2011. http://dangerousminds.net/comments/madonna_shills_for_adobe_photoshop_day_cream/.

Jefferson, Cord. "American Medical Association Officially Condemns Photoshopping – Helath GOOD." *GOOD Home Page – Good*. 28 June 2011. Web 6 July 2011. http://www.good.is/post/american-medical-association-officially-condemns-photoshopping/.

Killing Us Softly 4 Advertising's Image of Women. Dir. Sut Jhally. Prodl. Jeremy Earp. Perf. Jean Killbourne. Media Education Foundation, 2010. DVD.

Roberts, Darryl. "Darryl Roberts: The Ugly Truth About 'America The Beautiful'" *Breaking News and Opinion on the Huffington Post*. Huffpost Chicago, 25, Aug. 2008. Web. 9 July 2011. http://www.huffingtonpost.com/darryl-roberts/the-ugly-truth-about-amer_b_121153.html.

YouTube – DOVE Evolution. YouTube-Broadcast Yourself. Youtube, 5 Mar. 2007. Web. 8 July 2011. http://www.youtube.com/watch?v=sfAPT1_0TDg.

Peer Workshops

As a student in a composition course you will likely be asked to provide feedback on your peer's assignments. Perhaps you have had some classroom experience in a peer workshop. A peer workshop requires you to engage in exercising the skills you have learned in chapters 1 through 4, while also responding as a reader. Peer workshopping (this activity is also sometimes referred to as *peer editing* or *peer review*) is often misunderstood and therefore a frustrating activity in composition courses. It is often misunderstood by students who feel that they do not yet possess the skills to correct the work of a peer who is in the same level composition course. But, a peer workshop is not an activity that requires students to correct errors. Even your instructor's job when evaluating your work is not to correct errors, but to suggest where a paper is in need of improvement. A writer's job is to correct errors. A peer workshop is about sharing readers' experiences reading a text (essay) produced by a writer (a peer). A peer workshop should produce, for the writer, a sense of what areas need improvement, where the reader got lost or confused, in language or in structure or organization. A peer workshop tells the writer where to begin revising. The writer, since it is his or her thinking and expression, should be the judge of how to solve the problem and what changes will better serve their purpose.

To make a peer workshop effective, we must create an understanding of how to provide useful feedback. In a peer workshop you become the critic, one who examines the ideas of another. It all starts with an examination of how the writer has applied the basic rhetorical strategies to deliver a message, or create a meaningful purpose.

▶ How has the writer (a peer) established ethos?

▶ How has the writer (a peer) integrated pathos?

▶ How has the writer (a peer) used logos as a strategy?

Another set of questions that are valuable are the questions we use when we engage in any form of critique of a text:

▶ What is valuable?

▶ What is reliable?

▶ What is included?

▶ What is left out?

▶ Why was it left out?

▶ What questions remain after reading a text?

Remember that any text can be examined in parts. Recall this chart from chapter 3.

The Main "Parts" of a Text			
Whole Text	**Paragraphs**	**Sentences**	**Words**
The whole of a reading includes a **main idea** (thesis)— an idea, proposal, argument, or experience an author would like to share with the reader/ audience.	The paragraphs, units or blocks of writing are designed to offer a single idea in support of the main idea (thesis).	Sentences are individual units of writing that collectively support the main idea of the paragraph. Sometimes, it takes only one sentence to construct a paragraph.	Words, carefully selected, become sentences that directly link and connect to the ideas in other sentences in the same paragraph.

Once we understand the rhetorical situation assigned to a text produced by a peer, and examine the ways in which a peer writer applies rhetorical strategies, we can begin to examine how the peer writer produces the parts of their text.

- ▶ Do we understand the main idea (thesis/purpose) of the text?
- ▶ Are the paragraphs clearly offering evidence and support of the main idea (thesis/purpose) of the text?

Are the sentences focused on the topic of the paragraph in which it supports?

- ▶ Are the words descriptive, explanatory, and well chosen?

The purpose of a peer workshop is to provide a response, and reaction to the ways in which a text is produced, and to offer insights and suggestions. It is, in many ways, a conversation about how meaning is produced by a writer and how it is understood by a reader.

Below is a list of criteria often evaluated in a text, areas where peers are seeking the most feedback and input. Please note that where the term "essay" is used, these areas can be applied to any type of text.

- ▶ The text begins with an engaging title that clearly articulates the content of the essay.
- ▶ The introduction is engaging and clearly states the thesis and purpose of the essay.
- ▶ Each paragraph, segment, or entry clearly supports the thesis/purpose of the essay.

- ▶ Paragraphs, segments, or entries support the thesis with valid research and/or personal experiences.
- ▶ Each paragraph, segment, or entry clearly supports the thesis/purpose of the essay.
- ▶ Paragraphs, segments, or entries clearly engage in the use of ethos, pathos, or logos as a writing strategy.
- ▶ Sentence variety is evident (short, medium, long).
- ▶ Tone/Voice is appropriate to the subject matter and engages the reader.
- ▶ Research is integrated to support the thesis (do not merely include quotes that appear random and detached to the points being made in the project).
- ▶ Arguments are sound and support of thesis/purpose avoids bias and logical fallacies.
- ▶ Examples, details, and research support the thesis/purpose go beyond general explanations.
- ▶ Essay gives the reader a sense of fullness, completeness—and the topic/thesis/purpose has been fully explored.
- ▶ Essay goes beyond the "obvious" and engages in critical thinking—project goes beyond sharing information that may be considered cliché or part of general knowledge.
- ▶ Essay avoids stereotyping and displays regard for issues surrounding race, culture, and gender based–critical thinking.

Engaging the Gears: Activity for Practice

Classroom Activity

Carefully and critically read the peer workshop draft of "Maybe It's Maybelline, Maybe It's Photoshop" and respond to the following questions:

Criteria	Peer Response
Locate the thesis statement. Is the thesis statement carefully crafted? Does it allow you to predict the ideas that will be discussed?	
Does the writer successfully support her opinions? Is the main idea/thesis supported with reliable research? What specific suggestions would you make to assist the writer in improving evidence to support the analysis?	
Carefully review the topic sentences of each paragraph. Keeping in mind that topic sentences introduce an individual critical idea in support of the thesis statement, does this writer successfully support the ideas presented in the topic sentences? Does the organization of the essay fulfill the promise of the thesis statement?	
How or where does she/he apply ethos, pathos, and logos? Explain.	
Do the paragraphs successfully conclude and transition to the next idea? Are there conclusion sentences and transitions that can be improved? Where? Explain.	
Carefully examine language. Are there terms or concepts that can be better defined or explained? Which terms? Are there sentences that can be shortened, or made more concise? Locate an example and rewrite it. Are the sentence lengths and structures effectively varied throughout? Is the word choice accurate and appropriate?	
Imagine that you have been asked to write one additional body paragraph for this essay. The paragraph should present a critical idea that has not yet been introduced or discussed in this essay. What would you add to this essay? Explain with as many details as you can.	
In a brief summary of your response, tell the writer what you enjoyed, or thought well done, and the main areas where they should direct their revisions.	

First Writing Activity

For individual practice: After reading the student sample below, provide revision advice using the same evaluation rubric used in the above classroom activity.

Sample Student eJournal Entry
Chris Hernandez

A Response to: *The Joy of Reading and Writing: Superman and Me* by Sherman Alexie

Fortunately, our nation's history has been perservered over the past centuries, through assorted scriptures and paintings. American's have discovered countless personal diaries, letters, books, and works of art, which has gave us the marvelous opportunity to take a broad insight into the status of our nation, according to the individual's period of living. The ability to read and write, opened up a new window that allowed citizens throughout the nation, to record essential events occurring throughout the United States and beyond its boundaries. "The Joy of Reading and Writing: Superman and Me", composed by Sherman Alexie, passionately underlines the importance of being capable to read and write. The competence to carry out these certain actions has sustained and protected valuable cultural history and traditions, which Sherman Alexie, the world, and myself, can embrace and cherish.

Sherman Alexie was "a Spokane Indian [,] living with his family on the Spokane Indian Reservation in eastern Washington state" (15). Sherman Alexie's family was "poor by most standards, but one of [his] parents usually managed to find some minimum-wage job or another, which made [them] middle-class by reservation standards" (15). They would live "on a combination of irregular paychecks, hope, fear, and government surplus food" (16). Evidently, life on a reservation was no basic task. The formation of reservations was just another distinct way of segregating an underprivileged civilization from a modernized society. Native Americans were primarily the targeted group, who were forced by Americans, to live on these isolated reservations. The existing conditions on these reservations were extremely brutal. Americans chose isolated areas where no natural resources were at hand and basically, no human being could manage to live a decent life while situated there. The living circumstances within reservations could have been compared to the living standards of a third world country. As Sherman Alexie explained, Native Americans were deprived of their fundamental human rights, as a result of being placed in reservations. Not only did the establishment of reservations handicap Native Americans of their basic human rights, but it also demolished their self-esteem and identity. Native Americans would grow up with a mentality believing they "were expected to fail in the non-Indian world" (17). Millions of Native Americans died, as a result of the relocation from their original homes. Somehow all of this inhumanity was downplayed and concealed by Americans. The very history of the European colonization in America, which resulted in the relocation of Native Americans to reservations, was written out of the history books our younger students read and learn. Years of pain and suffering, diminished in a blink of an eye out of our nation's history. The harsh truth is absolutely sickening and appalling. Another similar case, the Slave Trade, millions of Africans were murdered but still no concrete facts are present in our adolescent student's history books. America is ashamed and embarrassed of its barbaric past, which is why we disguise the past. Sherman Alexie emphasizes the importance of being able to read and write, so that America's disgraceful actions won't relapse. By being competent to read and write, we would have the opportunity to record, understand, and expose the actual events occurring throughout the world. Sherman Alexie writes about his heritage and background, in order to reveal the actuality of how his people were mistreated and murdered.

On the brighter side, the endowment to read and write can also be utilized to preserve and pass down cultural traditions. My family has passed down delightful recipes, generation after generation. These recipes have been formulated by my ancient ancestors. By handing down these recipes, our family is able to keep our cultural history and traditions, alive and breathing. The essence of understanding and acknowledging you roots, gives you the opportunity to recognize and appreciate what your family has been through, to stand where you are now. Genuinely speaking, how we came to have our very own place at the table, in America.

In conclusion, the ability to read and write executes a tremendous factor in our society. It grants us the liberty to conserve and protect our cultural history and traditions. We are given the opportunity to acknowledge and treasure our own roots. Reading and writing behold a double-sided authority, which can be used for good or bad. We chose the destiny our words will possess and direct to. As Sherman Alexie affirms the power of reading and writing, "the words inside a paragraph [work] together for a common purpose. They [have] some specific reason for being inside the same fence" (16).

Second Writing Activity

In a peer group, or a whole class, revise an assignment produced in class using Google Docs (or the site your instructor selects). Post your text in Google Docs and invite members to revise or add comments about what could be improved. If you are in a computer lab classroom, revise the text during class in "real" time, to see the changes students might make to improve a text.

CHAPTER SIX

Editing and Proofreading:
Style, Voice, and Polish

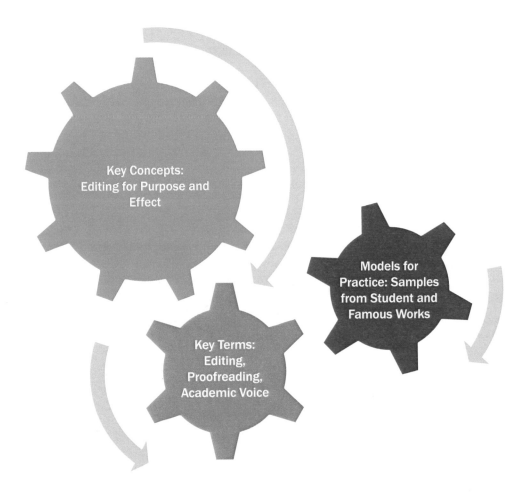

So the writer who breeds more words than he needs, is making a chore for the reader who reads.

—Dr. Seuss

The difference between the right word and the almost right word is the difference between lightning and a lightning bug.

—Mark Twain

Editing and proofreading are distinct activities, and they are also distinct from revision, in that the focus shifts among the three. The previous chapter on revision demonstrates that when we revise, we discover better ideas, or better arrangements of ideas, and we also examine the whole of the composition to decide if it meets the conventions of that genre (see chapter 9).

But when we are **editing**, we are looking directly at the language that expresses the ideas we examined while revising: the sentences, in terms of style, syntax, and arrangement toward a rhetorical purpose, the diction, in terms of meaning and tone, and the voice that is created by all of those components.

When we **proofread**, we are also looking at language, but we are focused on polishing the prose to be sure that words, grammar, and mechanics are used correctly. We also proofread for formatting consistency, such as margins, font size, and other formatting according to genre and audience expectations. For academic writing, consult the guidelines written by the Modern Language association (MLA), or the American Psychological Association (APA) for correct formatting.

If we approach these activities similarly, as most students often do, then none of them are done well, or sometimes even adequately, and at best, our audience is confused, or mistaken in their interpretation of our ideas, and at worst, we may have lost their trust in us, and so our ethos is undermined by the lack of clarity and correctness in our language.

Genre has much to do with this, and chapter 9 discusses that quite a bit, but we can understand it simply when we compare the expectations we have of the academic essay against the expectations we have of a text message, an e-mail, or a tweet on Twitter. Needless to say, the level of editing and proofreading required for each of those genres varies.

Let's now look at all of the terms related to editing and proofreading in order to better understand them.

Editing	Proofreading
Sentence Style/Syntax • meaningful variety of sentence patterns, length and rhythm • use of rhetorical devices (see rhetorical device list in addendum) • passive voice to active voice	Grammar • subject (or noun) to verb agreement in number • fragments • run-ons • possessive and plural confusion • verb tense accuracy and consistency
Word Choice • diction • tone • voice	Mechanics • punctuation • abbreviations • capitalization • spelling

Editing	Proofreading
	Formatting • page margins, title, numbering • citations • works cited page
	Typographical Errors (typos)

Editing

Sentence style includes several elements. We'll take a look at two you can work on to improve in your own writing.

Develop a **variety of sentence patterns**. Sentences that have different patterns intermingled with the standard sentence pattern (a subject, followed by a verb and its object or SVO) create a vibrant rhythm for improved readability.

Here are a simple and a compound sentence in the Standard English pattern, SVO:

Simple	Rebecca ran to the store very quickly.
Compound	Isabella likes ice cream and cake for dessert, but she loves apple pie too.

Variations of these sentences could read:

Quickly, Rebecca ran to the store.

(opens with an adverb)

Rebecca *quickly* ran to the store.

(moves adverb before the verb it modifies)

Although Isabella likes ice cream and cake, pie is her favorite dessert.

(complex sentence)

Pie is Isabella's favorite dessert, yet she also likes ice cream and cake.

(compound sentence)

In these very simple examples, the syntax, the order of words, is rearranged to develop a different pattern. This can help to alleviate the monotony of similar sentence patterns.

In addition to alleviating monotony, varying your sentence patterns can also emphasize certain ideas. In the first sentence about Rebecca, "Rebecca running" is emphasized, where in the second and third it is *how* she ran, *quickly*, that is emphasized. And in the case of Isabella and her desserts, "Isabella" is the focus in the first sentence, but in the second a contrast to pie is offered with the *although clause* at the beginning, and in the third sentence, it is *pie* that is emphasized.

Below is an example of a paragraph that is composed with sentences that have a similar, or consistent sentence pattern.

> The creation of the pockets on our pants, jackets, and shirts has a history. In the 1400s European men and women had girdle pouches. In the 1800s women started holding the girdle pouches with their hands. In the 1900s luggage makers started producing small bags they called purses. In the 2000s purses became expensive fashion accessories. Many designers create purses individually customized for each woman.

Below is an example of a sentence level revision that has changed sentence pattern by offering more sentence variety.

> The pockets on our pants, jackets, and shirts have a history. In the early 1400s men and women had "purses" called girdle pouches. By the 1800s women started holding girdle puches with their hands. As fashion trends changed, with men using wallets and women becoming the sole consumers of purses, luggage makers began producing purses specifically for women in the 1900s. Today, purses can be expensive, fashion accessories, and designers are now working on custom-crafted purses for individuals, shaping fashion in the coming century.

As you can see from this brief example of editing, the edited version is more interesting to read. It is important to look at the way that your sentences flow together in a paragraph and how those sentences affect the style of your writing.

Wordiness is defined by having too many unnecessary words in a sentence. Developing a concise style is the mark of "good" writing, no matter the genre you write in. Wordiness is often mistakenly used to demonstrate knowledge, with the idea that the more words, and especially "big" words you use, the smarter you sound to your reader.

Yet, wordiness just obscures your ideas.

Ideas are what demonstrate knowledge, and delivering them in clear and specific language helps your readers or listeners understand those ideas clearly. This can often be solved by precise diction, or precise word choices, which is addressed below, but can also be solved by reducing abstract nouns, or redundant words.

A wordy sentence might look like this:

Students will need to fulfill course work in order to complete graduation requirements. The idea above is repeated in both halves of the sentence by the redundant idea of completion.	13 Words

An edited version of this sentence might be:

To graduate, students must complete all required coursework. This five-word reduction is much more clear, and concise, while losing nothing of the intended meaning of the original sentence.	8 Words

But remember, wordiness is not in how many words there are in a sentence, but how many *unnecessary* words there are. A long sentence can be more concise than a short one: it's all in how much work a word does. If it is a lazy word, get rid of it, and replace it with a word that works harder to express your idea.

Wordiness is often characterized by redundancy. This occurs when either within a sentence, or within a paragraph of many sentences, ideas are repeated. Yet, do not mistake it for merely the repetition of words, which is also something to be edited away. Redundancy occurs when you repeat the ideas using different words to say essentially the same thing.

For example, phrases like the "color blue" or "advanced planning" are redundant. But so are sentences like these:

> *The audience was pleased with the performance. They liked it very much.*

As you can see, this writer should pick one of these sentences, and add ideas instead.

> *The audience was pleased with the performance. Artful lighting, music and costumes made the performance stand out as one of the best of the year.*

In the sentence above, details were added that supported the idea that the audience was pleased.

Sharing ideas is the reason we write, in any genre. Avoid wordiness in any form; it only detracts from your ideas and limits your ability to communicate clearly.

Diction

Diction is word choice. Your audience, and your genre, will help you to make this choice, but even within those helpful guides you have a wide range of language choice at your disposal.

As implied by the quote from Mark Twain at the beginning of this chapter, the *right* word is often hard to find. But, it is precisely because you have so many words to choose from that have so many effects on the reader, that you must take the time to consider this.

But what makes a word the *right* word? Well that depends on all of the areas of composition we have discussed at length in this book: Ask yourself about your purpose and your audience and make the choices accordingly. But generally speaking, the right word is the one that specifically and immediately, like Mark Twain's lightning bolt, transmits your idea so clearly that it could never cause your reader to become confused, or misled, or allow them to misinterpret your ideas.

One way to do this is to ask these questions of your writing:

▶ Will my reader see what I see?
▶ Does this word specifically illustrate my idea, or is it too vague and open to other ideas or interpretations?

If the answers to these questions suggest that a better word might help, then consult a thesaurus. But be careful! We have synonyms in our language because each of those words in a thesaurus entry has their own meaning and tone associated with them. So, don't just pick any word from a thesaurus and assume it is better; instead, look it up in a dictionary too, and check its connotative meaning and usage.

Tone refers to the words you choose from your own vocabulary, or those you choose from a thesaurus, and their denotative and connotative meanings. Denotation and connotation are important concepts to understand, because they can deeply affect how a word's meaning is conveyed.

Denotative meaning is the meaning that we find in a dictionary. That meaning can often be shared by other words too, but the connotation will change from word to word. **Connotative meaning** is the attitude or feelings we associate with the meaning.

For example, let's say your friend saw you at the mall one day, and later she asks, "Who was that elderly lady you were with at the mall last week?" You will likely respond explaining that she was your grandmother, and likely would think nothing of it, since the term "*elderly*" and "*lady*" are neutral in attitude or feelings, or even somewhat positive in that they are respectful terms for a woman who is of an advanced age.

But what if that friend had asked you "Who was that old bag you were with at the mall last week?" Now, the speaker is showing disrespect by using those words, and you might become offended. The denotative meaning of these words is the same: a woman of an advanced age. But the connotative meaning is quite different. Choose your words carefully!

Now, when you have chosen a genre, that genre's conventions will largely dictate what connotative language might be allowed. If you are tweeting, you will use the shortest word that can convey the thought, and since it is a casual communication, even slang, or colloquial language can be, and is often used. But, if you are writing a long research paper for your philosophy class, slang is inappropriate, and the majority of your words should have neutral, or objective connotations, with very little feelings attached to the words. Remember the ethos, pathos and logos lessons. Objective or neutral genres like the academic essay expect appeals to logos, and very few emotional appeals, and keeping your diction neutral satisfies that expectation. If you fail to use the correct words, it also undermines your ethos as a writer, just as your friend calling your grandmother an "old bag" would undermine your faith in them, too.

Voice: Most of us understand voice as a sound—voice is something we hear. Many of us can recognize each other simply by the sound of our voice. Voice can tell us how a person is feeling. Think of when you call someone on the phone and immediately detect that the person you are talking to is not feeling well? Perhaps they had a bad day at school or work. How do you know this? You make this assessment because you are familiar with the individual's normative or regular patterns of speaking. You can also make this assessment based on the volume and speed of speaking.

Writing works in a similar fashion. All writers have an individual style. A writer's personality can emerge from a text. Writers create a voice that is all their own, and this sometimes occurs naturally and often without thinking. But, most writers develop their style by crafting together their own sense of language with the expectations of an audience, or the conventions of genre. They can adopt different "voices" in writing to satisfy those expectations.

For example, Martin Luther King Jr. delivered his famous "I Have a Dream" speech while considering his own style, that of a minister, and his purpose, to persuade people to see discrimination on the basis of race as morally wrong, and his audience of thousands of Americans from all racial and ethnic backgrounds. In that speech, and in others he made, his voice is distinct: he uses parallel structure and repetition, and allusion (see glossary of rhetorical devices) to important American events. He frequently uses the elements of ethos, and pathos, to reinforce his ideas. King used a voice and style that matched both his purpose and the expected needs of his audience.

Listen to the speech and read the transcript at:

http://www.npr.org/templates/story/story.php?storyId=122701268

Like King, you will develop your own voice and style by making conscious and thoughtful choices. These choices will depend upon the rhetorical situation (what are you writing and why) and the needs of the audience, as well as your own personality.

The Academic Voice

The academic voice is the voice most frequently required for college writing assignments, and this voice is characterized by the use of Standard English grammar, formal structures and sentences that are complex, and require logical thinking to understand. The academic voice also includes college level vocabulary, including technical words, and abstract, conceptual language. All of this produces an informed voice that illustrates not only a clear understanding of its subject matter, but also establishes itself as reliable. It is language that appeals primarily to logos and ethos. Pathos is set aside, or limited because academics prefer reason over emotion in regards to study and discovery.

Delivering an academic voice while also maintaining your own voice takes practice and patience, but it is a powerful tool once you become accustomed to its use.

Proofreading

Grammar: The word "grammar" describes the logical structure of language. So when you are proofreading for grammar you are essentially applying the rules for how sentences, clauses and phrases can be used, and how words can be used within those sentences. Essentially, grammar includes the parts of speech, and the forms those parts take and where in a sentence they can be placed. Knowing the rules, and how to apply them correctly, and later in your studies, even artfully, can help the proofreading process.

But, in addition to knowing the rules you should also understand what common grammar mistakes arise not only in writing in general, but specifically in your own writing. You will likely have a set of grammar mistakes that you make frequently. Know what they are and proofread specifically for those errors. Some people have a tendency to mix up verb tenses, or use incorrect subject/verb agreement. Others write run-on sentences, or fragments. Some people have vague pronouns in their writing, or confuse adverbs and adjectives, or plurals and possessives. It is always good to know what your particular mistakes commonly are, and read your writing to look for those especially.

Mechanics are the conventions we use to manage the structure of language: punctuation, capitalization, spelling, and abbreviations. The same advice applies here too: know these conventions, and know how you make mistakes in these and proofread just for those errors. Be sure you use the apostrophe correctly, or understand the difference between the semicolon and colon usage.

Formatting is altering the shape our composition to fit the expectations of the genre we chose to write in. A story is shaped differently than a poem, and a newspaper article is formatted differently from an essay, and a report is formatted differently from a Power-Point presentation.

Typographical errors: These are the obvious errors made when we type our drafts. Be careful that you do not rely on spell-check or other electronic aids to proofread your paper. Often these aids are only flagging a *possible* error, or they will miss an error that in another context is not an error; the words "form" and "from" are good examples of this. You must check your paper for these errors. And like grammar and mechanics errors, we also have our own unique typos that we repeat. Notice them, and look for them when you read to proofread.

Your instructor has probably required that you buy a reference guide for writers. These types of books cover common grammar, mechanics and usage errors, as well as including sections on formatting. There are many such reference guides widely available, and strongly recommended. Your instructor or your librarian can help you choose a reference guide book if one was not assigned to you. Alternatively you can also visit one of the many websites available on the web for help.

Experienced writers treat editing and proofreading as separate tasks; they know that it improves the quality of each task, therefore improving the quality of the composition as a whole work.

Editing: A Model

Let's take a look at a famous writer's attempts to develop clarity and voice. Thomas Jefferson's edits change for the better the famous document, *The Declaration of Independence*. Today, it might strike us as strange to know that the words Americans take for granted as true and unchangeable, were words that emerged from earlier drafts, and not the writer's first choice, and stranger still that a document of such importance, maybe precisely because it was important, was altered to suit its purpose and audience(s).

Below are two columns depicting excerpts of the opening paragraphs of *The Declaration*. Column one is the rough draft and column two is the final draft. Note the changes well, and discuss among your classmates what the changes did to the tone, the meaning, and the voice of the document. Write a critical response in your class blog, or post in a class media page, a critical comment regarding how these changes affected the ideas and how those ideas were communicated, and how we, as a different audience than the one intended (in that time and circumstances separate us), might perceive these ideas today.

Thomas Jefferson's "original Rough draught" of the Declaration of Independence*

A Declaration by the Representatives of the UNITED STATES OF AMERICA, in General Congress assembled.

When in the course of human events it becomes necessary for a people to advance from that subordination in which they have hitherto remained, & to assume among the powers of the earth the equal and independent station to which the laws of nature & of nature's god entitle them, a decent respect to the opinions of mankind requires that they should declare the causes which impel them to change.

We hold these truths to be sacred & undeniable;

that all men are created equal & independent;

that from that equal creation they derive in rights inherent & inalienable, among which are the preservation of life, & liberty, & the pursuit of happiness;

prudence indeed will dictate that governments long established should not be changed for light & transient causes:

and accordingly all experience hath shewn that mankind are more disposed to suffer while evils are sufferable, than to right themselves by abolishing the forms to which they are accustomed.

but when a long train of abuses & usurpations

begun at a distinguished period, & pursuing invariably the same object, evinces a design to subject them to arbitrary power,

it is their right, it is their duty to throw off such government, & to provide new guards for their future security

such has been the patient sufferance of these colonies; & such is now the necessity which constrains them to expunge their former systems of government.

the history of his present majesty

is a history of unremitting injuries and usurpations, among which no one fact stands single or solitary to contradict the uniform tenor of the rest,

all of which have in direct

object the establishment of an absolute tyranny over these states. to prove this, let facts be submitted to a candid world, for the truth of which we pledge a faith yet unsullied by falsehood.

*This is a transcription of Thomas Jefferson's "original Rough draught" of the Declaration of Independence, June 1776, before it was revised by the other members of the Committee of Five and by Congress.

First printed version of the Declaration of Independence**

In Congress, July 4, 1776.

A Declaration by the Representatives of the United States of America, in General Congress Assembled.

When in the course of human events, it becomes necessary for one people to dissolve the political bands which have connected them with another, and to assume among the powers of the earth, the separate and equal station to which the laws of nature and of nature's God entitle them, a decent respect to the opinions of mankind requires that they should declare the causes which impel them to the separation.

We hold these truths to be self-evident,

that all men are created equal,

that they are endowed by their Creator with certain unalienable rights, that among these are life, liberty, and the pursuit of happiness—

That to secure these rights, governments are instituted among men, deriving their just powers from the consent of the governed, that whenever any form of government becomes destructive of these ends, it is the right of the people to alter or to abolish it, and to institute new government, laying its foundation on such principles, and organizing its powers in such form, as to them shall seem most likely to effect their safety and happiness.

Prudence, indeed, will dictate that governments long established should not be changed for light and transient causes;

and accordingly all experience hath shewn, that mankind are more disposed to suffer, while evils are sufferable, than to right themselves by abolishing the forms to which they are accustomed.

But when a long train of abuses and usurpations,

pursuing invariably the same object, evinces a design to reduce them under absolute despotism,

it is their right, it is their duty, to throw off such government, and to provide new guards for their future security.

Such has been the patient sufferance of these colonies; and such is now the necessity which constrains them to alter their former systems of government.

The history of the present King of Great Britain

is a history of repeated injuries and usurpations,

all having in direct

object the establishment of an absolute tyranny over these states. To prove this, let facts be submitted to a candid world.

**This is a transcription of the first printed version of the Declaration of Independence, July 1776.

Engaging the Gears: Activity for Practice

Classroom Activity

Coordinating Sentences / Sentence Combining:

Below is a list of sentences. Combine the sentences to form a single compound, complex, or compound-complex sentence. Be mindful of punctuation and avoid wordiness.

The dancer is a master of ballet.

The dancer dances on a stage.

The dance is elegant.

The dance is strong.

The music is inspirational.

The music is passionate.

The stage is dark.

The dance is masterful.

Eliminating Wordiness

Practice composing precise and concise sentences by editing the sentence below for wordiness.

A group of concerned, caring, and compassionate citizens living in Park Meadows have asked the city council to clean and landscape several empty lots on Main Street that have been neglected for over a decade and are now a health concern and safety concern for concerned residents that are currently living in the area.

Word Choice

Practice editing for word choice. Read the paragraph below and determine where word choices can be improved so that the main idea of the paragraph is clearly articulated with an academic voice.

It isn't fair that students who live in low-income neighborhoods have to go to schools that don't have enough funding for books and other educational stuff. When students don't have enough resources their learning is impacted in a negative way. For example, every student needs to have a copy of all their textbooks to complete homework. In some schools students cannot take home their textbooks because there are not enough. Textbooks are the basic tools for learning. To increase learning and education schools must be funded in a way where each student has enough resources to succeed.

First Writing Activity

Below, two students wrote academic summaries of the same text, "Turkeys in the Kitchen" by Dave Barry, and both are attempting to achieve an academic voice while maintaining their own style. Note how each student employs sentence structure, diction, and tone to develop their voice.

If you were her or his peer editor, what edits might you suggest, using the guidelines in this chapter, to help each of them achieve their goals?

On the essay, Turkeys in the Kitchen, Dave Barry identifies a typical "American" scene on Thanksgiving Day: women in the kitchen and men watching the football game. Automatically as a reader you can determine the vast differences between the gender roles. Although the authors tone is humorous, it is purposely made this way because some men do not like the idea of not being able to do something so they laugh at their horrible behavior. The humor can be revolved around the idea that men like to be the dominant ones without having to say that and applying the humor to it. For many years if a man and a woman get married, the woman is more likely to get his last name and if they have children then they are his children. Times are changing and you get that idea with Barry's essay. His essay is not intended to make men look bad, even though it does, but to prove how independent women have become. The gender roles have ultimately been restated, in which women can now work independently without the help of men. Now that women are more independent there are more men that are stay-at-home dads. (Kimberly Cabrera)

Barry portrays a stereotype of the woman's knowledge in the kitchen compared to the man's lack of knowledge and suggests that a man's expertise does not comply with those of the woman. Barry's tone of the essay was very humorous as he depicted the roles of the woman compared to the man. He made men seem as if they were insubordinate to the woman when in a kitchen setting. His analysis is based on his own experiences. Men fall under the category of sports, cars, and other masculine activities whereas the women fall under the category of chores, makeup, and fashion. "His style of writing is informal as he writes in a conversational tone. He speaks to the readers as if he were speaking to us presently. His perceptions are arguable for some men acquire certain skills to do the same women and vice versa. (Lee Cua)

Second Writing Activity

It is March 1925, and you and your team have been hired to revise, edit and proofread the inaugural address for President-elect Calvin Coolidge. Below is a three-paragraph excerpt from his speech. You and your team must revise and edit this speech for the president to deliver at the inauguration. You must maintain the ideas he presents, but use the guidelines on revision, editing and proofreading in chapters 5 and 6 to improve Coolidge's speech. You should also become familiar with the president's rhetorical situation. Each group should present their edits so that everyone can see the variety of ways a document can be improved upon.

Inaugural Address

Calvin Coolidge

March 4, 1925

My Countrymen:

No one can contemplate current conditions without finding much that is satisfying and still more that is encouraging. Our own country is leading the world in the general readjustment to the results of the great conflict. Many of its burdens will bear heavily upon us for years, and the secondary and indirect effects we must expect to experience for some time. But we are beginning to comprehend more definitely what course should be pursued, what remedies ought to be applied, what actions should be taken for our deliverance, and are clearly manifesting a determined will faithfully and conscientiously to adopt these methods of relief. Already we have sufficiently rearranged our domestic affairs so that confidence has returned, business has revived, and we appear to be entering an era of prosperity which is gradually reaching into every part of the Nation. Realizing that we can not live unto ourselves alone, we have contributed of our resources and our counsel to the relief of the suffering and the settlement of the disputes among the European nations. Because of what America is and what America has done, a firmer courage, a higher hope, inspires the heart of all humanity.

These results have not occurred by mere chance. They have been secured by a constant and enlightened effort marked by many sacrifices and extending over many generations. We can not continue these brilliant successes in the future, unless we continue to learn from the past. It is necessary to keep the former experiences of our country both at home and abroad continually before us, if we are to have any science of government. If we wish to erect new structures, we must have a definite knowledge of the old foundations. We must realize that human nature is about the most constant thing in the universe and that the essentials of human relationship do not change. We must frequently take our bearings from these fixed stars of our political firmament if we expect to hold a true course. If we examine carefully what we have done, we can determine the more accurately what we can do.

We stand at the opening of the one hundred and fiftieth year since our national consciousness first asserted itself by unmistakable action with an array of force. The old sentiment of detached and dependent colonies disappeared in the new sentiment of a united and independent Nation. Men began to discard the narrow confines of a local charter for the broader opportunities of a national constitution. Under the eternal urge of freedom we became an independent Nation. A little less than 50 years later that freedom and independence were reasserted in the face of all the world, and guarded, supported, and secured by the Monroe doctrine. The narrow fringe of States along the Atlantic seaboard advanced its frontiers across the hills and plains of an intervening continent until it passed down the golden slope to the Pacific. We made freedom a birthright. We extended our domain over distant islands in order to safeguard our own interests and accepted the consequent obligation to bestow justice and liberty upon less favored peoples. In the defense of our own ideals and in the general cause of liberty we entered the Great War. When victory had been fully secured, we withdrew to our own shores unrecompensed save in the consciousness of duty done.

CHAPTER SEVEN

Research: Finding a Topic and Discovering the Arguments

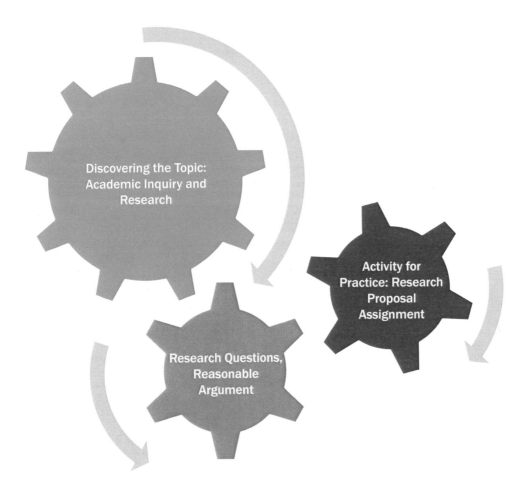

The art and science of asking questions is the source of all knowledge.

—Thomas Berger

Judge a man by his questions rather than by his answers.

—Voltaire

You have been assigned the dreaded research paper. As students, we often dread this assignment because we know it is a complex project, and we often feel ill equipped to handle it well, or even at all. But learning to do successful research and then interpret and communicate the results is an important task to master because for many other classes, and likely for your work, you will do some research, and write about it in some form.

If you are enrolled in a graphic arts program, or a nursing program or headed to medical or law school, you will need to know how to narrow, or broaden topics, how to develop research questions, locate/research sources for analysis, and develop an argument; these are universal skills for all professions and walks of life. And having these skills may even help you choose the right plumber or mechanic, or the right doctor or lawyer simply because you will know the right questions to ask and the right sources to consult.

In this textbook, three chapters assist you in learning the steps to a successful research paper: chapters 7, 8, and 13. We start the research paper with chapter 7, to learn how to choose a topic, narrow it to a specific focus, and develop a thesis statement. Chapter 8 helps you navigate the labyrinth of information sources by giving you tools to determine the value and quality of sources. Working on these tasks will keep you busy for a few weeks, until you finish researching and are ready to begin drafting. Then chapter 13 discusses the do's and don'ts of writing the research paper, reminding you that writing the successful research paper also requires that you apply the fundamentals of composition, such as your rhetorical situation and the elements of rhetoric, and that you have the skills of summary and critical analysis among others introduced in this textbook.

In some cases your instructor will assign a research topic, and then, usually, he or she also will provide a prompt. When this is the case, your instructor will have done the work of developing a research topic and a research question for you. But frequently, you will be given the opportunity to choose your own topic and develop your own research question. This chapter is dedicated in part to helping you develop those areas.

Choosing your own topic, and writing the research paper puts you well on the path toward becoming a person who can self-teach. You will learn how to learn whatever it is you want to learn. And truly, that is one of the goals of higher education: to help you become a lifetime learner by becoming your own teacher! Knowing how to ask the right questions, and to evaluate reasonable and plausible answers that you can successfully argue with reasonable people are marks of an educated person. Research papers, especially those where you must develop your own topic and argument, help to teach you those skills.

How to Find a Topic

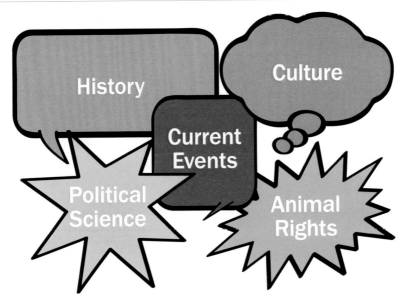

There are literally thousands of topics to choose from, so how does a student narrow it down to one topic he or she can write a substantive argument about? Luckily, there are a few ways to do so. Chapter 1 (refer to process chart) offers some general approaches to idea generation such as free writing, journaling, lists, visualization, brainstorming with peers, webbing, mapping, clustering, graphic organizers, or topic and word charts. For research paper topics, we'll focus on brainstorming.

Brainstorming: Discovering a Topic for Your Research Paper

When you are given the choice of topic, you may feel overwhelmed and ask yourself: What do I know enough about in order to succeed in this assignment? But it is not necessary to have a pre-established wealth of knowledge on the subject you will exploring. Your task in a research project is to *become* informed about a topic, and communicate that knowledge to others.

You may find it helpful to brainstorm as a precursor to making a final topic selection for your research paper. The goal of brainstorming is to allow yourself the space to think about what interests you and what inspires you. Brainstorming will help you to develop a research paper topic and it is often considered the first step in any writing process.

Below are some questions, or a personal inventory, for brainstorming. While the questions may seem "non-academic" they have been designed to allow you the opportunity to think freely without worrying about being "correct." Complete the questions with enthusiasm. Think critically and creatively. Take adequate time to address the questions.

Revisit the questions and your responses two or three times, as allowing time to pass to develop your ideas often produces detail and refinement, and ultimately will result in more meaningful work.

- ▶ What interests you?
- ▶ What are your abilities? Or, what are you good at?
- ▶ What issues concern you?
- ▶ What subject/topic/field would you like to know more about?
- ▶ What would you like to be doing five years from now? Ten years from now?

Remember, you are not able to deal with thousands of topics; even veterans succumb under such a huge array of ideas. Your job, then, is to narrow the topics. If your instructor left the choice entirely up to you, and you have no focused subject, such as a psychology or philosophy course guiding your topic, then you could choose a topic of personal interest, and turn it into a topic of academic interest.

For example, if you love video games, ask yourself what is important about video games.

- ▶ Who uses video games?
- ▶ What makes them important to others who enjoy them?
- ▶ What problems, real or perceived, arise with the use of video games?
- ▶ How might those problems or perceptions be addressed?

Answering these basic questions can provide you with the questions needed for focused research, and we'll address that a little later in the chapter.

If the topic is generally assigned, such as in a history or biology course, finding a topic of interest can feel harder unless that course is part of your major and you are already invested in that subject. But even then, you can find a topic of interest. Look through your textbook, instructor-recommended readings, notes, and exams, or other essays, and find a few facts you learned that surprised you, or left you with some questions.

For example, in a history course on the American revolutionary era, you may have learned about how the major forces in the area (Americans, British, and French) reacted to each other. But you became curious to know a little more about what role Native Americans played in regard to each of those three powers. You could use that as your first research question.

What role did Native Americans play in the politics of the revolutionary era?

Or, to help jump-start ideas, and you are in a particular subject's course, like history, biology or philosophy, you can look up your topic in a specialized encyclopedia where that subject is examined closely. Look over the entries in the encyclopedia for one that generates curiosity or questions. From that information begin asking the questions listed above that help guide you to research. You can find this kind of encyclopedia in your campus library.

Additionally, you can examine current events broadly, or within subjects:

▶ Read recent issues of several major newspapers online, specifically the "Editorials," "Opinion" or "Commentary" sections, or look for sections focused on topics such as the "Business" or "Politics" section.

▶ Read recent issues of academic journals related to your subject. Both newspapers and journals can be found online in your campus library databases.

▶ Listen to a current-events related show on your local National Public Radio (NPR) affiliated-station, or other local news program. Your local NPR station's home page will likely contain links to its broadcast schedule, with shows such as "Airtalk," "Marketplace," "Fresh Air," "All Things Considered," "This American Life," and "The Tavis Smiley Show" among others.

Take note of two or three stories that you find interesting. For each story you hear, write a paragraph noting where and when you heard or read it, and identify the main points you find interesting. These should include some indication of different viewpoints, and help you develop the critical questions that will lead you to a focused research question. Or you can use a preliminary topic chart, rather than writing it in paragraph form.

For the chart, let's take a moment to examine a few headlines from reliable sources, online or in journals or newspapers. These are the ideas, or stories that struck you as interesting. The titles of the articles are on the left side of the chart below. Based on the titles, what are your immediate opinions and reactions? How might these opinions and reactions become a springboard for ideas for research papers?

This chart, once you devise one of your own from the ideas and materials you gathered while brainstorming, should give you an indication of which topic is best suited to you and your rhetorical situation.

Preliminary Topic Chart

Title of Article	Response/Opinions	Does this interest me, why?
Privacy in the Workplace: Is Your Employer Reading Your E-mails?		
Getting Tough on Crime: Tougher Prison Sentences for First-Time Offenders		
Tax Breaks for Hybrid Car Owners		
The Minimum Wage Debate: Increasing Minimum Wage for Los Angeleans		

Narrowing a Topic to Fit the Task

Once you find a topic that suits you, you will still want to narrow it further to fit the task you have been assigned. For instance, let's say you are concerned about the effects of global warming, and your research paper assignment requires a minimum of eight to twelve pages. What problem might arise here? Since entire books can be, and have been written about global warming, the size of the topic is too large for the length of the assignment.

So you must ask yourself narrowing questions:

- ▸ What is most important about global warming?
- ▸ What makes that important to others?
- ▸ What problems, real or perceived, arise with increased global temperatures?
- ▸ How might those problems be addressed? Are they being addressed adequately? If not, why not?

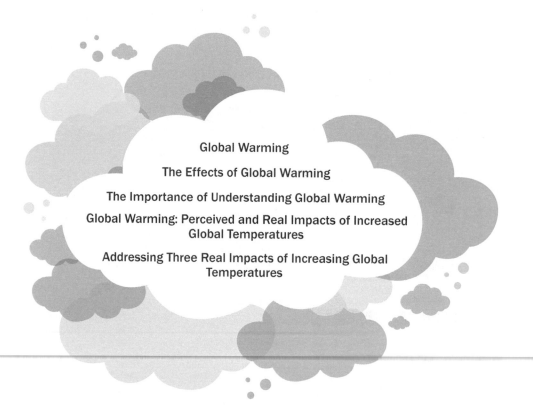

Global Warming

The Effects of Global Warming

The Importance of Understanding Global Warming

Global Warming: Perceived and Real Impacts of Increased Global Temperatures

Addressing Three Real Impacts of Increasing Global Temperatures

The answers will help you to narrow the focus of your topic to a manageable size for your task. And notice, with any topic, such as in the case of video games, or global warming, the questions were largely the same type of question: Who cares about this topic? Why do they care about it? How does this topic affect others? Answering these questions helps to narrow the topic to something more manageable.

Asking the Research Question

The research question is, in the end, the question that gets answered by the thesis statement you develop from your research. It is essentially you, the student, coming up with your own essay prompt. So, once you have generally inquired about a topic and narrowed it to fit the task you are assigned, you can now start asking the more detailed research question that will lead you to analysis and then later to develop an argument. The questions we asked to narrow the topic will be asked again, but they will become more focused, having come from the answers of the earlier and broader topic inquiry.

Once you have chosen your topic, you can turn to another chart that helps you see the many angles, or approaches to the topic you might take. Below, a student has chosen video games as a topic, and narrowed the topic into a few possible sub-topics suitable for his 8–12 page research paper (column 3).

ONE	TWO	THREE
Let's return to the topic of video games and the questions we developed:	You then might answer these questions with the following:	These are examples of narrowed topics which will become more focused when we develop the research question:
Why are video games important?	Video games are entertaining, and even educational if they use accurate history, for example.	Video games and school-aged children
Who uses them?	Young people, and increasingly, middle-aged and older people.	Video games and college students
What makes them important to others who enjoy them?	Many gamers believe the games improve hand-to-eye coordination and encourage friendships around the world.	Video games and entertainment

Video games and education |
| What problems, real or perceived, arise with the use of video games? | Some people think too much gaming makes you anti-social, or undermines education. Others complain about the violence and worry it negatively affects society. It is an expensive and time-consuming activity. | Video games and physical impact

Video games and violence

Video games and social skills |
| How might those problems be addressed? | Provide research to counter-argue the problems as real, or to suggest solutions to managing the problems. | Video games and the economy. |

Once you find, and read background information, you are now armed with enough detail to formulate that focused research question. Here is an example of a research question you might ask about video games:

> How do video games affect the intellectual and physical development of children and young adults?

Taadaa! You now have a working research question to focus on, and you can see that it also functions as a prompt for your argument/persuasive research essay. Still, it is always a good idea to test your question by turning it into a statement:

> Video games (describe or predict how) affect the intellectual and physical development of children and young adults by (insert results of your analysis of sources/ evidence).

You can see how this is the beginning of a "working" thesis statement, and therefore the beginning of your argument. Be careful: though you may already "feel" or have a "hunch" about the position you might take about how video games affect children, you should avoid becoming too attached to this "hunch." Let your research question guide your research so that you are exposing yourself to all available facts, positions and ideas about the topic. Later, as you synthesize the research, your thesis will develop with the compelling details discovered by your research. Then your argument will be well-reasoned and thoughtfully developed, and both are needed to develop your ethos.

The research question above is a successful research question because it took a personal interest and expanded it to an academic interest: one that examines the impact of video games on young people. But it is also successful because it focused your research to one specific and manageable idea.

Research and Argument/Persuasive Essays

What is an academic argument? How does it differ from the arguments we navigate at home, with friends, at work, or in our communities? We must approach argument as we would constructive criticism (see chapter 4). The word argument often stirs up negative emotions—argument is viewed as an event or activity that occurs when two or more people cannot reach an agreement.

The word argument also leads to the erroneous notion that there is a clear "winner" at the conclusion of an argument, which is not always true. Instead, think of an argument as a well-reasoned position about the topic and the underlying assumptions we discuss later in chapter 11. It is a proposition, and assertion about an idea. Any argument that you might make might also be one of many reasonable positions to take. But all arguments must, by definition, take an arguable position, one that others could also reasonably oppose.

For example, you could not reasonably research and argue the topic and position that "child abuse is wrong." It is, by definition of *abuse*, wrong. Therefore, no one could ever reasonably argue in opposition: "child abuse is right." It defies logic. So, does that mean you cannot write a research paper arguing about child abuse? Of course not, but you must find a position that can be argued for your argument to be well-reasoned. A solution to the problem of the child abuse topic could be:

> Although all agree that child abuse is wrong, we do not do enough to prevent it; reducing stress on young families, and increasing parent education, as well as adding harsher penalties could decrease the incidents of child abuse dramatically.

This argument acknowledges the problem is one all can agree upon, but reasonable people can disagree about how to solve it.

So, to write a research paper with the purpose to persuade, or argue a position, you must find an arguable topic, do preliminary research to narrow or broaden the topic to fit your task, develop a research question, use the research to attempt to answer that question as the formation of your argument. Chapters 8 and 13 will show you how to research correctly and efficiently, and how to approach writing an extended argument dependent on research. Chapter 12, though it focuses on debating skills, will show you how to develop counterargument in the form of preparing for debate.

Engaging the Gears: Activity for Practice

Classroom Activity

For this classroom activity you will brainstorm and narrow a topic for a research paper.

Part One:

Take some time to create a list of three topics you are interested in researching. You may actually have more than three topics. List all topics that interest you and select three.

Here is a reminder of the questions from earlier in the chapter that can help you brainstorm topics:

- ► What interests you?
- ► What are your abilities? Or, what are you good at?
- ► What issues concern you?
- ► What subject/topic/field would you like to know more about?
- ► What would you like to be doing five years from now? Ten years from now?

Part Two:

Once you have created a list of three topics for your research paper you will be paired or placed in small groups. The goal of the paired or group work is to discuss the three topics you have selected and form some preliminary questions you might want answered to develop your choice.

As a class, or as homework, go to the library and using the advice for developing a preliminary topic chart like the one on page 115, find articles in scholarly journals, newspapers, broadcast or other sources, and create a chart of your own topics, articles, and responses:

Preliminary Topic Chart		
Title of Article	**Response/Opinions**	**Does this interest me, why?**

Choose your topic from one of these ideas, and narrow it using the questions given earlier in the chapter:

▶ Who cares about this topic?

▶ Why do they care about it?

▶ How does this topic affect others?

Writing Activity 1

Now that you have had the opportunity to brainstorm, to visit the library and to narrow a topic for a research paper you can develop a research question. Use the process on page 117. Remember that successful research questions, when not prescribed by an instructor or course subject, will take a personal interest in the topic and expand it into an academic interest. Also, the research question should focus on one specific and manageable idea.

Writing Activity 2

Writing the Research Proposal

Below are questions to assist you in preparing the research paper proposal. Since the focus in this chapter is discovering topics and arguments it is a good idea to carefully outline your thinking and submit it to your instructor for review before you devote time to the research.

In MLA format, provide a proposal of approximately 200 words that addresses the following:

▶ The topic of my research paper is:

▶ My research question is:

▶ My argument (preliminary thesis) is:

▶ The opposing argument or counterarguments) are:

▶ I have selected this topic because:

▶ This topic is important because:

If you require more research to answer some of these, indicate that.

CHAPTER EIGHT

Research: How to Strategize, Evaluate, and Manage Sources

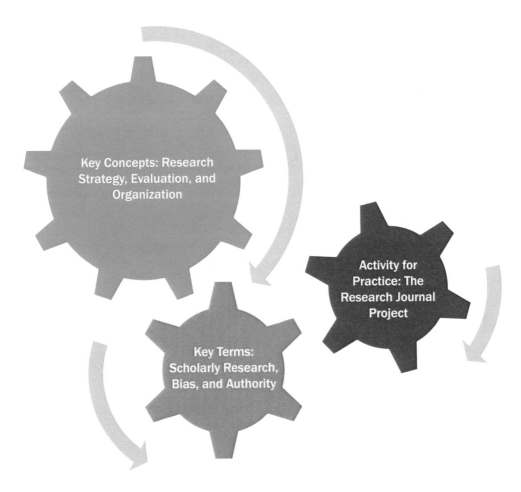

The library is not, as some would have it, a place for the retiring of disposition or faint of heart. It is not an ivory tower or a quiet room in a sanitarium facing away from the afternoon sun. It is, rather, a command center, a power base. A boardroom, a war room. An Oval Office for all who preside over their own destinies. One does not retreat from the world here; one prepares to join it at an advantage.

—Eric Burns, *The Joy of Books*

"Google" is not a synonym for "research."

—Dan Brown, *The Lost Symbol*

Researching the Issue

Your paper, your thesis—your argument is only as good as the research it rests upon. Hasty research may appear to support the thesis and purpose, but if not carefully qualified and applied, it can be detrimental to your logos and your ethos. Of course, we have to begin with a solid, well-thought-out, well-articulated thesis statement that has a specific and identifiable purpose. And, as explained in chapter 7, be sure to have your questions ready—they will guide you through your research. But your research is where the support, the very foundation of your argument, rests. If you have a great thesis, and not-so-great research, all was for naught.

In chapter 7 we explored developing a topic and shaping questions that will map out our researching needs. Once you have your topic and your research questions, you have to plan your research so you are not in the library or online for hours . . . and hours . . . and hours . . . in a mapless direction.

Creating a Research Strategy: A Model

Over the course of the next few weeks in preparation for the research project, you will be researching your question. It is important that you design an outline to strategize research. An outline, or strategy, creates a roadmap of where you are going so you can plan how to get there in the most effective way possible. So, in chapter 7, we chose and narrowed a topic, and created the research question and answer in the form of a thesis statement.

Let's take a moment to review the process of topic selection and narrowing the topic. This will help us create a research strategy for our chapter 7 topic, video games.

You have met with your instructor to discuss your topic. Your instructor has worked with you to develop a few questions to help you develop an argument and focus on your subject. Together, you have designed a set of basic questions:

- ▶ Who uses video games?
- ▶ What makes them important to others who enjoy them?
- ▶ What problems, real or perceived, arise with the use of video games?
- ▶ How might those problems or perceptions be addressed?

Based on your topic, and in response to a few exploratory questions, you have developed your research question:

> How do video games affect the intellectual and physical development of children and young adults?

Now that you have your question you can begin to organize the ideas that emerge as you begin to answer the question using your observations and experiences.

Video Games:

>What types of video games?

>What types of video games are typically played by young children?

Intellectual Development of Children and Young Adults:

>Are there video games that have a positive impact on intellectual development?

>What are the worst types of video games for intellectual development?

Physical Development of Children and Young Adults:

>How do video games directly impact physical development?

Preliminary/Working Thesis

Video games (describe or predict how) affect the intellectual and physical development of children and young adults by (insert results of your analysis of sources/evidence).

Think of the outline as a place to "think aloud." You need not have the answers for your questions, but there may be information that you already know, your satellite knowledge, or knowledge you have gained over your years of living and learning.

After developing your main ideas and main points you can begin your outline. But remember, this should *not* be a bullet point outline—but an extended outline that shows how you are thinking about your subject. Imagine that you are working with an outline that looks like the one below:

► Thesis

► Video Games

► Impacts

► Solutions

► Conclusion

Where would you begin your research? The key words in the outline are too general and broad. How would an instructor, librarian, tutor or peer help you?

While the bullet points above may provide some "mapping" of ideas, the ideas need further development. For brainstorming, a bullet list is adequate, but to prepare for research we need an outline that guides us much more specifically.

You have focused your argument, and preliminary thesis statement on video games and school-age children. Now you need to create a list of questions related to these two ideas, to drive your research strategy. Create a chart to help you document the answers to these questions, which will become the evidence for your research paper.

The chart below is a model of some questions that you could ask regarding these two ideas. The chart that follows provides some of the answers your research discovered using those questions.

Research Strategy

Area of Concern: Video Games

- Video games are rated for age appropriateness.
- Who is responsible for these ratings and how are they quantified or substantiated?
- Who is responsible for enforcing these ratings?
- Research how parents might feel about the effectiveness of the ratings.

Area of Impact: School-Age Children

- Look for consumer reports conducted by unbiased experts in the market; try to focus on specific types of video games for school-age children.
- Look for scholarly articles written on this particular topic by child development, behavior and psychology experts.
- Look for investigative news reports about the impact.

Once we focus the areas of research (above) and find sources to help us answer our questions, we might discover that the chart now looks like this:

Research Strategy Chart

Area of Concern: Video Games

Video games are rated for age appropriateness. Who is responsible for these ratings and how are they quantified or substantiated?	The Entertainment Software Rating Board (ESRB.org) is responsible for rating video games for school-age children. They are not regulated by government since the industry voluntarily rates their own products.
Who is responsible for enforcing these ratings?	The ESRB makes their own standards though they do take into consideration input from parents. (ESRB.org)
Who is responsible for enforcing these ratings? Research how parents might feel about the effectiveness of the ratings.	Apparently the ESRB offers free reports on ratings for parents and it appears that a very few number of parents actually read the report. (ESRB.org)

Area of Impact: School-Age Children

Look for consumer reports conducted by unbiased experts in the market; try to focus on specific types of video games for school-age children.	A 2012 *USA Today* news report indicates Nintendoland is popular amongst the younger children, and that Nintendo and Sony adventure games are popular with young teens.
Look for scholarly articles written on this particular topic by child development , behavior and psychology experts.	Wow! The list of "experts" is quite long. I think it would be best to ask a professor in the child development department for a brief list to begin research. I will send an e-mail right away. I could ask the librarian too.
Look for investigative news reports about the impact.	PBS has a documentary called *The Video Game Revolution*, and it informs consumers about video games. I will watch it and see if how I can expand my research areas.

This helps us refine our research strategy, and we should continue to look for more sources. But, while doing this we also need to determine the quality of the research we examine before we allow it to influence our thinking, our argument and our writing.

Evaluating Research

What Is Academic/Scholarly Research?

Academic (scholarly) research is information, data, tests, interviews, and surveys created and/or produced by experts in specific fields. Products that result from academic research are respected because the information provided must adhere to strict research methodologies. What are research methodologies? Each discipline (or subject area) sets standards (guidelines and rules) determining the best practices for accumulating trustworthy and meaningful information. Consult your instructor of subject-specific courses for those guidelines.

The Types of Sources for Consultation in Academic Research

- Peer-reviewed articles in scholarly journals
- Newspapers
- Periodicals
- Books or chapters in books
- Anthologies or collections of articles and essays
- Visual (photographic indexes or other images)
- Documentaries
- Films
- Broadcast news
- Online research (websites: .org, .gov, .edu, .mil, and so forth)

Many research sources can be easily accessed online. However, do not underestimate the necessity of a visit to your campus library.

Notice that Google searches and Wikipedia sources are not listed here. These are resources, but they often produce biased or otherwise unreliable sources. Use them with caution. Though, if you look at the sources those sites may have used, you might find a few that are reliable and unbiased.

Find the Experts and Authorities

Begin by looking for experts and authorities—people who author articles and books on your subject that are well respected in their field(s).

Verify who is an authority on your subject/topic. Ask around. Ask your instructor. Look at bibliographies or works cited pages of others who have researched and written about your topic.

- Who wrote the information?
- Why did they write the information/article?

▶ Are there others who have reviewed or evaluated this expert's work?

▶ How long has the expert "worked" in this field?

A good place to begin your research is online at your campus or local library. Using dependable databases (your college likely has many subscriptions to these databases such as EBSCOHOST, or JSTOR), and using carefully selected keywords (see your topic notes, or consult a librarian on how to use the search term criteria effectively), begin to search for experts and authorities in the subject area that you are writing about. Most college library resources will direct you to author information, full text or summary of articles, dates of publication and so forth.

There is also the old "shelf" method of research. Go to the stacks that house the books on the subject you are writing about. If you find a specific book that has articles that you find qualified and helpful—look at the books to the left and right of that book, and look at the works cited pages, or the suggested readings pages of the books you find.

Using Experts to Find the Experts (Credibility)

How do we determine when a source is credible and useful to our argument? One way to do this is to be sure that your source is from an expert in their field. Scholarly journals are where experts publish for other experts in their fields. They have their material reviewed, just like you do, in peer-reviewed publications. The editor or publisher of the article sends the article out to several other experts in the field. Those experts read the article, comment on it, ask questions, and evaluate it and send it back to the author, who reads the commentary and carefully considers the validity of the article they have produced before it is published.

Avoiding Biased Sources and Why Credibility is Important

Bias occurs when an expert or a source in a specific subject area may be motivated to report or make discoveries that support a personal goal or aim, or a specific position or belief.

Perhaps we can ask a credibility question about one of our intended sources for our research paper on video games and the impact on school-age children: The ESRB (Entertainment Software Rating Board). The ESRB writes annual reports explaining the rating of video games. What assumptions can we make about information from this particular source? We may discover that though the ESRB is self-regulated, they try to avoid bias by choosing to hire outside reviewers as part of their rating process. If they reported about their own products without an outside source, we could be skeptical of their credibility, in that they might be biased toward showing their products in a good light.

If we are to include research and information produced by the ESRB in our research paper we must understand the value and trustworthiness of the data and information produced. Why? Because we must explain to our audience that the inclusion of the research provides valid and legitimate support of the main argument. If we reveal that our own process and that of the sources we provide included biased information, our own credibility falters. In the case of a class research paper this could result in a lower grade, in the case of work-related research, this could lead to a poor business decision being made on faulty research, or even the loss of your job. Making sure that you use credible sources is crucial to developing a successful research assignment, but it can also be difficult, especially when doing research on the Internet where biased sources are easier to find than unbiased sources.

A Case of Mistaken Identity—Research that Poses as Academic or Scholarly

Earlier, a detailed definition of academic or scholarly research was offered. It is important to discuss what types of research is appropriate for academic work, especially if the research is used to support an argument or claim. Some publications implicitly claim authority when in fact they might employ logical fallacies such as testimonials, and masquerade as credible research (see chapter 11 for more discussion of logical fallacies). Below are some types of source material, either in whole or in part, that are susceptible to this kind of masquerade.

Personal Experiences

While personal experiences (or personal narratives), if properly placed at an appropriate moment can help the audience connect to the writer's ideas, such information is not effective in supporting an argument. This is not to say that a writer cannot use personal experiences and/or narrative to illustrate a point. Illustration, example and explanation are important to provide an audience with context, insight and perspective. Often, personal experiences and narratives can appeal to the audiences need for pathos—an emotional appeal. Keep in mind that manipulating the feelings or emotions of an audience is never an effective way to drive an argument forward, and can often, especially in an academic argument, undermine your ethos.

Anecdotes

Anecdotes are short stories that conclude with a lesson or value to teach a reader. Some anecdotes are dramatic, others are humorous, but the goal of an anecdote is to offer a reader a way to examine a dilemma. For example, Aesop's fables are often used to illustrate the various virtues that Western culture values. We might be compelled to include one of Aesop's fables to convince an audience that video game makers should be liable for producing games that are potentially harmful to school-age children because it is the moral choice to make. Using one of Aesop's fables may help you make your point, but it is not to be used with the belief that it is credible academic or scholarly evidence.

Blogs and Websites

Blogs and websites often contain a variety of opinions and experiences on a variety of subject areas. Keep in mind that blogs and websites are often created by individuals who have an interest on particular topics and subjects. Interest does not necessarily equate with expertise, and will often reveal bias. However, blogs and websites can be a good place to begin asking research questions. Some blogs and websites include links to academic and scholarly sources and thus can be used as a place to begin research. If you choose to use a blog or a website, be sure to locate the creator and the credentials of the creator, and again, only use these types of sources for illustration or supplemental support.

Internet Research

You can use a search engine, such as Google, Yahoo, Bing, or Duck Duck Go, to find credible sources as well. Yet, many of these search engines return paid sponsors first, before they offer more unbiased sources. To avoid this, you can refine your search to limit the types of domains searched. Domains such as .com and .net indicate "commercial" sites, and you should be careful with these domains. Bias is frequent in these domain sources since they are trying to sell a product or service, and so will often leave out information that might alter your view about their products, or provide alternative perspectives to the one they may think is in their own interest.

Here are some domains you can reasonably trust and use:

- **.gov** indicates a government agency site (for state governments, an abbreviation for the state before the .gov often occurs, i.e., www.dmv.ca.gov is the web address for the California Department of Motor Vehicles.
- **.org** indicates a site created by an organization with a specific non-commercial focus.
- **.edu** indicates an educational institution.
- **.mil** indicates military institutions (www.navy.mil, www.marines.mil, etc).

These domains tend toward scholarly standards when posting to their websites, but you should still look for other important contributor's credentials.

To get an Internet source to deliver these narrowed domains, you can set site delimiters in the search engine by entering the search terms this way:

Search Field: **video games site:.edu**

This entry will only provide search results about video games that come from educational institutions.

The format for this is simple: Search term + site: + .domain

You can do this with all of the above four "trusted" domains listed. This narrowing of your search will eliminate most commercially biased sources and keep the research to only those that are generally trustworthy. Yet, you still must evaluate the source once you get there. Don't let the source, or the search engine do your thinking for you.

You can also add terms together and use the site delimiter:

Google Search Field: **video games AND economy site:.edu**

This will return sources that deal with both topics and only from educational institutions. If you add "OR" instead of "AND" you will get only sources about video games, OR about the economy, but not any that deal with both.

If your search returns thousands of options, go back and narrow your search terms a little more. If you only get a few returns on this research, you must broaden the terms you use. If you are still having trouble, ask your librarian for help narrowing or broadening your terms.

Try it out. But, this is often a lot of work, and it is advisable to use your library's databases for this, as they have already sorted the data into categories using subject terms and scholarly sources for you. You can access subject categories by logging onto your campus library webpage.

Alternate Source Types

There are other ways to gather information besides scholarly books and articles. Students may decide to, or be instructed to conduct surveys and/or interviews. Both require students to formulate a very specific set of questions designed to generate data to support or refute their arguments. It is always best to speak to the instructor for specific instructions on how to formulate questions (the questions must be fair and generate unbiased and unrehearsed responses) and how to collect data (how interviews and surveys are conducted can affect results). Each discipline has a specific set of rules and standards.

Surveys

Surveys provide sample responses to questions in order to collect data, and are used to collect responses from a wide variety of sources and individuals. For example, after staying at a hotel for a vacation you may receive an e-mail from the hotel asking you to share your experience and to provide feedback for improvement of services. Such a survey may ask what your age range is, the number of days/nights you stayed at the hotel, and then rank the quality of room service, hospitality, and food quality. Sometimes corporations send out surveys asking you to try a product and respond to questions designed to help improve the product. Surveys can be administered online or in paper format.

Let's imagine you are asked to write a research paper on the topic of text messaging and young adults. What types of questions would you design to generate useful feedback/data?

Let's begin by examining survey questions that are neither effective nor useful.

- ▶ Do you like texting? Yes or No
- ▶ Does texting make your life easier? Yes or No

The survey questions above will produce data. But the data and information they provide will not necessarily be useful for a research paper because the responses will be general and subject to interpretation. The terms "like" and "easier" are vague, or relative to a person's unknown experiences.

Instead, consider survey questions designed to produce specific information that is not generalized or subject to interpretation. The survey questions below are designed to offer multiple specific responses that can be analyzed for the purposes of a research paper.

I am:

    A. between the ages of 15 and 18

    B. between the ages of 19 and 23

    C. between the ages of 24 and 30

    D. above the age of 30

I feel that texting: (check all that apply)

    A. helps me communicate with friends

    B. helps me communicate with my family

    C. is necessary for the type of work I do

    D. is unnecessary

In my daily routine, texting is:

    A. sometimes distracting

    B. often distracting

    C. an unnecessary distraction

    D. I do not text

In a regular 24-hour period, on average I send:

    A. 0–5 text messages

    B. 6–15 text messages

    C. 16–25 text messages

D. More than 30 text messages

In a regular 24-hour period, I receive:

    A. 0–5 text messages

    B. 6–15 text messages

    C. 16–25 text messages

    D. More than 30 text messages

These types of questions generate specific data, from specific groups, and through this specificity, your survey becomes a more useful source. Be sure to ask your instructor about the rules and regulations of administering surveys to individuals/people on your campus.

Interviews

Interviews are more complex than surveys. Interview questions are designed to keep the "conversation" focused on a particular subject, yet the interview responses can be unpredictable. Technology allows for a video/audio record of the interview, but some still use the traditional "pen and notepad" method of recording the interview.

Interview questions are designed for a specific topic, person, or a group of people, with common traits or experiences. For example, if you plan on interviewing a coach about basketball injuries, you would have to know something about the sport and the coach you are interviewing. You must also be familiar with some medical terminology. Be sure to conduct some academic research before interviewing. A "cold" interview (one done without proper research) can lead to confusion on your part.

Interviews have goals, and generally, they are framed around the following:

▶ asking others to share their knowledge or expertise

▶ asking others to share expert or informed opinions on an issue

▶ asking someone to explain a process

Interview questions should be designed to elicit responses beyond the "yes" or "no" answer, and engage the person being interviewed. Responses that are engaging come in the following structures (more on these structures in chapter 9):

▶ narrative

▶ specific information

▶ description

▶ analysis

▶ comparison

▶ contrast

▶ persuasion

Let's return to our basketball coach and our interview regarding basketball injuries, and design questions that will elicit engaging responses from the coach.

Narrative:

How did you become a basketball coach?

Information:

In your experience, what types of injuries are the most common, and which types of injuries are the most rare?

Description:

Some coaches recognize that smaller, or lesser injuries can lead to larger, more problematic injuries in the future. Can you describe how a lesser injury becomes a larger injury?

Comparison:

Some people feel that basketball players have become more physically aggressive on the courts. Have you noticed any change in court aggression in your years as a basketball coach?

Analysis:

Basketball players have started to wear some protective gear such as braces. Some players wear clear masks to protect their noses. In your experience, are these protective devices effective in preventing injuries, or at least reducing the number of injuries?

Contrast:

Do you feel that basketball players face a higher possibility of injury than a tennis player or any other athlete in a non-full contact sport?

Persuasion:

At which point in a basketball player's career would you recommend retirement as a way of preventing a debilitating or life-changing injury?

If you will be conducting an interview, the following chart offers some hints to facilitate the preparation and delivery of an interview.

Preparing for the Interview	Conducting the Interview
Contact the individual you would like to interview.	Ask permission to record the interview. If permission is not given, you will have to take careful notes.
Give them an option of times to meet should they agree to the interview.	Get your interviewee's permission to use responses in an academic paper for class.
Let the interviewee know what the focus of the interview will be (some may ask you for the questions in advance).	Start with the questions you created for the individual you will be interviewing.
Let the interviewee know the purpose of the interview and how responses will be used.	Stay focused on your main questions, but allow for some impromptu questions and responses.
Find a neutral or comfortable location to conduct the interview.	Be sure to thank your interviewee for their expertise, and their time.

Now that we have explored a variety of research sources and how to strategize and evaluate sources we can take one more step; managing our research.

Managing Research

Managing your research begins with annotating for research specific information and summarizing sources. Some students use note cards to complete this process. However, it is also perfectly acceptable to keep your research online in document form. You may already have a process of managing research that works well for you. This section details two different ways to manage research. Careful summary, organization, and analysis in the management of research will make integrating your research into your project or paper a more organized and less stressful experience.

First, you will collect your research (articles, data, interviews, visual sources, and so on).

Second, you will closely and critically read your sources (refer to chapter 2)—and underline or highlight passages you may want to cite when you compose your research paper. Be sure to annotate why you thought that information will be useful to you. Later, when you turn to that research for your project, and only see highlighter marks, you may experience frustration when you cannot remember why you had thought the information was useful, leading you to waste time rereading to look for that information.

Here is a brief review of annotation:

- ▶ Annotate in the margins or on a separate sheet of paper/computer page.
- ▶ Annotate areas that interest you or confuse you.
- ▶ Annotate questions that arise.
- ▶ Annotate areas you agree or disagree with.
- ▶ Annotate ideas you may discover or create.
- ▶ Annotate information that is new to you.

Third, you will write a **summary** of the research source after you have closely and critically completed the reading and annotating.

Finally, write an **analysis** of the research source and determine the quality (helpfulness) of the source in relation to your objective/thesis/argument. This is especially helpful if you are required to develop an annotated bibliography or works cited list as part of your assignment.

Below is a student example of managing research. Paula,the student writer, wants to know how Disney films and characters impact psychological development in young children. Paula has evaluated several scholarly articles on her topic. To help manage her resources she carefully reads and annotated the articles, then writes a brief summary and analysis. This type of research management will help her successfully apply her research as she writes her paper.

Student Sample

Source Publication Information:

The Role of the "Princess" in Walt Disney's Animated Films: Reactions of College Students

Author: Alexander M. Bruce

Source: Studies in Popular Culture, Vol. 30, No. 1 (Fall 2007), pp. 1–25

Publisher: Popular Culture Association in the South

Summary:

This article explains how children who grew up watching Disney films were impacted by the plots and the endings of the film. Disney has been criticized, especially by feminists in regards to how their films leave young girls waiting for the perfect man who will give them the perfect life. In 2005, Bruce interviews college students at Florida Southern College. Bruce asks them questions about their favorite Disney films. Many of the female students admitted being influenced by the princess films. Of the male students who participated in Bruces' study, they pointed out that Aladdin was the popular "guy film". Almost all of the men and women interviewed believed that Disney films reinforced traditional gender roles.

Analysis

This article was produced after a series of interviews with college students to demonstrate the effect Disney films had on individuals. Even if they did not initially notice, they concluded that Disney films has an impact on their identity and values. This article will be useful to my research paper because it explains, through interviews, how the films impacted psychological development. For example, when asked to describe a princess, the males focused on the appearance of the princesses. Females focused less on appearance, and more on how the princess finds her perfect prince. Times have changed, and gender roles have changed, but Disney focuses only on old fashioned gender roles. This article concludes the difficulty young boys and girls have when learning how to distinguish between fantasy and reality. When they grow up, males and females have to reconcile and change the beliefs and value they absorbed when watching Disney films - and this can cause conflict in their real lives and relationships.

As we can see from the model above, it is important and valuable to manage our research. Managing research allows us to document the relevance of our research materials so that they may be properly connected and applied to the writing of the research paper.

If you do this organizational work for each source you find for your project, integrating the sources into your research project becomes an easier task precisely because you can now use this document, rather than comb through the research, while writing, or developing your research project. Additionally, you can also copy the quotations you intend to use in your project to help avoid hunting for them when you write.

Additional Tips for Organizing Research

Keeping your research tidy and organized will help you immensely when it comes time to prepare, write, and develop a works cited page. It is important to keep careful record of your research so that you can effectively write your paper, and properly cite your sources (giving credit where credit is due). Chapter 13 includes an important section on plagiarism.

Keep a research notebook, or chart, that keeps the citation information handy, as well as a notation about why you chose that source and its value to your project. This is also especially handy if you are assigned an annotated bibliography. Do this even when you aren't yet sure you will use the source. If you decide later you need it, all of its information is at your fingertips instead of in a foggy memory from three hours of researching you did several days ago. Plus, if you need to find that source again, you will have the necessary information to find it instantly. Going back and redoing your search often will not yield the same results or sources.

If you use an electronic database, they usually have an automated citation generator. Choose the appropriate format (MLA or APA) and generate the citation. Cut and paste the citation into your chart, and add notations. It could look something like this (MLA format):

Source	Type/Location	Date Found	Notes
Cixous, Helene. "Sorties," Literary Theory: An Anthology. Ed. Julie Rivkin and Michael Ryan. Massachusetts: Blackwell, 1998. 578–584.	Book from library catalog	12/1/07	Chapters from this book support my argument that culturally determined gender differences set up the sexes as adversaries. Useful quote on 2nd page of chapter 6.
And so on . . .			

This kind of careful note taking can help you locate a source again, keep track of why it was useful or important to your argument, and manage the information all in one space. Imagine the insights you could develop by looking at and synthesizing all of your fourth column notes at once?

Final Suggestions

Application—Proper application of research is important—keep research directly connected to the focus of the paper (don't abuse or modify research to fit the needs and goals of the paper). Don't skew your research to inappropriately favor one side of an argument.

Timeliness—The research must be relative to the time period—outdated information weakens the validity of the argument. Be sure that any research that is included as evidence has been collected over a relatively fair time period. If it is a study that is being conducted, allow for sufficient time to conduct surveys, research, and tests. Research that is older than five or more years sometimes is out of date. Check with the instructor for your specific subject area, or project, for guidelines on suitable time frames for source materials.

Evaluate research for its authority, truthfulness, validity, timeliness, and accuracy as soon as you find it. Doing so immediately will save time and allow you to focus on research that is valuable.

And don't forget to ask your research librarian for assistance—they will be happy to review your research questions and guide you in the right direction.

Engaging the Gears: Activity for Practice

Classroom Activity

Below are some potential topics for research papers (broad topics). Working individually, or in groups (your instructor will decide) make a list of potential keywords to "search" on a search engine. The goal of this activity is to create concise keywords to successfully navigate the Internet for quality research information. Then, using those search terms, locate two unbiased and reliable online sources: one article, and one interview or survey.

- ▶ Toxic Ingredients in Nail Polish
- ▶ Sleep Deprivation and College Students

- ► Hybrid Automobiles and Environmental Protection
- ► Public Service Animals: The Canine Officer
- ► 21st Century American Women in Space Science

Writing Activity

Select one of the research sub-topics listed below (from chapter 7/Video Games) and complete the research strategy chart as modeled earlier in this chapter.

Research Strategy Chart

Area of Concern: Video Games	Area of Impact: College Students

Research Strategy Chart

Area of Concern: Video Games	Area of Impact: The Economy

Research Activity: Preparing for the Term Paper or Research Paper

This assignment can be tailored to meet the requirements for your course, but is generally designed to allow you the proper amount of time to develop research, and document and manage your sources regarding your topic. Chapter 13 will provide information on writing strategies for the research paper and properly citing sources.

Since research takes time, it is always a good idea to get started early, so that you can consult as many sources as is necessary to successfully support your thesis, make a plan to avoid last minute research work, and determine which research is most useful for your particular rhetorical situation.

The Research Journal Project

Chapter 7 guided you through the research questions and developing a thesis. This chapter modeled the next steps. Now you will being to apply those ideas in your own project. Outline your ideas, as modeled, and use the research strategy charts for your specific topic.

Then begin exploring the topic through research. In this activity you will gather your research, summarize, and analyze your sources. All research journal entries will be clearly and critically connected to that goal. This assignment should be completed over the course of several weeks, and according to the research parameters (number and types of sources) your instructor requires for your project.

This project begins now. Avoid the last minute crush of work, and experience the process of writing a culminating research paper due at the end of the term. This is meant to help you do this complex assignment, step by step.

The Research Journal Project should include the following source types and format (for a total of nine separate journals done over the remaining weeks of your course):

1. Five Scholarly or Professional Articles on Your Research Topic.
    a. Each journal will document one article and include a proper citation in the format required by your instructor.
    b. Include one hard copy or electronic copy of each article, carefully annotated.
    c. Summarize each article in 200 words or less.
    d. Compose a 300-word analysis that connects the article to your project proposal.
    e. Include your summary and analysis in your journal.

2. Two Visual or Audio Sources
    a. Each journal will document one video or audio source and include a proper citation in the format required by your instructor.
    b. View any combination (video clip, documentary, TV or cable show, radio program, and so on).
    c. Compose a 100-word summary and 200-word analysis of each source.
    d. Include your summary and analysis in your journal.

3. One Survey
    a. Students will write a survey to be administered in-person or online.
    b. Survey must include at least five well-formulated questions.

    c. Survey must be administered to at least fifteen individuals.

    d. Compose a 200-word analysis of the survey results and impact on your research ideas.

    e. Include your survey questions, results and your analysis in your journal.

4.   One Interview

    a. Write a script of at least ten questions you will ask during the interview.

    b. Interview at least one individual who can provide useful information that meets the goals of the research paper.

    c. Compose a 200-word analysis of the information you gathered from the interview.

    d. Include your analysis, the script and the interviewee's answers in your journal.

CHAPTER NINE

Writing Technologies, Composition, and Genre

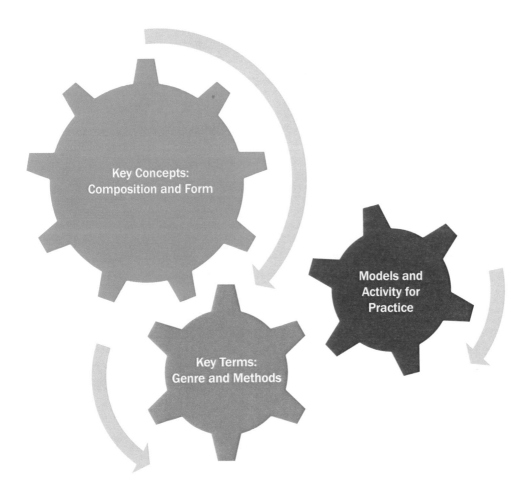

Good writing is good writing. In many ways, it's the audience and their expectations that define a genre.

—Rosemary Clement-Moore

The medium is the message.

—Marshall McLuhan

Writing, as discussed in chapter 1, is a technology, and it began in earnest with a stylus and clay tablets. Much later it became the revolutionary quill and ink on parchment, followed by the even more revolutionary moveable type presses, typewriters, and the keyboard. All of these technologies have had an impact on the ways in which we read and write. Keyboards and computers have changed the way we write in that once we write *it*, there are many ways in which that writing can be presented. Some form of paper had been a common denominator in earlier technologies, but emerging technologies allow us "print" on our cell phones, on our personal computers or other devices, or augment the writing with images, moving or still, with or without sound. Books can now be purchased in downloadable online formats and be read from electronic tablets instead of clay tablets. A few decades ago students carried several heavy books to school in a backpack. Today, students can carry hundreds of digital books downloaded on a lightweight computer or tablet. Social networking sites like Twitter, Facebook, Google+, or Instagram are also technological media that shapes the way we communicate with each other in written form.

Technology allows us the ability to integrate other mediums of information that make our compositions come to life. Through computer technology we can create personal websites and blogs, where, along with our written words (text), we can include sounds, moving images, and static images. Technology allows us to visually record ourselves—allowing us to appear (through pictures and sound) in our own compositions. In short, technology allows us to augment our texts by making them more alive. No longer is text, or writing, offered to an audience on a white sheet of paper that is one-dimensional and static.

It may be hard to imagine life without computers, word processing programs, research databases, and smart phones. Perhaps most of the information above is not new to you; it may seem obvious because these technologies are around us everywhere we go. However, it is important not only to be aware of the different forms of technology that is commonly available to most students, but also to be aware of how they affect us, and therefore how to use it effectively.

Technology and Access to Research	Technology and the Writing Process	Technology and Presentation
You might brainstorm and write your drafts on a tablet or computer.	You might brainstorm and write your drafts on a tablet or computer.	Your instructor may ask you to submit an electronic copy of your written assignment.
Technology allows us access to databases designed strictly for academic or professional purposes.	You can revise your work on a computer, and use e-mail to send your document to a peer for a peer edit.	You may be asked to design a website and the website will include writing(s) about a specific subject.
Technology allows us to access archives of images that can be used as research for a writing assignment.	You can store your work on a USB drive and transport your work to the library or the campus tutoring center for editing and proofreading.	You may be asked to work in a group to design a purpose-specific blog. A collection of your group research and writing in the form of posts will be submitted to your instructor.
Technology allows us to access videos, films, and documentaries when it is most convenient for us to do so.	Your instructor may ask you to post your writing assignment to a class website, or, send the final draft by e-mail for evaluation.	You may be asked to write a short response to a prompt or question to post on a forum. You might also be asked to read the forum posts of your peers and write responses.
Technology allows us to record our own voices and images, as well as the voices and images of others to use as research for writing assignments.	Your instructor may give you feedback, or an evaluation of your work via an electronic document. You might ask for feedback, co-author a writing assignment as a peer and complete the assignment on an interactive site such as Google Docs.	You may be asked to create a video or mini-documentary based on research you are doing on a particular subject or topic.

Technology has clearly improved the speed at which we can read and write. A writer who is familiar with a keyboard can write much more quickly than a writer using pen and paper. But speed should never be confused with quality or depth. Texting has become the technological tool for the genre of the "short note," but we certainly would not text an essay to an instructor because the medium does not support the purpose. So, you must learn to choose from a wide array of options, according to your rhetorical situation.

Composition and Genres

Composition offers you, as a writer, a variety of genres to choose from to suit your rhetorical situation. We must first look to our rhetorical situation: our topic, audience and purpose, but then, how we choose to display or compose our writing is still based on further **genre choices.**

Academic/Scholarly	Entertainment	Public or Arts
The Essay	Scripts	News Reports/Articles
• Persuasion/Argument	Lyrics (for music)	Literary Arts
• Expository	Documentaries	• Fiction
• Analysis	Films	• Nonfiction
The Research Paper	Television	• Poetry
Literary Critiques		• Drama
Scientific Genres		
Professional	**Personal**	**Electronic**
Business Report	Letters	E-mail
Executive Summary	Notes	Text
Visual Presentation	Journals	Website
Medical Logs and Records		Blog
		Social Networking

Of course, this is not a complete list, nor are the "categories" above that neat and orderly in real writing situations. These different genres will often bleed into one another, for example, a scholarly or academic writing might also use a film, or a visual presentation, or other types of electronic genres too.

What Are Genres?

In a traditional English class students read and analyze (and research) literary genres. **Literary genres** include fiction, nonfiction, creative nonfiction, drama, and poetry. In a traditional English class, one would not expect to read a report on capital punishment.

Yet, composition courses examine different types of genres and the conventions, or the characteristics, of each genre. Composition courses ask you to become a writer, where traditional English courses that you may be more familiar with offer you opportunities to examine literature, and learn to become a critic.

In a composition course, instructors offer a wide variety of readings to provide a launching place for ideas and critical writing. Reading assignments can include the literary genres, but will also likely include other academic genres, as well as professional and personal genres. Genre is also important to understand when considering the discipline in which you are writing. What genre we select to write in depends first upon our audience, and secondly, on the goals, or purpose of the writing task.

An instructor may assign the most common or familiar form of composition—the academic essay. Perhaps the instructor's prompt asks you to compose an essay about the topic of online shopping, or making purchases through the Internet. The instructor may not indicate what your purpose in writing this essay might be, and when you ask your instructor "what" to write about, you may be told to develop a unique approach on the subject.

This is where an understanding of genre and the **conventions of genre** are helpful. The simple definition of an essay is a focused piece of writing that engages in the discussion of one particular area of a subject. Essays can range from the basic five-paragraph essay to graduate level dissertations of several hundreds of pages. In most cases, college students are required to compose essays of between five and fifteen, or twenty pages. Yet, a good place to focus is not on word or page number requirements, but rather on genre, as that has an influence over how you will develop and employ your rhetorical strategy toward your purpose.

The most common essay genres found in a composition course, or other academic classes are:

- ▶ Persuasion/Argument
- ▶ Expository
- ▶ Analysis
- ▶ Research
- ▶ Literary Critiques
- ▶ Narrative

Let's review for a moment what makes each of these genres unique and different from the other listed genres in the same category.

The **persuasive** or **argumentative** genres are writings that take a position on a controversial issue or topic in an effort to explain a specific viewpoint. Persuasion can also ask the reader to act or take action to create or cause change. Persuasive essays rely heavily on logical reasoning, reliable evidence, and clearly presenting the benefits of a change of thinking or the need for taking action.

The **expository** essay is a genre that seeks to explain and inform a reader about a particular topic. This genre requires a writer to carefully explain one particular subject. For example, a student may write an essay that explains the difference between financial aid and college tuition bank loans. Such an essay requires a writer to be direct and concise in a language that is accessible to the intended audience. This type of essay avoids the use of opinions and focuses more on explanation. Such an essay would not advise readers which funding is best. This type of essay would not try to encourage students to take out student loans. Instead, it seeks to give the reader sufficient information so that the reader can reach her/his own conclusions based on their understanding of the topic and their specific needs.

The **analysis** essay is a genre that provides a reader with a critique of a specific text, object, process, person, idea, or event. Often an analysis essay may appear to share similar conventions and characteristics of the argumentative essay in that an analysis seeks to make a critical point that must be supported by valid and reliable evidence. For example, you may be asked to read an article on the mass production of beef for the fast food industry to prove the process is safe and does not need further regulation. Here you will apply your skills in critical thinking and critical analysis in order to prove the reliability of the article. This would require you to examine the validity of all the evidence presented to you and take a position on whether the evidence is trustworthy, or should be reexamined from another perspective.

The **research paper** is a paper that asks students to investigate and analyze, then claim a position (like an argumentative/persuasive/analysis paper) on a particular subject area and present data and facts and in an organized manner. In some cases an instructor will ask students to gather research from primary and secondary sources. Some instructors may ask students to conduct interviews or create surveys and polls. All research would then be carefully organized, analyzed, and presented. Of course, all research must be focused on a particular subject. In some cases, an instructor will ask students to form a conclusion from collected research, thereby mixing the genre of persuasion with research. For example, a student may be asked to research a particular vitamin, like vitamin A. The goal of the research might be to examine dosage, consumption and long-term effectiveness of vitamin A in the daily diet, and then draw and present a conclusion/argument about the use of vitamin A in our diets as a supplement.

Literary critiques are much like critical reading responses in that your task might be to evaluate the importance of a piece of literature or text through theoretical perspectives, or look at structure and form as a literary concern. As explained in the opening chapters of this text, critiques can include unique interpretations and determination of quality of meaning, and of craft. Literary critiques primarily involve the skills of analysis, synthesis and evaluation.

The **narrative** genre allows writers to use the conventions of storytelling to deliver a main idea. The narrative need not be a first-person account of an event. Narrative can be a collection of stories from various experiences. The narrative can be fictional or hypothetical, or factual and reportive. A writer may compose one complete narrative, the narrative essay. Or, a writer can employ shorter narratives to emphasize or support a single point in an essay, or include a narrative in police or other official reports.

Choosing a Genre

Inquiry into a subject matter provides us with questions that can help us decide how to use genre in our writing assignments.

Let's look at the assigned topic of online shopping. We may find that online shopping is a broad topic that can have many "angles" to expose. We could talk about the convenience, or the environmental impact of online shopping, or we could talk about its effect on the economy or on the unemployment rate. We could talk about how online shopping affects the psychology of shopping, and spending rates. Finding this focus is necessary: it refines the type of information we will research, and if not assigned, which purpose we pursue, and therefore, in which genre we write.

Let us assume we decide to write about the impact online shopping has had on unemployment rates. We must decide which of the genres below would best suit our writing needs. We might not get to the one choice yet, because we still have not determined our purpose. But let's narrow the choices:

▶ Persuasion/Argument?

▶ Possible choice, because once we have gathered enough information to evaluate, we could determine, or **propose** a different way of writing unemployment policy.

▶ Expository? Also a possible choice, if our purpose is to **inform** people of, or **explain** how to benefit from online shopping.

▶ Analysis? Also a possible choice, if looking at the relationship between unemployment rates and online shopping, one may have to analyze many factors to develop a **critique** of the impacts of online shopping on employment.

▶ Research? Marketing firms, policy makers and business will all be interested in research data about online shopping, so if your purpose is to inform, analyze and develop marketing, business or policy ideas from the data, this genre will work too.

▶ Literary Critiques? The subject of online shopping's effects on unemployment is not qualified as literature, thus a literary critique would be wholly invalid.

▶ Narrative? Unlikely, unless used as anecdotal evidence in a persuasion or analysis paper.

Well, because we have not identified our purpose yet, we have eliminated only two. So now, let us assume that as we study and discuss the topic we find that online shopping has contributed to unemployment and many Americans find that they cannot find other types of work, thus they are unable to support their families. Perhaps you decide that you would like to ask your readers to think about the impact they have on families and employment rates each time they shop online. Which of the genres above would best suit your writing needs now?

- ▶ Persuasion/Argument? If we want to persuade them to change their shopping habits, this would be a good choice. But in perspective, this seems like an argument doomed to fail, as online shopping appears here to stay. So, better to find alternative ways to raise awareness and influence change.

- ▶ Expository? Also a possible choice, if our purpose is to inform people of, or explain how particular shopping habits affect the economy and unemployment rates, and allow readers to become aware and reflect on this information.

- ▶ Analysis? This choice is best only if your audience needs a thorough breakdown of the multiple ways that unemployment rates are affected by online shopping. Otherwise, you must do this work, but not necessarily write in that genre.

- ▶ Research? If you want people to understand how their behavior might be affecting unemployment rates, you should become knowledgeable about this topic by researching it, but choose only a few key sources to illustrate. As with analysis, for this topic and purpose, a little could go a long way in developing ethos and logos in your essay.

So, it looks like an expository essay is best for our purposes here, with a little analysis and research to help your ethos and logos along the way.

Keep in mind that a strong essay or a strong writing assignment carefully considers genre use and/or a combination of genre uses. An argument can contain analysis and narrative. A narrative can include research and argument. Choosing the right genre to support the thesis of a writing assignment is the goal.

Additional Genres and Brief Descriptions

Literary

Literary texts are generally defined as fiction, nonfiction essays, creative writing pieces, drama, and poetry. Students are often asked to read novels and analyze the plot and characters. We often are asked to read poems and engage in a discussion on artistry and meaning and write **literary critique** essays (much like the critical reading responses from chapter 2). Aside from literature that is assigned for class work, we often engage in reading literature that sparks our imagination or is entertaining.

The Article

Popular Articles

The most popular form of the article is the texts we read in newspapers and magazines. Articles can be general and speak broadly about a general subject or topic. In newspapers we read articles about current events, fabulous places to visit, and important people in our local or state communities. In popular magazines we read articles about celebrities and culture.

Scholarly Articles

Articles can also appear in professional and subject-matter magazines, journals. For example, a magazine on men's health may be full of focused articles written by professionals in the fields of nutrition, exercise, and medicine. Groups of professionals often publish journals that contain articles that focus on their particular specialization. Students are often required to research and consult scholarly and professional articles for writing assignments.

The Essay

There are several genres under this broad category.

- ▶ The Persuasion (also called argument)
- ▶ The Expository Essay (an essay that informs or explains a particular topic)
- ▶ The Analysis (also called critique)

The Research Paper

The research paper is usually a lengthy "essay" that focuses on utilizing scholarly source material as evidence and support for a focused thesis, hypothesis, analysis, or argument.

The Blog or Webpage

These spaces on the Internet are highly visual. Text is usually accompanied by color, sound, video clips, music, and animation of some form. The important point to understand about blog or webpage creation is that the text, or information, can be viewed by many people from many different corners of the world. Because the Internet is a public space, writers must keep in mind that what they read and/or produce is subject to validation by others. Blogs and webpages are used to post all genres of writing.

Social Media

Social technologies like Twitter, Facebook, and Instagram (to name a few) are primarily used to communicate with a select group of individuals. However, social technology spaces can be very public too. These spaces are usually informal spaces where people post a wide variety of information. Some social networkers use these spaces to transmit or share other genres of writing (such as articles or news reports). Social technologies are informal in that there is no clear defined theme for usage. Blogs and webpages often focus on specific subject areas, whereas social network sites contain a wide variety of themes and interests.

Composition Methods and Genre

Once a genre is selected to best suit the writing goals assigned, students must select a method suited to the genre and purpose.

Contractors who build homes and carpenters who build furniture use similar tools and practice similar methods as they build. Both contractors and carpenters need hammers, saws, and screwdrivers. But contractors and carpenters use different types of hammers, saws, and screwdrivers. A carpenter that is building a wood-and-glass display cabinet would certainly not select a hammer that a contractor uses for roofing. In short, every task has the proper tool, and those tools must also be modified to fit the task.

The Composition Toolbox

Below is a chart of the tools you can use when composing. Each tool is defined with an example provided, using this topic and thesis: Students should use the campus recreational center rather than a private gym to improve their health.

Composition Tool & Definition	Example
Description to describe using facts (size, color, weight) or using senses (sight, sound, smell, taste, feel)	At the campus recreation center all I see are monstrous glass doors and people rushing about. Women are dressed up cutely or wearing heavy sweat suits. The men wear sleeveless shirts and show off their muscles. Some people are struggling to climb a rock wall. Near the locker rooms I smell everyone sweating.
Observation to witness or share experiences from the first-person point of view	There are all types of body shapes at the gym. I see people on my left in a room dancing Zumba. Up on the second floor I see a Ping-Pong table and a court filled with people playing basketball. On the third floor people are running on the indoor track.
Explanation to dissect an idea, process, action or object into parts, then present them in an orderly arrangement	The gym is a place where people go to stay fit and meet new people. It has equipment and people to help you design a fitness plan. Fitness instructors, food nutritionist, zumba instructors, yoga, and kickboxing experts help you stay motivated to succeed.
Definition to draw a line or boundary around the meaning you want your readers to understand; to pronounce the scope of your meaning	Personal trainers, coaches, and nutritionists are hired to advise those using the recreation center. Professionals are individuals with extensive education, training, testing and certification in a specialized area of health and fitness.
Anecdote a short story or narrative used as illustration of an idea or event	One day I went to the doctor's office for a physical and learned I wasn't as healthy as I thought. My doctor told me that my blood was iron deficient and my bones weren't as strong as they should be. I have suffered from knee pain for a few years. He also told me I should be taking advantage of the energy I have because as I get older my body must be stronger.
Example/Analogy to provide a model; to illustrate a point	What happens if you buy a car and ignore maintenance advice? You never check the oil, the tire air pressure, or take it in for a tune-up. Eventually the car will become inoperable. Of course, you can always buy a new car to replace the one you did not take care of. You cannot do the same with your body, if it breaks down and is irreparable, you do not get to buy a new one.
Hypothetical Scenario to invent a situation to assist in modeling or explaining	What would happen to my health if I did not follow my doctor's advice? I am focused on my studies, but I cannot make school an excuse for being lazy. Lack of exercise could potentially lead to a weight gain of twenty-five pounds over four years. That twenty-five pounds would wear away my knee joints, and by the time I reached graduation, I might need knee replacement surgery.

Composition Tool & Definition	Example
Compare/Contrast to show similarities and/or differences	While diet and exercising are necessary for good health, they work in two different ways. A proper diet fuels the body, allowing exercise to be much more efficient. Exercise uses the fuel to burn fat and build muscles.
Cause and Effect to explain how one event can be assumed to cause a secondary event	The lack of a healthy diet made me lethargic and unmotivated. I changed my diet and found I had more energy. With more energy (and a higher level of iron in my body) I was able to exercise, build muscle, burn fat, and I felt better.
Process or Procedure shows how something occurs	I attend the gym daily and I want to learn more. My trainer started me out slowly. I cut a few bad eating habits a week and started with low impact workouts. After three weeks I moved to aerobic exercises. At six weeks I started lifting weights. Two months later I lost fifteen pounds. Sometimes I cheated on my diet, but my trainer said that is part of the process. We have to lose bad habits and replace them with positive behaviors.
Evaluation to critique for value using a set of specific criteria	The campus recreation center and the professional staff help students stay healthy and fit. The membership is $60 a year. Most gym memberships cost $40 a month and they do not have all the amenities the campus has. The campus center is convenient for students because students can go there before, between, or after classes.
Classification to sort information or ideas into groups to facilitate understanding	There are three types of people at the recreation center. The first type enjoy the company and motivation of others. The second type of people are like me, shy and uninformed, but willing. The third type are the experienced who have made fun, health, and fitness a part of their lives. These three types make the center effective and enjoyable.
Analysis to divide, or break up the subject into its parts to show your readers how something works; to explain how you arrived at a conclusion	Learning about exercising and how good it is for physical and mental well-being is important. For good results people should know the type of exercise best for their fitness level. No one should ever begin a diet and exercise program without the help of a trained professional because the consequences can lead to permanent injuries. My experience has taught me not to take my health lightly and that it takes a little courage, determination, and an open mind to manage health properly.

There are additional rhetorical situations, and genres not commonly found in composition classes, but that might be found in other disciplines such as business, criminal justice, medicine, science, or athletics, among many others. In each of those disciplines, the genres chosen might be a memo or quarterly report, or a police report, a scientific paper, or a patient record. The composition toolbox above will help you write in those genres since it is meant to help you write across the curriculum in every class you attend. Understanding the rhetorical situation that exists in any discipline you may encounter in college and beyond can help you, as a reader, decipher the information you need, and as a writer, make your writing more effective and powerful.

Engaging the Gears: Activities for Practice

Classroom Activity

Below you will find prompts asking you to practice using your toolbox in small groups. Your instructor will decide how many peers should be in a group. Each group will select/or be assigned one or two of the prompts below and spend some time responding to the prompt by practicing the tool indicated (refer to the chart on pages 155–156). Once this is completed, share your group work in class and see how well each tool is demonstrated in the shared work.

1. Imagine you are majoring in design and you have been asked to write an essay that tells readers the difference between design and efficiency. You decide to begin your essay with a description of your own kitchen. In 200 words, **describe** your kitchen at home. Be sure to include concrete and sensory details.

2. You are taking a public speaking class and have been asked to observe two people talking in a casual environment. Your instructor has asked you to observe body language. Your assignment is to share your observations. In 200 words, describe your **observations**.

3. Your friend wants to enroll at your campus, and e-mailed you asking you what steps she must take. Write a 200-word response that **explains** the most important steps.

4. Your cousin has been reprimanded for cheating on a test at school. Write a 200-word **anecdote** that will sympathetically and compassionately tell your cousin why this type of behavior in the present might cause problems in the future.

5. A peer is confused about how the planets orbit. Despite all other efforts, this peer still does not understand. Write a 200-word letter that provides an **example or analogy** of how the planets orbit. The only catch is that you cannot refer to the planets, because that is confusing to your peer. What other example, or analogy, can you provide to explain?

6. The class is debating capital punishment. You feel that capital punishment is unfair. Your instructor asks you to provide evidence supporting your point. You do not have access to the Internet for research and you have five minutes to provide an example. Create a 200-word **hypothetical scenario** to support your position.

7. Which makes for a better pet? A cat or a dog? Write a 200-word opinion piece for your local newspaper. Use **comparison and contrast** to illustrate your position.

8. As a college student you have been informed about The Freshman Fifteen (the notion that college freshmen gain fifteen pounds during their first year in college). You are trying to avoid the weight gain. You are writing yourself a 200-word "warning" about what might **cause** you to gain fifteen pounds.

9. When you visit a doctor or a dentist, you might notice that each office has a particular set of procedures. From the moment you walk in, until the moment you walk out, procedures are put in place to ensure that you have received the best service. In 200 words, explain the **procedure** at your doctor or dentist's office.

10. Think about a recent film you have watched and that you did not enjoy. Write a 200-word evaluation explaining why you did not enjoy the film.

Writing Activity 1

Choosing the Right Genre for the Task:

Consider writing an essay on online/Internet shopping. Which genre would best support our ideas about online shopping? Below are three different prompts about online/Internet shopping. For each, in less than 200 words, write a brief proposal indicating which genre best suits the needs of the prompt and why.

1. Create a debate or ask your readers to begin shopping online.

2. Review reports regarding online shopping and report on a variety of responses, reactions, and experiences on online shopping.

3. Share personal stories from your friends and family about their online shopping experiences.

Writing Activity 2

Using the Toolbox in a Specific Genre:

For this activity you will be writing a 200–300-word police report about a car accident. To do this you will first need to know the genre conventions of police reports.

Police reports begin with a synopsis, or a very brief summary of what happened.

For example:

> A car traveling on Elm Street struck a pedestrian after she entered the intersection against the traffic light.

The synopsis is followed by a concise and detailed report about the incident that includes the following:

> On April 1, 2014, at approximately 12:15 a.m., in light rain, Maliq Smith (35 years old), the driver of a dark blue, 2012 Ford Fusion, while driving east on Kester Rd., struck pedestrian Penelope Diaz (27 years old) as she attempted to cross Kester Rd. at the intersection with Orange Blvd. Maliq Smith proceeded east through the intersection on a green light, while Diaz entered the intersection without a walk signal. Skid marks indicate that Diaz was struck at approximately 25 mph, and she reported that she was thrown to the north side of the street. She walked to the sidewalk where she awaited medical care. Smith removed his car from the intersection to the side of the road, called emergency services from his cell phone and attempted to assist Diaz as she waited for medical care. Henderson Valley Paramedics arrived at approximately 12:45 a.m. and transported Diaz to Henderson Hospital. Maliq Smith was questioned by Officer Alexander Johnson, and released at 2:00 a.m. There were no witnesses to the accident and no traffic camera at the intersection.

The police report then requires you to use the following composition tools:

- ► Narrative (chronological narrative of what happened)
- ► Description (describe in concrete details: location, time, involved persons, location and description of surrounding area relevant to the incident)
- ► Observation (observe what you see—who was involved and what happened before, during, and after the incident)

These composition skills will be used to:

▶ Write an objective report

▶ Write an informative report

Remember to engage in understanding your rhetorical situation:

▶ What is the subject of your police report?

▶ What is the purpose of your police report?

▶ Who is the audience of the police report?

Now for this Assignment:

Watch the following video of a car accident, pay close attention as you watch it because your observation is important to the report.

https://www.youtube.com/watch?v=0L41AdmLijo

Writing Task: Write a police report with a one-sentence synopsis followed by a 200-word detailed report. Do not exceed the word count, and do not leave out important details.

CHAPTER TEN

Images and Visual Rhetoric: Interpretation and Analysis

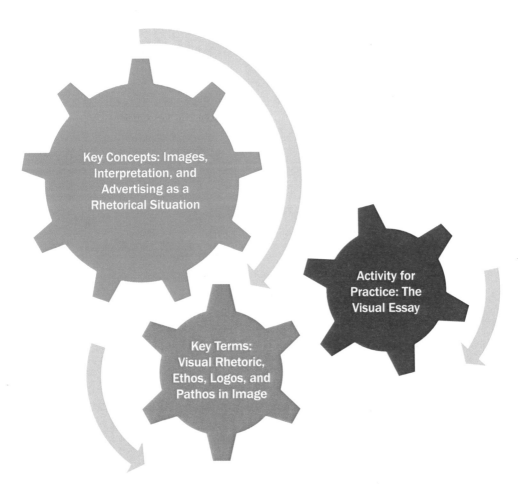

A visual image in the hand of an artist is merely a tool to trigger a mental image.

—Roy H. Williams

It did what all ads are supposed to do: create an anxiety relievable by purchase.

—David Foster Wallace, *Infinite Jest*

Images as Messages

We are exposed to hundreds of images on a daily basis: one-dimensional images, moving images, and three-dimensional objects. These images are in our homes, our schools, our workplaces, our markets, malls, and museums. Some images persuade us to act or react through suggestive political campaign posters or through advertisements aimed at recruiting consumers. Other images attempt to please us through a sense of beauty and art.

All day long we see images and interpret them almost without thinking. Yet, visual or aural (heard) images, as Roy Williams suggests in the epigraph above, create mental images, and it is with mental images that we shape our thoughts. Images, then, have the power to shape our values, our beliefs, and our attitudes, and so shape us as individuals, groups, and communities. Therefore it is important to understand the power of the image and then develop critical skills to "read" an image and shape our interpretations more consciously and critically.

In the first few chapters of this book, you learned that the rhetorical situation exists whenever you read or write. Images and objects are like texts that can be read, but instead of using only words, they also, sometimes exclusively, use a visual appeal, or in the case of moving images, often include aural (or heard) images. If that is true, then images also ask us to consider the rhetorical situation.

Our sensory system is the way that we receive messages, and when we see an image, or when we hear a sound (aural image), it engages our senses and creates an emotional response or reaction. This response or reaction is the intended message of the image, or its purpose, in terms of the rhetorical situation. So, in addition to sharing a rhetorical situation with reading and writing, images and objects also appeal to the rhetorical elements of ethos, pathos, and logos. We call this visual rhetoric.

Visual analysis is the basis of many disciplines and professions. If you are majoring in art, you must write papers analyzing how a specific culture during a specific time period evaluated images in art. Likewise, history students will analyze how paintings, photographs, and other visual materials recorded history—and how those images are understood today. Film majors will evaluate how the movie industry interprets popular culture, history, religion—and a wide range of global issues. Business majors will analyze the impact of visual images in marketing and on consumers. Health majors will examine how images of food, drugs, or behavior impact our health. Physicians are educated to first look at how a patient appears—does the skin tone reflect illness or health? How do the eyes look, what is the patient's posture? Learning to thoughtfully engage in visual analysis in order to understand and apply visual rhetoric will allow you to practice critical thinking skills that will become vital to any profession.

You've seen the image below before, in chapter 2, where we discussed the way to analyze a text. Just like a textual analysis, an image analysis begins by peeling off the first layer— a layer that can be defined as an initial reaction. We ask ourselves: What is the intended message? What is the purpose of the image? What must a viewer know prior to seeing the image to understand it? Then, we think about who might be the audience and how might they respond to the image. In the final layer, we perform a close reading of the composition of the image, and we analyze what elements of the image's composition create that the response.

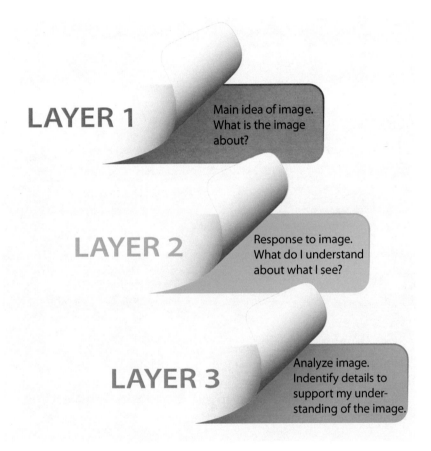

Messages and Analysis

Let's begin a visual analysis using these strategies. We will begin with simple images that will allow you to record your ideas and think about your own reactions and responses. The chart below, modified from chapter 2, should help you with that. Keep referring to it as we walk through these more simple images, and later, on to more complex images.

Pre-Reading	Developing Understanding	Interpreting	Reflecting
Have a look: what is familiar about this image?	What does this image mean?	How does this information relate to prior knowledge and outside texts, or ideas?	What are the effects of these strategies?
Scan image for clues about what message is there, and for the genre of image: advertisement, road sign, product packaging, film, art, vlogs, etc.	Annotations: what might each component imply, or express?	Summarize, infer, analyze, synthesize, evaluate (see chapter 3).	What meaning is present? Do you agree? Why? Why Not?
Take note of components: color, lighting, sound (if present), text (if present), shapes, arrangement, size, foreground, background, etc.	Who is the source of the image? What do you know about that source?	Structural and organizational analysis: Why are those components chosen? Why are the components arranged this order? What effect do these choices have on the audience?	Does it contrast with other knowledge? What details were left out? And why? What would change if those components were included? How does that change the message?
Can you predict meaning and purpose?	What might be the purpose? Who is the audience?	Rhetorical strategies: what parts of the image appeal to the elements of ethos, logos and pathos?	What questions do I still have?

What is your initial reaction to the simple image below? What initial associations do you make? How does it make you feel, or what does it make you think? As mentioned earlier, an image prompts mental, emotional, and physical responses from you, the viewer (audience).

Use the chart above. What kind (genre) of image is it? Take note of the components: What is familiar? What association(s) can you make with this image? Can you predict meaning?

We might associate the color of the image above with the reaction "to go." This initial association or reaction might be caused because we most commonly, almost on a daily basis, see such a shape and color on an intersection street signal.

Layered or Multiple Reactions

A layered reaction is a reaction that causes successive reactions, each one leading to a new (or different) reaction. For example, initially we might associate the green circle with a "go" light—and then our next reaction might be to think about a button, like an "on" button that we might push with a finger. We might have a third reaction, another layer, that might make us think of a planet or a face. Layered reactions happen because we have individual reactions to all the elements of an image; the color, the shape, the size, the possible connections to our experiences. Understanding and interpreting an image often happens in this layered way. We have an initial reaction or response that leads us to think more deeply about what we are seeing, and what the possibilities of meaning are.

Now, let's look at another image:

It is just like the first image, but now has changed color. Answer the same questions you answered for the green circle, and then answer this question: How does your reaction to the yellow circle differ from, or is similar to, your reaction to the green circle?

Each element of an image adds another layer of response or meaning. Understanding develops as an aggregate experience; each image creates meaning by building one component on another. Our responses to an image can become complex when we become aware of how the parts impact the whole image. We can not only understand the message, but also its implications, as well as predict the response, and impact of the image on audience.

If we combine both of the images and colors above, and add one more component, we might find ourselves analyzing a familiar visual object with an intended message.

Above is a familiar and "understandable" object to analyze and we can begin to break down the parts of the whole. A green light indicates to drivers and pedestrians who has permission to "go." An amber or yellow light indicates to drivers and pedestrians that traffic must slow and prepare to stop. And of course, we understand that a red light means drivers and pedestrians must stop.

But these colors mean more than go, slow, and stop. These colors have a language that we have come to understand. Green means, "the coast is clear." Yellow indicates "caution," and red indicates "danger." When we analyze an image we look at shapes and colors and ask ourselves what meaning comes with those shapes and colors and how those meanings have developed.

What happens when those meanings are not understood by all who read the image? For example, how does an individual who is color-blind and cannot distinguish the three colors of a stoplight come to understand what this image/object means?

What happens if the structure or the organization of the image changes?

Would pedestrians and drivers unfamiliar with a horizontal stoplight experience hesitation at reading and interpreting the meaning? Would this cause traffic problems for those only familiar with the lighted messages of a vertical stoplight?

Pedestrians and drivers understand that stoplights are designed to create order and to promote walking and driving safety through common understanding of the image. Yet even with this common understanding, accidents at stoplights occur. Pedestrians "walk against the light," ignoring the meaning of a stoplight changing from yellow to red. Drivers who "run red lights" and cause intersection crashes might say, "I thought I could make the yellow light, " interpreting the yellow light to mean "proceed with caution" rather than "prepare to stop for red light."

Stop lights are fairly simple images whose purpose is clear and non-controversial. Let's take a look at what happens when the image becomes more complex.

Visual Rhetoric: Advertising Analysis

Advertising is everywhere and in many different forms persuading us, educating us, shocking us: all to serve the primary purpose of calling us to act by purchasing a product, or donating to a cause, committing to a program or contract, voting for a candidate, or simply changing our behavior, as public service announcements do. Those who create advertisements design them to influence us. Yet, they know they have only a matter of seconds to appeal to us, so they strive to make those few seconds memorable.

How do ads, or visual arguments, accomplish this task? Well, they use the *elements of rhetoric* with images and text—sometimes alone, sometimes combined. It is your job and goal, as a critical reader, to detect, and evaluate the quality of the argument presented in the advertisement. After all, since they are calling on you to act, you should understand the underlying assumptions advertisers make about you, the consumer, the product's real value, as well as your own values before you part with that hard-earned cash, sign a long-term contract, or vote for that candidate.

Think back to the last three purchases you made. What did you purchase and why? What influenced you to decide upon that purchase? Can you connect your decisions to a print advertisement or commercial? While people (our friends and family) can influence our decisions when making a purchase, it is highly likely that whatever the source of influence, that source was also informed or influenced by an image.

In advertising, images come in many forms. Chances are, if asked, you can describe the design of several product logos off the top off your head. Images, like product logos, create what is called brand recognition. Brand recognition makes the product more familiar to us, so the next time around, our attention falls to the same product, and causes us to repurchase it. Television commercials work in the same way static or print images work, except they have the added features of movement often choreographed to sound.

Here are some beginning critical questions to ask yourself as we begin analyzing an image for persuasion. You will find that these questions are similar to the questions we have covered in other chapters in this book, and to the earlier chart, but modified to focus on persuasive elements.

What is the rhetorical situation? *(topic, purpose, audience)*

- ▶ What are they advertising? *(topic)*
- ▶ What is their argument? *(purpose)*
- ▶ Who is their target audience? *(audience)*

What makes up the image, what is the rhetorical composition of the image?

- ▶ What images are present and why?
- ▶ How do the images and text support their argument? Or help you understand the argument? Summarize the main components.
- ▶ What specific supporting details (components) are used? Why did they choose these details? Why not other details?
- ▶ What types of evidence, if any, support their claim? How does the evidence support the claim?
- ▶ What might be left out of the image? Why did they leave it out?
- ▶ If it is a television or Internet advertisement, with sound and/or music, why did they include that particular sound or music? How does that shape your perceptions as a viewer?

Then identify the appeals to rhetorical elements:

▶ Which elements of the advertisement appeal to *logos*?

▶ Which elements of the advertisement appeal to *ethos*?

▶ Which elements of the advertisement appeal to *pathos*?

▶ Are these appeals legitimate, or do they employ any *logical fallacies?* (see chapter 11)

▶ Are these elements used in balance, or are one or two elements relied on more than the others? Why did they choose that strategy? What effect does this have on the reader/listener/viewer of the ad?

Now let's take a look at an advertisement and apply these critical questions:

Courtesy of Molly Nguyen

What is the rhetorical situation? *(topic, purpose, audience):*

What are they advertising?

> *They are advertising the harmfulness of cigarettes to the quality of life, or promoting non-smoking behavior.*

What is their argument? Purpose?

> *The ad's purpose is to persuade people to quit smoking, or not start at all.*

Restate the ad's purpose as a thesis statement:

> *"Smoking cigarettes will 'burn up' your chances for love and happiness."*

Who is their target audience?

> *The target audience is young people beginning their lives.*

Then look to the rhetorical composition of the image:

How does the image/text support their argument? Or help you understand the argument? Summarize the main components:

> *There is a cigarette in someone's hand with a cartoon-like image of lovers smiling at each other. The cigarette has burned up half of the image, and the hot embers are approaching the young lovers. There is no text; we can see the danger the lovers are in.*

What specific supporting details (components) are used? Why did they choose these details? Why not other details?

> *The hearts all around the young lovers show us they are in love and floating in happiness. They represent "love and happiness." These details are "cute" and cartoon-like, appealing to young people. Also, the burning embers are very close to the lovers to indicate danger, so all of that on the cigarette implies that it is cigarettes that will destroy this happy couple's life. No need for any other details, as the picture is complete, even without text it is a very effective message.*

What types of evidence, if any, support their claim? How does the evidence support the claim?

> *There is no "evidence" such as facts, or statistics, so the image "burning up" is the only evidence the ad supplies.*

What might be left out of the image? Why did they leave it out?

> *Text is absent because the image is so effective delivering the anti-smoking message, it isn't needed. Adding text might have distracted from the effective image.*

Then identify the appeals to rhetorical elements:

Which elements of the advertisement appeal to *logos*?

> *The burning ember approaching the lovers is a weak appeal to logos: it is logical to avoid danger when it is present, but there is no direct or strong appeal to logos.*

Which elements of the advertisement appeal to *ethos*?

> *There is also no direct appeal to ethos, but even the weak appeal to logos brings a little ethos to the image.*

Which elements of the advertisement appeal to *pathos*?

> *The image appeals almost entirely to pathos: there is a happy (emotion) image of young lovers in the clouds, followed by the danger (emotion—fear) approaching. "Happiness is in danger of burning if I smoke" is the resulting idea from this emotional appeal.*

Are these appeals legitimate, or do they employ any *logical fallacies*?

> *There is no deceptive or fallacious use of any of the elements. Everyone already knows smoking is bad for your health, but this image seems to provide a context that young people might relate to better, as it shows an immediate kind of danger, rather than the long-term dangers of smoking (no one immediately dies from smoking). But this shift in danger from long-term to short term doesn't seem deceptive or misleading, especially since the burning embers are burning up "love and happiness," and both are long-term quality-of-life states.*

Are these elements used in balance, or are one or two elements relied on more than the others? Why did they choose that strategy?

> *This image relies mostly on pathos to convey the message that smoking is danger-ous. It does this because appeals to pathos are needed to call people to action. In this case acting to quit, or refuse to smoke. By threatening danger to love and happiness, it is threatening not just life itself, but the quality of life, and this might appeal to young people who often see themselves as invincible because they are so young.*

The analysis above is meant as a model for you to use when you develop your own image analysis, or to consider when you need to create an image of your own. The skill of visual analysis, as exemplified in the model above, shows us the importance and value of understanding why an image is created, and how it is created. Understanding how an image influences our thoughts, ideas, and beliefs allows us to think more criti-cally about what we see, and how it changes our ideas or perceptions.

Engaging the Gears: Activities for Practice

Classroom Activity

Below are several images. Form small groups of approximately four to five people, and using the guidelines in this chapter, analyze one of the images below. Develop answers to questions found in the chart, and from the list of questions for visual rhetoric. Pres-ent your findings to your classmates.

Image 1

Image 2

Image 3

Image 4

Image 5

Image 6

Image 7

Image 8

Image 9

Compare two images: Analyze each image below, then discuss how the differences affect the meaning, and/or purpose.

Image 10

Image 11

Writing Activity 1

Advertisement Analysis Assignment

For this assignment, you will choose an advertisement from a magazine, newspaper, or the Internet (YouTube ads are OK too) and analyze (using the list of questions on pages 167–170) the advertisement you chose for its rhetorical situation and its rhetorical elements in 1–2 pages, completing the tasks below.

Writing Task:

► **Summary:**

Summarize the reason for the advertisement and its visual and textual elements in 1–2 paragraphs.

► **Rhetorical Situation:**

Identify the rhetorical situation for the advertisement (its purpose and audience only—topic is part of the summary above).

► **Elements of Rhetoric:**

Identify and explain the elements of rhetoric (ethos, logos, and pathos) present in the ad; start a new paragraph for each element, labeling the paragraph accordingly.

► **Analysis:**

Explain why you think the authors of the advertisement made the choices they made and write your conclusion in the form of a thesis statement.

► **Response: A Summary Analysis:**

On your class website or blog, in class as a presentation, or as a printed document, produce the ad itself (or the link to the online ad) and one paragraph that summarizes your response(s) to all of the above tasks. Revise, edit, and proofread this paragraph for unity, clarity, and concise language. This last task is your analysis, summarized for others to read.

Additional resources for advertising techniques:

► A link to "Dove Revolution" a video essay on ad making techniques
   http://www.youtube.com/watch?v=iYhCn0jf46U

► A PDF for other advertising techniques
   http://medialiteracy.net/pdfs/hooks.pdf

► A website about media deconstruction by author and teacher, Antonio R. Lopez
   http://www.world-bridger.com

Writing Activity 2

The Visual Essay

For this assignment you will create a visual essay. Instead of analyzing an image that is produced by someone other than yourself, you will be the creator of the image and your peers will have the task of analyzing the message in your visual essay.

Your visual essay may be a drawing, a painting, a collage, a video, or an object, like a sculpture.

The image or object that you create should consider your rhetorical situation, and the elements of rhetoric (ethos, pathos, and logos).

Brainstorm—Freewrite

To begin this assignment think about who you are, your life experiences, and what is important to you and why it is important. This can be anything from family traditions to environmental protection. There are no word minimums or maximums—just write. Some free-writing prompts are offered below to help you get started, or gear you back up if you become "blocked."

Free-writing prompts: Fill in details as you think of them to help generate a topic.

> My greatest dream is . . .
> People think I am . . .
> If I could do anything I would . . .
> My destiny is . . .
> I excel at . . .
> When I was seven years old I . . .
> I would like to change . . .
> Happiness is . . .
> My most valued possession is . . .
> When I am fifty years old the world will be ...

Focus—Purpose

When you have finished freewriting, carefully read and review your work. Select one idea to focus on and expand upon. For example, if you found you wrote much about family traditions you might ask yourself which traditions are most important to you and your family, or if other families share similar traditions, and are these traditions connected to culture or religion?

Now you can begin to create the parts of your visual essay. What are the parts of the family traditions; who is involved, what happens, what does the preparation for the ritual or event "look like," what is valuable about the tradition? Remember, you will be producing an image, and that image and each part of it can function as a paragraph or sentence might. As the creator of this image you will provide the clues that help your audience understand your message.

Visual Medium

Choose the medium that is best suited to your topic, or to your skills. In any case, a strong visual message is much like a strong essay—the details are important. Be sure to include the important components that provide your message and the supporting details to deliver that message. The visual essay may be produced in the following mediums: drawing, a painting, a collage, or video. It can also be an object, like a sculpture.

Presentation

Your visual essay will be shared with your peers in an informal presentation. Your peers will analyze the visual rhetoric in your production and look for clues about your meaning or purpose.

You will then facilitate a conversation with your peers. This conversation will be shaped largely by their observations and questions to you, about what they see and understand in your work. Be prepared to explain your work to your audience.

Tips

If you create a visual essay that is too large or cumbersome to bring to class, you may be permitted to take a photograph of it and create an electronic presentation. Or, if your visual essay is created online using some form of production technology, the tips below will be useful.

Here are some tips to keep in mind for PowerPoint or Prezi presentations:

▶ PowerPoint slides should be uncluttered. They should not have a lot of text or images crammed onto the slide; slides are meant to supplement your oral presentation, not replicate it word by word.

▶ The PowerPoint presentation should be dynamic and interesting, but be precise in your choice of "bells and whistles" to make sure that your slides do not distract from the content of your presentation and your ideas.

▶ When choosing font styles, size, and color for slides, think about the room you will present in, the size of your audience and how far away some of your audience might be (again, be considerate of your audience!) Don't choose hard-to-see colors, or font size. Make sure the important ideas are not obscured by faded or poorly contrasted colors, or sizes, or complicated fonts.

If your presentation has a time limit, practice it before your presentation date to be sure you aren't short of time, or too long, to avoid embarrassing moments. Presentations are difficult enough without having to fill in empty space or get cut off by your host or instructor. See if you can present in front of some peers for practice to get revision feedback before presentation day.

CHAPTER ELEVEN

Logical Reasoning and Logical Fallacies

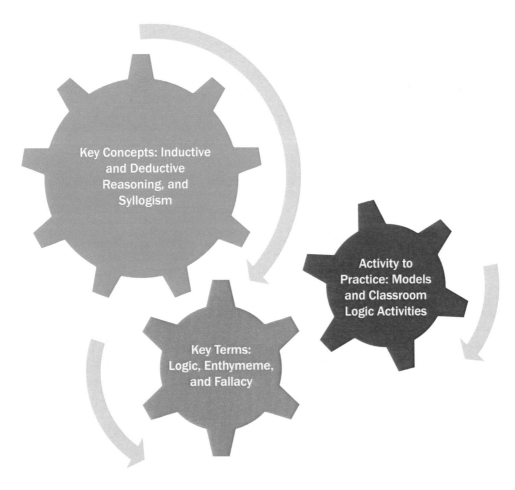

It is reason, and not passion, which must guide our deliberations, guide our debate, and guide our decision.

—Barbara Jordan

He that will not reason is a bigot; he that cannot reason is a fool; and he that dares not reason is a slave.

—Lord Byron

We have been discussing the concept of reason in general terms in many of the chapters in this textbook. Here, in this chapter, we will discuss the concept of reason, specifically the concept of logic, and false, or fallacious logic. In order to think and write well ourselves, and to critically evaluate others' thinking and writing, we must be able to understand how reasoning works. We must ask, what does *reasoning* look like, how is it structured, and why is getting it wrong so common, and yet so avoidable?

Logos, the Greek word for logic as an action, or a way of thinking, is an important tool in the pursuit of arguments that are sound and that promote understanding. It is the topmost of tools for the purpose of persuasion, whether for your career, or your finances, or your politics, but especially for your immediate future as a college student.

Developing strong reasoning skills, *critical thinking*, is the primary benefit of an academic education. And strong reasoning skills that can use specific criteria to evaluate information, and then communicate that evaluation clearly to others, are needed in all fields, from communications to engineering, and from science to politics. The modern world is a complex web of information and ideas, and students who work to develop nimble skills of thinking and communicating about that complexity will find the modern world easier to navigate.

There are many types of reasoning: Classic, or Aristotelian logic, Toulmin logic and Rogerian logic; inductive, deductive, and abductive; and within all of those ideas about logic, there is also modal, mathematical, and symbolic logic, and the list could go on. This is because there are many ways to *see* an idea, or an object. What the larger umbrella term, *logic*, implies is that despite the many ways to *see* an idea, there is a structure, a method to use to be sure that your thinking is clear, and correct in form, so that if you were to place another idea in that structure, that idea will also be clear and correct in thought. Some academics are experts in all types of logic, and these thinkers are usually found in the field of philosophy. The word *philosophy* itself means, "love of," *philo*, "wisdom, thought," *sophy*, and so it is plain to see why that field examines many of the different modes of logic.

For the purposes of introducing the concept of logic, and logos in rhetorical composition, we will look closely at inductive reasoning, deductive reasoning, the syllogism and enthymeme, and a short list of common logical fallacies (false logic in either structure, or premise), and likely, you will learn other types of logic, and other forms of fallacy as you progress toward your degree(s).

Inductive Reasoning

In chapter 2, we discussed the idea of inference, a conclusion we make about what is not known by examining what is known, or what is factual. Inference is part of what inductive reasoning does. Inductive reasoning moves from the specific details to a broader *inference*, and when the connections themselves can be tested and repeated, as in the scientific method, *conclusions* can be made. These conclusions are then held as reasonably true, or reliably true, but never absolutely true, since the introduction of a detail not previously known can alter the conclusion irrevocably. Yet, the conclusion will often be used to further another type of argument by becoming the major premise in deductive reasoning—see below.

For example, if you work as a barista in a local coffee shop, and you notice that for the six months you have been a barista, a man comes in at the same time every weekday morning, and orders the same thing each time: a mocha latte and a chocolate chip bagel, you can draw a number of inferences from these facts:

- ▶ The man either works or lives nearby the shop
- ▶ The man has a regular schedule during the week
- ▶ The man likes chocolate, coffee, and bagels

We can also reasonably predict that the man will come on the next weekday. Induction is drawing a conclusion that follows from the details or experiences we know.

Deductive Reasoning

Deductive reasoning is the opposite of inductive reasoning, but they are closely related. Deductive reasoning is reasoning that takes a general principle, and reasons the details from it. That general principle is often a conclusion drawn from inductive reasoning.

For example, if we used the details of the man and the coffee shop from above, we can infer that he is a chocolate lover, and then form this inductive argument that:

People who eat chocolate every day are chocolate fans.

If we then take a specific example, Jane eats chocolate donuts every day, we can deduce that Jane, too, is a chocolate fan. Here, the specific example of Jane, and the general principle that chocolate fans eat chocolate every day combine to conclude that Jane is a chocolate fan. This is how we deduce facts, and in formal logic this is referred to as syllogistic reasoning.

The Syllogism

Syllogisms are formal logical structures that take two premises to conclude a third idea. The general principle is called the **Major Premise** (MP), and the specific example is called the **minor premise** (mp), and the conclusion is **C**. The formal structure of syllogism allows you to think through a claim and test it for soundness and reasonableness.

A famous syllogism deals with a universal truth: death.

Major Premise (MP):	*All people are mortal*
minor premise (mp):	*Alexandra is a person*
Conclusion (Therefore):	*Alexandra is mortal*

Here the MP is formed from a conclusion formed by inductive reasoning: every person who has ever lived has died, therefore, "All people are mortal": the many specific examples support a general principle.

Then a specific example, the mp, "Alexandra is a person" is provided, and combined we determine that "Alexandra is mortal."

In the case of chocolate lovers, let's see how this works:

> **MP:**   People who eat chocolate every day are chocolate fans.
>
> **mp:**   Alfredo eats chocolate every day.
>
> **C:**   Alfredo is a chocolate fan.

Placing our ideas into these forms can often help us see where our ideas are illogical or unreasonable. We can look at the premises as the assumptions on which the conclusion is based. In most communications however, we don't engage in these formal arguments. They would become very burdensome and tedious indeed! Instead we only deliver the conclusion, or one of the premises and the conclusion. This is the formation of the enthymeme.

The Enthymeme

The enthymeme will be more familiar to you if think of it as a thesis, or a thesis statement, or the main idea in an argument, without its premises revealed. We call this phenomenon the *underlying assumption* because it is a hidden, or underlying, idea on which the argument rests.

The enthymeme, *Alexandra is mortal,* forces you to think through the logic that led to this conclusion: *All people are mortal and Alex is a person.* And often we can see the logic clearly, especially when the premises that form those assumption are well known, such as human mortality.

But when those premises are obscure due to complexity, or not examined by questioning, it is hard to see if the conclusion is sound.

For example, let's create the enthymeme:

> *Lexy loves to cook.*

On the surface, this is a simple claim. One that would go unexamined for its assumptions because it might seem obvious that the person making this claim might know that to be true. You might just assume he or she had a conversation with Lexy about cooking. Or you decide that how this person knows that Lexy loves to cook is just trivial information that is irrelevant to you. Though, if you examine the logic that led to this conclusion, by questioning the person making the claim, you might be surprised, or in this case dismayed, by the logic he or she used.

So, let's examine the enthymeme to see the logic he or she might have used:

MP: All women love to cook.

mp: Lexy is a woman.

C: Lexy loves to cook.

This conclusion, delivered as an enthymeme, is deduced using a false premise. The **MP** (major premise) in this syllogism is false: All women love to cook is a general principle drawn from poor inductive reasoning, as there are many examples of women who don't cook, or who don't love to cook.

In making claims, arguments, or conclusions, when one of the premises (assumptions) is untrue, or illogical itself, the conclusion does not follow, and therefore the conclusion is *necessarily* false. Even if it turned out to be a fact, and Lexy does love cooking, the *reasoning* that got us there is indeed false.

This faulty reasoning demonstrates the logical fallacy of *hasty generalization,* or what we often refer to as *stereotype,* a certain kind of *hasty generalization.* And while knowing whether Lexy loves to cook is likely irrelevant to you, the logic is not. All people should be concerned about conclusions drawn from poor or false logic. The implications of the casual acceptance of false logic are troubling. Imagine that the person using stereotypes to come to conclusions is also a senator in the U.S. Congress voting on women's issues. What other important conclusions might the senator claim using stereotypes about women? Or any other type of faulty logic?

It is the job of a critical reader to expose the assumptions on which arguments are made, and to become aware of how certain assumptions, both true and false, shape our own thinking. You should be able to identify the reasoning that leads a writer, or yourself, to claim an argument. You will more effectively persuade when writing because your logos will be sound, and you will more effectively understand arguments that could affect you because you will look for the veracity, or the accuracy, of the assumptions those arguments rest upon.

Logical Fallacy

Logical fallacies come in all shapes and sizes. Generally defined, fallacies are breaks in logical thinking, misrepresentations of facts, or sometimes a combination of these errors that can occur in persuasive and argumentative speaking and writing.

Below is a short list of the most common logical fallacies used when making arguments. Look out for them in obvious places where the purpose to persuade is the main focus of the communication: advertising, political speeches, editorials in newspapers and magazines. But also look for them where the goal of persuasion doesn't seem important: discussions about life decisions, Facebook posts, Tweets, and other social media.

Fallacies are important to notice and challenge, as they can often lead to poor policies, decision making, and beliefs.

Circular Logic or Begging the Question

This kind of faulty reasoning runs in circles because it asks you to see the argument as also the fact that supports it. In its most obvious forms, we can see it here:

I am a good swimmer because I swim well.

Here the conclusion, *I am a good swimmer,* is the same as the fact that supports it, *because I swim well.* In more complicated examples though it is harder to spot:

Netflix is a popular website for watching TV shows and movies because many people watch it.

If we focus on the words "popular" and "many" we can see the conclusion and the facts that support it are synonymous.

People become poor because they have little or no money.

Here we can see that "poor" and "little or no money" are two ways to make the same statement.

Teenagers are often wrong because they are young.

Ever hear of an old teenager? This illogical statement is also based on stereotypes, but the most glaring problem rests in the words "teenagers" and "young"—one word refers back to the other.

Either-Or Fallacy

An either-or logical fallacy sets up a false argument limited by only the two options given, when other options are likely available.

You are either with us, or you are against us.

Either attend class today, or you will fail.

America. Love it or leave it.

Making these types of statements will certainly "turn off" your audience if you are attempting to be persuasive, for they leave no room for rational discussion.

These examples are often used to limit your thinking to the more acceptable option, and usually that acceptable option is the conclusion the speaker or writer wants you to assume. When, in fact, there are often many plausible alternatives.

Slippery-Slope Fallacy

A slippery-slope fallacy claims that one action will cause something else to happen.

Banning tobacco will reduce premature death rates.

Give someone an inch, and they'll take a mile.

If we ban off-shore oil drilling, we might as well get ourselves a horse and buggy.

This fallacy rests on the assumption of inevitability of the outcome, where no evidence is produced for that inevitability.

Hasty Generalization

A hasty generalization is a fallacy that concludes an outcome based on insufficient evidence. A small example is used to prove the larger idea, or only one aspect of an issue is addressed.

This year, the news reports several instances of pit bull attacks.

You conclude that all pit bulls are dangerous.

This is a hasty generalization. It is a logical fallacy because the evidence is a small sample of reports you have heard and is not based on more comprehensive reports before a conclusion is reached.

A form of hasty generalization, stereotypes about people are formed by taking the fallacy of generalization and applying it to an individual. It is a crippling false logic to apply: it cripples the thinker by limiting his or her broader cultural experience and limits the receiver of this logic (the person who is stereotyped) by ignoring the details of their individuality and assigning them with an identity of generalization that is falsely created.

Think of the example about women and cooking: The premise *all women love to cook* is a fallacy of generalization. To then assume that Lexy loves to cook because she is a woman is a stereotype formed from the false premise.

Post Hoc Ergo Propter Hoc Fallacies

Post hoc fallacies assume a cause-and-effect relationship in reverse or false order. It claims that *because* of B, A must occur. When in fact, it is simply a coincidence, or unrelated entirely.

Every time I wash my car, it rains.

If you go outside with wet hair you will catch a cold.

Here, there is no relationship of cause and effect; washing your car does not influence weather, and wet hair does not cause a cold, a virus does.

Straw Man Fallacy

A straw man fallacy ignores the opposition's actual position, then claims they hold a position that they don't actually hold, and then attacks that position. Essentially, when this fallacy is used, it misrepresents an opponent's argument to make it easier to attack. For example:

Teenager: I want to attend Sally's birthday party next Saturday.

Parent: Not this time, we have plans to visit your grandmother.

Teenager: Why must you keep me prisoner? I should be allowed out once in a while!

Ad Hominem Fallacy

The name-calling fallacy (ad hominem) engages in personal attacks, rather than attacks on the argument presented.

The leader of the anti-gun movement is an ignorant fool who does not understand constitutional rights.

Non Sequitur Fallacy

A non sequitur is an error in the connection of two events or ideas. It means *"it does not follow."*

If we change the legal drinking age to eighteen, then teenagers will become alcoholics.

Bandwagon Fallacy

Bandwagon appeals are emotional appeals to your sense of belonging. Everyone else does it, so why shouldn't I? Or, no one does anything so why should I? Here your loyalty to the group is at play, rather than the morality of the action/inaction itself.

Rationalization Fallacy

Rationalization occurs when a writer creates an excuse for action (or inaction).

I can never be on time for my 8 a.m. class because it is hard to wake up early.

This writer doesn't accept the idea that while difficult, it is possible to wake up on time.

There are many more instances of faulty logic. Use your search engine to find more, or consult a textbook dedicated to logic and logical fallacy for more information.

Engaging the Gears: Activity for Practice

Classroom Activity 1

Identify the underlying assumptions (or the absent premises) in the following enthymemes:

Since it rained yesterday, the golf course must still be wet.

MP:

mp:

C:

We pay taxes so there should be no highway tolls.

MP:

mp:

C:

Snowboarding is a dangerous sport.

MP:

mp:

C:

Cars older than twenty years are unreliable.

MP:

mp:

C:

Employers hire competent workers, so students should care about their grades.

MP:

mp:

C:

Be sure to be on the lookout for logical fallacies!

Classroom Activity 2

Using classroom activity 1 as a model, create a set of five different syllogisms that use correct deductive reasoning.

Classroom Activity 3

Carefully read the composition below. It is a first draft of an argument. The student has outlined reasons why grading should be eliminated. As you read, carefully underline arguments that are illogical, or represent a logical fallacy. Be sure to annotate each fallacy by indicating what type of fallacy is committed. Remember that poor inductive and deductive reasoning also leads to illogical conclusions or statements. Also keep in mind what you have learned about enthymemes. Some logical fallacies may be difficult to categorize or label because they are caused by poor inductive and deductive skills or are a combination of two types of logical fallacies.

Eliminating Grading

The grading scale. It is a scale used by public and private schools to determine whether the students meet the school's requirements, but also to test students on their ability to be responsible. We need to eliminate the grading scale because we don't need it, earning an A, B, C, D, or F doesn't really determine intelligence, and it just promotes competition between students.

The grading scale indicates responsibility and how obedient you are in following directions. If an 'A' is earned it means that directions were followed with excellent performance. A 'B' means that the student did what they were told with good performance, but not great. A 'C' means the performance was fair and the minimum requirements were met. A "D" followed by an "F" means that the student did not attempt to make any effort in meeting at least the minimum requirements, and the performance was unacceptable.

People who support the grading system are trying to keep young people from succeeding. Grades do distinguish who takes their work more seriously and who is committed, but it does not mean that one student is smarter than the other. There are lots of people who succeeded in life but had poor grades in school. If we eliminate the grading system, more students will graduate from high school because they won't feel the pressure of the grading system.

My nephew John who goes to Cathedral College Preparatory high school is a D and F student because he doesn't feel like doing homework and reading assignments is necessary. When it came down to take the College Standardized Test (CST) he scored advanced, which means that he exceeded the state's requirement. How can someone who scored well on a state test not doing well inside the classroom?

When applying for college, grades are important, but some teachers are tough and do not give high grades because they are mean. This is why colleges also look at test scores. Since test scores are important, we do not need the grading system.

Writing Activity 1

For this activity you will select one of the argumentative topics below and take the position indicated. You will then compose a 200-word defense of your position. In your defense you must include at least three of the logical fallacies introduced in this chapter. You may not use the fallacies in an intentionally humorous way because the next part of this activity is to see if your peers can spot the logical fallacies in your composition.

► The government should require computer companies to put a warning label on computers that read, "Warning; excessive use of this product can cause loneliness, isolation, and poor health."

► The city should give all university students free public transportation passes for buses, trains, and subways.

► Products containing caffeine or energy stimulants should not be sold to anyone under the age of eighteen.

CHAPTER TWELVE

Developing Ethos in Argument and Debate: Counterargument and Concession

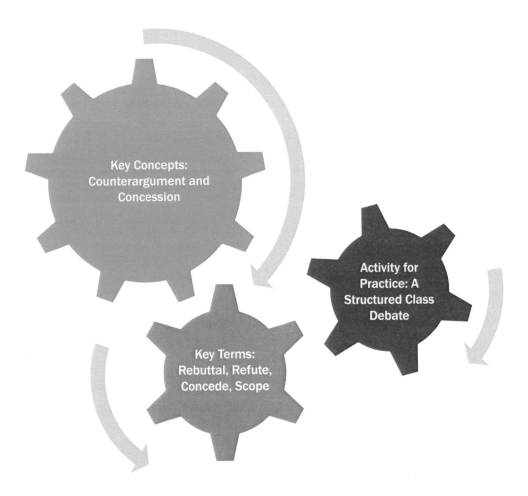

She used to pride herself on her refusal to see two sides of an argument, but increasingly she accepts that issues are more ambiguous and complicated than she once thought.

—David Nicholls

It is better to debate a question without settling it than to settle a question without debating it.

—Joseph Joubert

When making claims, or taking positions on substantive topics, and in order to be persuasive, you must appeal to a balance of ethos, logos and pathos. In argument, especially academic argument, (which can take many forms, as we described in chapter 9), we rely more heavily on logos than pathos, because our purpose is largely to expand knowledge and understanding, and by definition, appeals to logic are required. Appeals to pathos, as you may remember, make us feel things. Academia, however, is committed to learning and understanding. So to create a persuasive argument, you must appeal to ethos, and for a solid argument to be persuasive, to appeal to ethos, logos is the primary choice.

So, when evaluating an argument's credibility, logic demands that we consider all reasonable aspects of a claim, or an argument, and evaluate its logical strength. An argument is considered invalid, or underdeveloped if it fails to take into consideration all of the reasonable claims and positions and analyze them for their logical strength.

Your job as a writer of credible arguments is to demonstrate that you have considered the pertinent information, make concessions where logical to do so, and develop counterarguments that indicate why (and how) you disagree with the strength of those ideas.

Debate has a formal structure that demands counterargument and concessions. So to illustrate these concepts for you, this chapter focuses on those formal structures in a model, and later, in an exercise where you and your classmates can practice these skills in a live debate. But these skills are not just for use in formal debate, in fact, they are required each time you make a claim or take a position, because taking a position that is valid and considered requires you to examine the whole of an argument, and choose the strongest, and therefore, most logical position.

Debate: Preparing for Counterargument and Making Concessions

What is debate, the noun? What is debate, the verb? *The debate. To debate.*

The noun, "debate," is usually defined in formal legal, legislative, or political circumstances. Political candidates must participate in political debates on issues that concern the welfare of citizens. Debates between candidates reveal their position and opinions on issues, and reveal important details about themselves, and their opponent(s). Debates also happen at city council meetings, where community members are often invited to voice their experiences, opinions, and suggestions regarding changes that need to be made to benefit their communities. These are formal, structured rule-driven debates for a particular purpose.

Yet, for most of us, "debate" is a verb; we debate whenever more than one perspective exists in a particular situation, which is nearly every time you communicate. We engage in smaller and more frequent arguments every day. Sometimes the argument or debate is with ourselves, sometimes with another person, or with a larger group. Sometimes we are alone in our debates, and sometimes we have supporters. Your new skills for determining your rhetorical situation will help you to understand how to approach these more common (and frequent) debate circumstances.

In either case, whether under formal or informal debate circumstances, the same skills will apply: you must develop a position on a substantive topic, prepare your support, anticipate both the objections to your own position, and your opposition's, and finally prepare rebuttals to the opposition's objections and counterarguments.

For example, imagine that you feel you deserve a pay raise at work. You have worked diligently for over a year, have never taken a sick day, arrive early and meet all deadlines successfully. A request for a pay raise might compel your employer to say, "Sure, you've been working hard and that hard work has been noticed." There's a good beginning, but debate has not yet occurred. The next response may be a question from your employer asking, "How much of a pay raise are you requesting?" Let's imagine you ask for a two-dollar an hour raise, and your employer appears rather surprised by the amount and asks you to explain why you feel such a pay raise is reasonable. While this marks what may be defined as a "negotiation"—you will engage in a debate with your employer. How much do you feel you deserve and why? Will your employer find your reasons justifiable? Is a compromise necessary, and if yes, what will the terms of that negotiation include?

Asking for a raise requires preparation. You must anticipate questions such as: What are the possible reactions and outcomes? How will you support your argument? What evidence will you use? How will you appeal to ethos, pathos, and logos in your negotiation? How will you respond to counterarguments?

The debate activity in this chapter will help you to practice argumentation (persuasion) skills in debate format and will ask you to engage actively in preparing for a debate with your peers. Below is a list of points to consider as you prepare for the debate. Detailed explanations for these list items will follow.

- ► Select a debatable topic or a persuasive topic.
- ► Narrow the scope of the debate and focus the thesis.
- ► Define the parameters (rules) of the debate.
- ► Recognize the stakeholders (consider multiple perspectives).
- ► Research the issue for defense (support) and counterargument.
- ► Analyze and organize evidence (determining the quality of your defense/ evidence).
- ► Create claims (organizing your ideas).
- ► Anticipate counterarguments and prepare rebuttals.
- ► Consider concessions.
- ► Create an opening and concluding statement.

Preparing for Debate

In a debate, persuasive language is performed *live*. Yet, it is different than casual or spontaneous discussions. Even if you find yourself in a discussion that *feels* like debate, you should only engage in that debate if you are prepared. You must understand and know what supports your position and what arguments you can use to refute any counterarguments that could weaken your position.

Debates require preparation and prediction skills that draw from multiple perspectives. Since issues are often more complicated than they first appear, debates involve more than one individual argument. You must be able to understand your own position well enough to know its strengths *and* its weaknesses, and be able to respond with a plausible idea, or response that reveals, or explains those weaknesses as stronger than they appear.

This is true for preparing for formal debates in your coursework or in your career. But it is also true whenever you are considering a topic that has many plausible perspectives. Even if your "opponent" is simply *yourself* engaging in a thoughtful attempt to make the right decisions in your own life.

You can use the debate structure as outlined in this chapter to help you focus a research paper as well as prepare for a debate. The time limits in a formal debate may not apply when writing, but the thinking you engage in to prepare for a debate is valuable in any form of argument, oral or written.

Part One—Planning: Questions/Concerns/Issues

Planning a debate begins with a discussion or exploration of the subject that is selected. It is inevitable in any debate that concepts will become the center of concern. Concepts are ideas, or thoughts about ideas. In the model debate plan that follows we begin with a discussion about online college classes. For this sample debate we should first explore our own concepts, or thoughts and ideas about what education *is*. In tandem with a discussion on defining the concept of education, for this debate we must also contend with our understanding and experiences with computer systems, the Internet, and social networking in relation to how we learn and experience through technology.

Before establishing the parameters and scope of the debate, all debaters (in large or small groups) should share initial concerns, questions, experiences, and observations of online or technology-based educational systems such as class websites, PowerPoint or other technology-based lecture or presentation approaches in the college classroom. Additionally you should share your experiences with online homework submission, online testing, or online courses or online group work.

Let's imagine that the topic that has been presented to the class is:

Colleges are moving toward more online education.

Below are the concerns, questions, and experiences shared by a class of twenty-five students as they discuss the topic, or concept, of online education. Note the variety of responses (and how the responses are related). Also note what is missing from the discussion. Remember that this is a preliminary discussion and that the scope of the debate has not yet been defined. Study the concerns, questions, and experiences below. Which responses do you relate to? Which responses share concerns that interest you?

▶ Students will experience less "live" classroom interaction.

▶ Instructors can teach more students with an online format, but students may not have the same amount or type of immediate aid/assistance that occurs in a traditional classroom setting.

▶ Technology is unpredictable. Several times this semester the university computing systems were shut down for maintenance. In a few incidents, student and faculty e-mail systems were "hacked" and electronic viruses spread, causing miscommunication and preventing access to online course pages.

▶ If a student is having difficulties in a course, where will they receive help? Instructors can provide "examples" of work online, but it is not the same as being able to ask immediate questions and receive immediate responses.

▶ Will cheating increase? Will students be tempted to use online sources and search engines to complete their work instead of reading the required materials for a course?

▶ Does an online education actually teach students to learn a profession well enough to be successful in that profession? Can a student who wants to be a doctor be successful if she or he supplements classroom education with online education?

▶ An online education doesn't provide an opportunity for sharing ideas and learning from peers. A classroom allows this type of interaction that is integral to academic success.

▶ Students who go to college expect to land a good career. Students network on college campuses and have the opportunity to meet important people. Does this happen at online colleges?

▶ What about students who need visual or audio assistance. Is an online education accessible to all students with a variety of needs?

▶ Would online degrees have the same value as traditional degrees?

▶ Attending class allows for a student to gain various life skills that cannot be gained by staring at a computer. These skills would be punctuality, arriving to class on time, taking diligent notes while listening to the professor—skills that are necessary for success in a profession after graduation.

▶ Older adults with many responsibilities want to finish school and an online education would be helpful.

▶ Obesity and health concerns (sitting in front of a computer all day—then doing homework on the computer all night).

- Some students may have financial limits and can't afford Internet, a high-speed computer, webcam, or microphones. Will there be funding available for these concerns?

- Online education could be beneficial to students who are sustaining a family or have certain financial problems which require them to work while taking classes.

This list of concerns, questions, and experiences is far too lengthy to cover in a single debate, but the list provides examples of how we respond to debatable topics. Through further reasoning and discussion, as well as research, this list should be narrowed to the strongest arguments, concessions and rebuttal to counterargument.

Part Two—Taking the Opposing Viewpoint: Counterarguments and Concessions

Students were asked to make a preliminary list of concerns connected to an online college education (above). While the scope of the debate has not yet been decided, we must evaluate initial ideas, experiences, and questions regarding online education. Note that creating a list of concerns in response to a proposed debate topic does not necessarily require research, but does require critical thinking. Note how many of the concerns above are presented as questions, and that in some cases, responding to these concerns may require research.

Below is a list of five concerns students agreed were the main concerns of the many presented regarding online learning formats. After each of the concerns listed below, students developed potential counterarguments, and wrote these in brief responses that explains or claims the opposing perspective of each idea.

Counterargument

Counterargument asks students to take, or understand, the OPPOSING perspective, so that you can defend your position against it, or develop an appropriate concession. Counterarguments require including evidence to refute the original argument (claim). We cannot merely be disagreeable. We must explain, illustrate, or support the reasoning behind potential disagreement logically and within reason.

Usually, at this point, students become concerned that if they expose counterarguments to their own position, they will weaken their position. But the opposite is true: when you expose the counterarguments and either make a concession to that argument or rebut it, you demonstrate that you fully understand the topic and its complexities, and chose your position carefully; you have in fact developed a strong ethos, and a stronger argument.

If you don't have confidence in your position, or hide potentially strong evidence against your position, either your position *is* weak, and you should consider one that is stronger, or your argument *appears* weak, and you will fail to persuade your audience.

Therefore, identifying strong counterarguments to your own position and finding the right approach to them is crucial to creating a persuasive argument. Remember, opposing a perspective is much like making a claim—both must be clearly and fully thought out. There is no room for generalities and vagaries in debates. Be sure to avoid committing logical fallacies as they invalidate claims and counterarguments (see chapter 11 and logical fallacies).

Below are five claims related to online education. Immediately following each is a counterargument. Note how the counterargument to the claims are supported logically and with coherent explanation and details.

Claim 1:

While instructors can teach more students in an online format, students may not have the same amount or type of immediate aid/assistance that occurs in a traditional classroom setting.

Counterargument to Claim 1:

Accredited online courses require instructors to meet online for virtual office hours and assistance. Students have different schedules and many cannot meet with the instructors during scheduled office hours. Online office hours can be scheduled in the evenings or on weekends.

Claim 2:

Online education could be beneficial to students who are sustaining a family or have certain financial problems which require them to work while taking classes.

Counterargument to Claim 2:

Many college students work part-time or full-time. Over the decades the need to work has increased and students have been managing. Many colleges offer evening and weekend classes for those who must work during the day. Many colleges offer reduced daycare services to full-time enrolled parents. Colleges have increased student resources over the years based on the changing economic needs of students.

Claim 3:

Attending class allows students to gain life skills that cannot be gained by staring at a computer. These skills would be punctuality, accountability, listening, and verbal communication skills.

Counterargument to Claim 3:

Online courses have deadlines for homework assignments and tests. Students must be punctual with all online work. Online students will need to stay motivated, responsible for communicating online with instructors and peers, and must focus on class material that is presented in different formats. This develops skills that are necessary for success in any field.

Claim 4:

A student who wants to be a successful doctor should not replace classroom education with an online education. An online education cannot teach students to learn a profession.

Counterargument to Claim 4:

Clearly there are professions that require hands-on learning and practice. A surgeon would not be expected to complete her education online. Yet is possible for a future doctor to do online coursework to learn most other necessary skills. In fact, many doctors use computers in the field of medicine for testing, diagnosing, and researching.

Claim 5:

There are health concerns. Online education means sitting in front of a computer for extended periods of time.

Counterargument to Claim 5:

Students in a traditional classroom are seated during classes (except in courses requiring movement, such as physical education and lab classes). Students sit in libraries studying. Many courses require students to complete work online, even though they meet in classrooms for lectures and discussions.

Rebuttals

A rebuttal is a denial, contradiction or invalidation of the counterargument. It refutes the claim made in the counterargument. If you allow a counterargument to stand, without rebutting it, and explaining why it is a weak or invalid claim, you give it power to undermine your own argument. So, the next step in planning your debate is to create rebuttals to the counterarguments.

The following are the same claims and counterarguments developed above, with rebuttals prepared.

Claim 1:

While instructors can teach more students in an online format, students may not have the same amount or type of immediate aid/assistance that occurs in a traditional classroom setting.

Counterargument to Claim 1:

Accredited online courses require instructors to meet online for virtual office hours and assistance. Students have different schedules and many cannot meet with the instructors during scheduled office hours. Online office hours can be scheduled in the evenings or on weekends.

Rebuttal to Counterargument:

The dynamic immediacy of a teacher's and classmates' assistance in a classroom setting can not be replaced with an online chatroom/office visit, and with more students, the instructor's time is further divided, therefore limiting access to instructor guidance.

Claim 2:

Online education could be beneficial to students who are sustaining a family or have certain financial problems which require them to work while taking classes.

Counterargument to Claim 2:

Many college students work part-time or full-time. Over the decades the need to work has increased and students have been managing. Many colleges offer evening and weekend classes for those who must work during the day. Many colleges offer reduced daycare services to full-time enrolled parents. Colleges have increased student resources over the years based on the changing economic needs of students.

Rebuttal to Counterargument:

Evening and weekend classes do not provide relief to students who must work with inconsistent schedules. Nor do they help parents who must care for children on the weekend and in the evenings, since "daycare" services are by definition *day*care. Online classes allow parents to be in the home with their children and attend classes as their individual needs require, and still allow them to work during the day.

Claim 3:

Attending class allows students to gain life skills that cannot be gained by staring at a computer. These skills would be punctuality, accountability, listening, and verbal communication skills.

Counterargument to Claim 3:

Online courses have deadlines for homework assignments and tests. Students must be punctual with all online work. Online students will need to stay motivated, responsible for communicating online with instructors and peers, and must focus on class material that is presented in different formats. This develops skills that are necessary for success in any field.

Rebuttal to Counterargument:

While turning in assignments on-time is still required for online classes, the development of other skills, verbal and listening specifically, are not addressed by online classes. Online focuses on reading and written responses, and does not develop skills presenting ideas in oral form, nor allow for development of skills to evaluate ideas presented this way.

Claim 4:

A student who wants to be a successful doctor should not replace classroom education with an online education. An online education cannot teach students to learn a profession.

Counterargument to Claim 4:

Clearly there are professions that require hands-on learning and practice. A surgeon would not be expected to complete her education online. Yet is possible for a future doctor to do online coursework to learn most other necessary skills. In fact, many doctors use computers in the field of medicine for testing, diagnosing, and researching.

Rebuttal to Counterargument:

While this concession makes a strong point, universities should also require that online courses only be offered at the undergraduate level to maintain high standards in professional programs.

Claim 5:

There are health concerns. Online education means sitting in front of a computer for extended periods of time.

Counterargument to Claim 5:

Students in a traditional classroom are seated during classes (except in courses requiring movement, such as physical education and lab classes). Students sit in libraries studying. Many courses require students to complete work online, even though they meet in classrooms for lectures and discussions.

Rebuttal to Counterargument:

Asking students to add more time to their day in a seated position is not an argument. Conceding that sitting all day is bad for health is conceding that we should find healthier ways to provide education. Online classes perpetuate the health risks of being seated for too long each day. Additionally, sitting in front of a computer is not the same as sitting in a classroom. Sitting in one position for extended periods looking at a lit screen has other implications for health than merely sitting in a desk does.

Concessions

While debate appears to be about arguing (or persuading), it is also important to understand that no position is 100 percent fail-proof. It is important to concede, or to acknowledge the merits of an opposing perspective. For example, imagine that you are in support of online education because you are a self-motivated learner who is both eager and disciplined and you have a part-time job that is necessary to your financial well-being. Your "opponent" in the debate can concede to your narrative claim by simply acknowledging that some students have the skills necessary to learn from online education, and that online education is a time-saver in terms of commuting. Though your opponents might make that concession to your position, they can still form a rebuttal that limits the strength of your position too. For example they might argue that:

Although many students do have the skills necessary to learn from online education, and that online education is a time-saver in terms of commuting, there are many others who will learn better by being in a physical classroom, directly engaging with others, and will not mind commuting for this advantage.

Counterarguments, rebuttals and concessions should be developed and considered in advance of a debate, formal or informal. If you are not fully prepared, that is, having considered these important aspects, you may fail to persuade, even if your argument is truly the stronger argument, because you will have failed to *demonstrate* its strength when tested by your opponent's counterarguments, rebuttals and concessions.

Now that preliminary discussions have taken place and consideration has been given to address counterarguments and concessions, we can begin to shape the scope of the debate.

Part Three—Defining the Scope of the Topic and the Parameters of the Debate

Simply debating the "wrongs" or "rights" of online education will lead to a complicated and uncontrolled debate that could easily stray off into hundreds of directions. Therefore, it is necessary to identify the problem or concern that calls for online classes, and debate whether the online classes solve that problem appropriately, without causing further concern elsewhere. This is setting the rhetorical situation, or the purpose of the debate. Remember, arguments and debates rarely move toward a goal of complete victory. They work toward reasonable understanding among differing perspectives in order to find workable solutions to complex problems.

> **Topic: Online Classes—Presenting the Problem or Concern**
>
> Recent budget cuts have reduced student resources—class sizes have increased, campuses are running out of classroom space, students are unable to enroll in needed classes, graduation dates are pushed forward due to lack of class availabilities, and tuition increases every year. Administration proposes implementing a mandate requiring university students to complete 50 percent of all required general education courses online.

Creating a topic title as well as defining or explaining the problem or concern will help you remain focused on the debate at hand. Once you have determined the topic and the main problem you can establish the parameters of the debate. Parameters set the "rules" of the debate, or rather, clearly defines what may be argued. Any claim that does not fit within the parameters of the debate can be deemed irrelevant as they sidetrack the main problem or concern.

Establishing the Parameters

Debates, formal or otherwise, should remain on the topic and well defined because it is too easy to slip into fallacies of relationship (see chapter 11). The scope (the breadth, or narrowness of the topic), and the parameters (the rules that govern the structure and format of the debate), can be negotiated by the parties before the debate. Be sure to establish those boundaries, and define the terms carefully to avoid abstraction, or allow fallacies to remain unchallenged.

The debaters have decided to set the following parameters. These parameters, or measurable conditions, clearly define what is considered open for debate by listing the facts related to the debate:

The administration argues that these specific changes to courses will solve for the problem stated above in the debate topic:

- ▶ The average lower-division online class size will be 100 students.
- ▶ The average upper-division online class size will be fifty students.
- ▶ Online courses will be taught by one faculty member and one teaching assistant.
- ▶ Classes meet live online for seventy-five minutes per week—the seventy-five minute class session will be recorded and accessible for students who cannot meet during the live session.
- ▶ Faculty are required to maintain a minimum of two hours of online "conference" time per week.
- ▶ Online courses must meet the university requirements for student learning objectives and meet national accreditation requirements for four-year universities.

Part Four: Identify and Acknowledge Multiple Perspectives

Now that the scope of the debate has been established, you should form groups of the stakeholders, or the specific perspectives relevant to the debate. Carefully consider the perspective of the group to which you have been assigned. Here are some ideas for potential stakeholders for this proposed mandate for online courses:

Group One: College administrators

Group Two: College faculty

Group Three: College students

Group Four: Employers in various education professions

Group Five: State representatives

Once you form groups, members of each group must take on the point of view of that group by thinking in terms of its concerns about the online courses. To do this you must ask some basic questions:

- ▶ Determine position: Would your group support or oppose the proposal or argument?

- ▶ Determine reasoning: Why do they support or oppose it? (Draw from the early thinking, as well as find new ideas.)
- ▶ What research must be conducted to validate support and refute opposition?
- ▶ Provide detailed support for reasoning: What type of examples would assist in supporting the proposal?
- ▶ Provide detailed support for reasoning: What type of examples would assist in opposing the proposal?
- ▶ Provide detailed rebuttals to examples to refute ideas in opposition.

Once each group determines these ideas and provides the details, it is time for the debaters to prepare by:

- ▶ Writing an **opening statement** that clearly states your position and main arguments—this is the **thesis** statement of the argument.
- ▶ Preparing a minimum of three strong reasons that **support** the argument.
- ▶ Providing each claim of support with researched **evidence**.
- ▶ Anticipating potential **counterarguments** and preparing **rebuttals** or **concessions.**
- ▶ Integrating ideas or language specifically designed to appeal to **ethos, pathos,** and **logos.**
- ▶ Writing a **closing statement** that summarizes the argument and the evidence and explains the benefits of the position.

Part Five: Understanding the Structure and Format of the Debate

You may work with your instructor to format the debate according to the specific needs and time limitations. Below are formatting suggestions for consideration. This is a flexible activity that can be completed in a variety of ways. Be sure to establish clear time limits. For example, groups may be allowed only one or two minutes to make an opening and closing statements, or, groups may be allowed only two minutes to prepare a counterargument to a claim.

Opening Statements

All groups present opening statement.

Opening statements allow all participants (and audience) to present and understand the aim of the argument.

Round One

Group 1: Presents first claim.

Group 2: Presents counterargument to Group 1.

Depending on the format or preference of the instructor, counterarguments may be in open forum format, allowing any and all debaters to participate, or students and/or groups may be assigned to counterargue specific groups or individuals.

Group 1: Rebuts the counterargument.

Round Two

Group 2: Presents first claim.

Group 1: Presents counterargument to Group 2.

Group 2: Rebuts the counterargument.

Debates continue in this format until the reasoning, counterarguments and rebuttals are complete. This will largely be decided by the format and scope of the debate. In some debates, you can have separate debates in paired perspectives, such as the one illustrated above, or all groups could debate in turn at once.

Closing Statements

Each group (or student) makes a closing statement summarizing the main arguments. New arguments and counterarguments should not be introduced in the closing statement.

Once closing statements conclude, the debate is finished, and hopefully all stakeholders (groups) in this debate came to a closer understanding of the problem, the proposed solution, and possible alternative solutions to develop a number of workable solutions to this complex problem or issue.

Engaging the Gears Activity for Practice

As a class, explore potential topics and a format for a debate. Follow the suggested planning guide above and take into careful consideration the information provided about argument and persuasion to prepare a customized debate that offers everyone the opportunity to practice logical thinking skills, research skills, and argument (or persuasive) skills.

- ▶ Select a debatable topic.
- ▶ Respond to (through discussion or writing) to the topic.
- ▶ Narrow the scope and define the parameters of the debate by defining the main problem, and the facts of the debate.
- ▶ Consider multiple perspectives, or list the people or groups directly invested in the debate.
- ▶ Research the issue.
- ▶ Organize evidence.
- ▶ Create the strongest claims possible.
- ▶ Anticipate counterarguments.
- ▶ Consider concessions.
- ▶ Create an opening statement.
- ▶ Create a closing statement.

CHAPTER THIRTEEN

Writing the Research Paper:
Do's and Don'ts

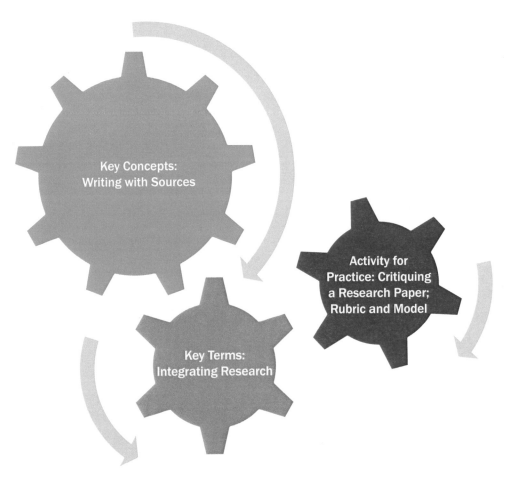

There is nothing to writing. All you do is sit down at a typewriter and bleed.

—Ernest Hemingway

The greatest part of a writer's time is spent in reading, in order to write; a man will turn over half a library to make one book.

—Samuel Johnson

Writing a Research Paper

In chapters 7 and 8, you learned how to find a topic, develop a research question, and then strategize, evaluate and manage your sources. Over the following weeks, you performed these actions in your Research Journal Project, so that you should now have multiple sources, annotated and organized.

The goal of this chapter is help you focus all of those efforts, and communicate them in a researched academic paper. The aim of a successful researched paper is to make an argument that is logically supported by reasonable, reliable and relevant evidence. As guidelines, here are the *Do's* and *Don'ts* of research papers:

DO:

- ▶ Develop a strong and arguable claim
    - ▷ Organize each supporting claim for the main argument in a topic-appropriate and logical order
- ▶ Provide background information for the subject of the argument
- ▶ Provide well-researched and well-reasoned evidence to support each claim
- ▶ Consider possible counterarguments for each claim
    - ▷ Develop a rebuttal (or response) to each potential counterargument
- ▶ Consider points of concession
- ▶ Examine the argument for logical fallacies (see chapter 11)
- ▶ Cite sources
    - ▷ Create a works cited page
- ▶ Edit and proofread carefully multiple times for clarity, concision and focus

DON'T:

- ▶ Don't Misunderstand:
    - ▷ A research paper is not merely a collection of quotes and data.
    - ▷ A research paper is not an essay that repeats the ideas of others.
    - ▷ A research paper is not impressive just because it has ten quotes on each page.
    - ▷ A research paper is not a book report, nor meant to simply inform.
- ▶ Don't plagiarize; that is, borrow, use, or change the ideas of those whom you research or interview without assigning proper credit—this includes both your paraphrasing and summarizing of others' ideas, not only the direct quotation of their words.

These two lists are guidelines for what are commonly considered parts of a well-researched and well-written research paper. To do this work efficiently and successfully, a developed outline can help.

Outlining a Persuasive Research Paper

Developing an outline is helpful and many students likely use outlines to write papers, but an outline for a research paper can be used in an intensive way to improve the efficiency of the writing. In short, if you use an outline to develop your ideas in detail, you no longer have to simultaneously tackle the two tasks of drafting—*what* to say, and *how* to say it. Instead, in the outline you plan *what* to say. Then when you draft, you only focus on *how* to say it.

But first, you must see what a research paper requires so that you build a good structure to put all that content into. Research papers have a general structure that you will shape to fit your specific rhetorical situation, and below you will find that general structure, followed by example outlines.

General Structure of a Persuasive Research Paper

- ► An engaging **introduction** (Why should the audience care?) and **thesis statement.**
- ► Background paragraph (provide **information** that forms the **grounds** for the argument).
- ► Definition paragraph—**define the argument** clearly and define all terms.
- ► Provide first claim. **Develop** paragraphs that **support**, **explain**, **illustrate** your claim in detail.
- ► Respond to a potential **counterargument** to the first claim.
- ► Provide a second claim. Develop paragraphs that support, explain, illustrate claim in detail.
- ► Respond to a potential counterargument to the second claim.
- ► Provide a third claim. Develop paragraphs that support, explain, illustrate claim in detail.
- ► Respond to a potential counterargument to the third claim.
- ► Connect the **benefits** of the position with the reader/audience.
- ► Conclude: reiterate for the reader the information and opinions developed in the essay, and **leave reader with important points/opinions/ideas to ponder.**

This list is meant to help you shape your research paper. Please do not imagine this list as rules that must be obeyed. If your argument could benefit from other strategies that build ethos, pathos and logos, do so. Your rhetorical situation should be your true guide: Ask what your purpose requires and what your audience expects. Ask how your topic shapes both purpose and audience.

Organizing Ideas and Developing Focus

Now that you have seen the general principles of a good research paper, we can now address early preparation of your draft. Below is a topic, and a very loose "list" outline of ideas. Then the items on the list will be expanded by freewriting what was learned during the research on those topics. This will help you see how to then sketch a focused, multi-level outline so that you can integrate specific details to further your argument. Once that is finished, drafting the essay will begin.

Imagine writing a research paper persuading city dwellers about the benefits of owning a fuel-efficient compact car (this is a complex issue that will be treated without great depth for illustration purposes here). Imagine that your research has delivered a few subtopics you can discuss, and you create a simple idea list that looks like this:

> Options
> Budget
> Navigation
> Environment

Now, we examine the list: perhaps it seems too broad and your mind begins to ask—*where to begin*? Or perhaps the outline appears limited—*is this going to be enough*?

Take a deep breath and begin what is popularly called "freewriting"—but focus the freewriting on the goal of the essay: *persuading city dwellers about the benefits of owning a fuel-efficient compact car*. Use words from the thesis or purpose statement, and the loose structure above, as often as possible (see model). This will keep the writing focused and moving forward. Any redundancy (or repetition) that occurs can be revised and edited later when you have a more detailed outline (see the expanded outline on "benefits of running").

Here are modeled results of a freewrite:

Options: Car manufacturers offer many **options** in compact cars. Compact cars come with two or four doors. Consumers now have the **option** of choosing the right size. Don't let the word "compact" appear misleading. Gone are the antiquated, tiny, cramped fuel-efficient cars of the 60s and 70s. Today, compact cars have been designed to fit five people comfortably. Some are even designed to transform into vehicles that can carry big packages, loads, even furniture by simply folding down the backseats. City dwellers will find that innovative design can also provide comfort, room, and convenience.

Budget: Let's face it—there are few people who live in the city that can say they are not concerned with budgeting money. Gas prices soar without notice and taxes for gas increase similarly. Citizens of large American cities pay more for gas. Compact cars cost less than larger cars. Compact cars usually cost less to maintain (unless it is a luxury model). Licensing, taxes, and registration is also cheaper for compact cars (non-luxury).

Navigation: Navigating the city can be difficult. Parking and parking spaces are also a problem in crowded cities. Compact cars reduce space congestion and are much easier to handle in those "tight" spaces and places. Compact cars do not reduce traffic, but they generally take up less space. Look at how parking space sizes have changed in the last ten years. Parking spaces have been redesigned (or repainted) to make more room for parking larger cars, taking up more and more precious space.

Environment: Cities are highly populated and the average family has two cars. If one of those cars was a compact car it would make a big difference. Compact cars emit less pollution and use less petroleum in other forms (oil, transmission fluid, brake fluid), thus reducing toxic waste in our environment.

Now we can see the paper taking shape. This student developed some ideas from what she has learned in her research. These ideas prepare us for the next step of integrating the research.

Integrating Research

As you are drafting your outline you should plan, add, and integrate your research. Remember that research is placed meaningfully and with careful consideration. Research should not be "cherry picked." Do not scan articles, websites, or other sources simply "looking for what looks good." Scanning research sources is a preliminary activity used to evaluate source material. Scanning and plucking out random source information can lead to faulty analysis and support. Be sure to refer to chapter 8 as you collect and evaluate your sources.

As you organize your paper you have several options to consider in regards to where and how you will most effectively use your research. Because you have spent a great deal of time, thought, and effort in gathering your materials, you will want to use it diligently. Summary, paraphrase, and direct quotation are the three ways in which you can strategically place your research. But first, you must plan which research will be suitable for each of your subtopics.

A modeled plan for integrating research into your paper is below. To do this for yourself, look at the freewrite you did, and ask, what types of support will be needed here? Where in my research notes do I have this kind of information? If it is not there, do a little more research and add it.

Options: Car manufacturers offer many **options** in compact cars. Compact cars come with two or four doors. Consumers now have the **option** of choosing the right size. Don't let the word "compact" appear misleading. Gone are the antiquated, tiny, cramped fuel-efficient cars of the 60s and 70s. Today, compact cars have been designed to fit five people comfortably. Some are even designed to transform into vehicles that can carry big packages, loads, even furniture by simply folding down the backseats. City dwellers will find that innovative design can also provide comfort, room, and convenience.

Include specific gas mileage on specific compact cars.

Research alternative vehicles—electric or hybrid cars.

Research measurements on interior room of these vehicles.

Budget: Let's face it—there are few people who live in the city that can say they are not concerned with budgeting money. Gas prices soar without notice and taxes for gas increase similarly. Citizens of large American cities pay more for gas. Compact cars cost less than larger cars. Compact cars usually cost less to maintain (unless it is a luxury model). Licensing, taxes, and registration is also cheaper for compact cars (non-luxury).

Research gas prices over the last year in major cities.

Research vehicle prices.

Go online to the Department of Motor Vehicles for licensing, tax, registration info.

Ask family, friends, neighbors (for paraphrase) about their budgets.

Navigation: Navigating the city can be difficult. Parking availability is also a problem in crowded cities. Compact cars reduce space congestion and are much easier to handle in those "tight" spaces and places. Compact cars do not reduce traffic, but they generally take up less space. Look at how parking space sizes have changed in the last ten years. Parking spaces have been redesigned (or repainted) to make more room for parking larger cars, taking up more and more precious space.

Visit a strip mall downtown that has ten businesses. Count the parking spaces and write down observations on what the car-to-parking space ratio looks like.

Environment: Cities are highly populated and the average family has two cars. If one of those cars was a compact car it would make a big difference. Compact cars emit less pollution and use less petroleum in other forms (oil, transmission fluid, brake fluid), thus reducing toxic waste in our environment.

There is a lot of information on this particular topic. Stick with one major city and studies conducted in that city.

Consider comparative research with other cities, but be sure the studies have been conducted by experts without bias.

The student above decided, based on his ideas, what types of research would be best suited to each of his subtopics. Now this student must use this plan to provide the specific evidence that each area called for, and choose how best to integrate it into his own argument using summary, paraphrase, or direct quotation.

Summary

In the early chapters of this textbook you were introduced to the skill of summary. Remember that summary is not used to analyze material, but rather to present your reader with a condensed version of a large(r) body of work. You may summarize a novel, a lengthy journal article, a television show, a documentary, or even a YouTube video. Anytime you offer a summary of a source, that source must also be cited and be included in your works cited page.

When you provide a summary of a source you must be careful to offer key source information. For example, if you are including a summary of a documentary you should follow a format similar to this:

In 1991 director Peter Wilton released a documentary titled *Going Green and Compact*. In this documentary three families share how they feel they are saving the environment by driving compact, gas-efficient cars.

The key source information being provided to your reader is the title of the documentary, the director (or creator/author), and the year it was made public (released/published).

Paraphrase

Paraphrasing is taking a large "chunk" of text that is useful to your thesis, but condensing and restating it in a shorter or more direct phrasing. Essentially, you are placing the ideas of another into your own words. Like summary, paraphrase must attribute the original source and must be properly cited in your works cited page. Remember, plagiarism is using the words or *ideas* of another without proper citation and credit.

> Consumer analyst Sarah Taylor implicates media in promoting the "bigger is better" material culture. In 2010 the Hudson Chronicle published her article, *Driving Ourselves into Poverty: An Examination of Waste and Vehicle Purchases.* In this article, Taylor blames television shows, print advertisements, and popular culture for offering up a value system that insists on luxury over moderation and social status over the environment. Taylor contends that American drivers spend needlessly and without consideration to the long-term impact of driving large vehicles in urban communities. Americans tend to believe what they see, hear, and read through popular media, and yet fail to recognize how it applies on a personal and global level. What they see does not match reality. This cognitive dissonance often leads to poor decision making with possible irreversible consequences.

Notice how the author is completely credited for her ideas and her work. As a writer it is your responsibility to ensure that a reader is not misled about the source of ideas or information. A good research paper includes your ideas and the ideas of others. Just be sure to give credit where credit is due.

Direct Quotes

You are probably most familiar with using research in direct quote format. The basic rule when quoting directly is to avoid "floating" a quote. A quotation cannot exist on its own and is not a substitute for a sentence. Additionally, since this research paper is to be written by you, you should keep direct quotes to approximately 10–15 percent of your word count, and should only be used when the original is stated so perfectly that any paraphrase or summary you might offer would reduce its effectiveness as support for your argument.

Once you decide to use a quotation, it must be introduced, embedded into your own sentences, and justified. Introducing your quotation allows you to present the information as a valid source. Embedding the quote allows your reader to take in the information in a sentence relevant to your essay's ideas. Justifying the quotation allows you to explain, evaluate, or connect it to your main idea or thesis.

Here is a brief illustration of how Taylor's passage can be integrated in your essay:

> Consumer analyst Sarah Taylor uses the term cognitive dissonance to explain why Americans who live in major cities purchase expensive (and expensive-to-maintain) vehicles that contribute to environmental pollution. Taylor contends that:
>
> *Cognitive dissonance is mental confusion caused by two seemingly contradictory ideas or messages. TV commercials laud the power and social status behind driving S.U.V.s and gas-guzzling vehicles. Yet, public service announcements ask us to recycle and reduce waste in an effort to preserve the environment. Consumers are confused between making a popular choice, or a money-saving, environment-protecting choice. (265)*
>
> Taylor clearly wants to make the point that consumers have two things to protect: their financial well-being, and a fragile environment. This, Taylor believes, can be achieved if American consumers can recognize the consequences of their decisions regarding their financial choices.

Notice that because a lengthy passage (more than three lines of your own essay) was taken from the source, the quoted material is placed in block form.

But, perhaps you decide to use a shorter part of the text. Your quote might appear like this:

> Consumer analyst Sarah Taylor uses the term cognitive dissonance to explain why American consumers who live in major cities insist on buying expensive and environmentally unsound vehicles. Taylor defines cognitive dissonance as "two seemingly contradictory ideas or messages" (265). Taylor clearly wants to make the point that consumers have two things to protect: their financial well-being, and a fragile environment. This, Taylor believes, can be achieved if American consumers can recognize the consequences of their decisions regarding their financial choices.

However you choose to integrate and use your source material remember that everything must be diligently cited and credited. If you have questions about proper citation you can always ask your instructor.

Once a research plan is complete, and you have chosen the summaries, paraphrases and direct quotations, all of that material can then be placed in a highly detailed outline as illustrated in the section on "The Benefits of Running."

When you begin, be sure to have your research organized so that the information is accessible and easy to integrate into the structured outline. Having research in several locations (in a notebook, on cards, on an electronic document) can cause disorder that will interfere with the writing process (see chapter 8, Managing Sources).

Here is a basic, yet slightly more detailed outline for a paper on the benefits of running. It is much like the freewritten structure above, but provides a more detailed approach to "see" the overall organization of your ideas in a listed format. To build this kind of outline, you can take the details from the above outlines, and add to them as modeled below. This exercise uses a more simple topic than the compact-car topic, in order to highlight the structural details.

Working Title "The Benefits of Running"

   I. Introduction
      A. Running has become an extremely popular sport for all ages.
      B. Running is a great form of exercise because it helps people control their weight, develops muscles, and improves mental and physical performance.

  II. Claim/subtopic 1—Weight Control
      A. Aids self-control
      B. Burns calories
      C. Encourages a healthy diet
      D. Suppresses appetite

 III. Claim/subtopic 2—Muscular Development
      A. Improves tone
      B. Enhances contours
      C. Increases strength
      D. Improves endurance

 IV. Claim/subtopic 3—Psychological Well-being
      A. Aids sleep
      B. Inhibits depression
      C. Intensifies vitality

  V. Claim/subtopic 4—Cardiovascular Fitness
      A. Strengthens heart
      B. Lowers blood pressure
      C. Changes blood lipids
      D. Improves circulation

 VI. Conclusion
      A. Benefits of running make it an excellent exercise
      B. People who want to improve their health should consider running

Once you have this basic outline prepared, you can now take the *specific* research you have decided to use and add it to the outline along with your commentary regarding the evidence. So, look at the outline again, this time focusing on the first section about *weight control*, and look at how developing and adding the research and commentary deepens the levels of detail:

Working Title "The Benefits of Running"

I. Introduction
- A. Running is becoming an extremely popular sport for all ages
- B. Running is a great form of exercise because it helps people control their weight, develops muscles, and improves mental and physical performance

II. Claim/subtopic 1—Weight Control
- A. Aids self-control
    1. Provides a regimen to follow
        a. Introduce evidence:
            - i. Insert the intended evidence from your research, (quote, paraphrase, summary, illustration, examples etc.) and cite it here
            - ii. Add comments to justify the evidence and its connection to your subtopic, or your thesis
            - iii. Transition to next evidence
        b. Introduce evidence:
            - i. Insert the intended evidence from your research, (quote, paraphrase, summary, illustration, examples etc.) and cite it here
            - ii. Add comments to justify the evidence and its connection to your subtopic, or your thesis
            - iii. Transition to next evidence
        c. Introduce evidence: (quote, paraphrase, summary, illustration, examples etc.)
            - i. Insert the intended evidence from your research, (quote, paraphrase, summary, illustration, examples etc.) and cite it here
            - ii. Add comments to justify the evidence and its connection to your subtopic, or your thesis
            - iii. Transition to next evidence

         d. Introduce evidence: (quote, paraphrase, summary, illustration, examples etc.)

            i. Insert the intended evidence from your research, (quote, paraphrase, summary, illustration, examples etc.) and cite it here

           ii. Add comments to justify the evidence and its connection to your subtopic, or your thesis

          iii. Concluding sentence

          iv. Transition to next paragraph on burning calories

  B. Burns calories (repeat structure above)

    1. What are calories and how do they help with weight control

      a. Introduce evidence:

         i. Insert the intended evidence from your research, (quote, paraphrase, summary, illustration, examples etc.) and cite it here

        ii. Add comments to justify the evidence and its connection to your subtopic, or your thesis

       iii. Transition to next evidence

    (Repeat structure above)

  C. Encourages a healthy diet

  D. Suppresses appetite

  E. Address/respond/rebut potential counterarguments to "weight control" using a similar pattern of evidence/example/commentary etc. (if necessary)

III. Claim/subtopic 2 (repeat structure above)

Notice how section A. *Aids self-control* is developed. In the first outline example, each of the letters represents an idea that supports *weight control*, which is a claim/subtopic supporting your thesis.

In the second example, *weight control* remains the claim that supports the thesis, but the ideas of support such as *A. Aids self-control, becomes* the topic of a section, and each of those ideas of support, such as *1. Provides a regimen to follow*, becomes the topic of its own paragraph.

So, with an expanded outline format, it is not only the paper's structure, but also each paragraph's structure that is outlined, with the details that support and refute the claims explicitly placed in the outline, along with your commentary that is relevant to each piece of evidence.

Now, imagine the entire research paper outlined at this level of detail. Sure, this kind of outline takes time to develop, but when you draft, you will no longer have to worry about *what* to say, or where to say it, instead you only concern yourself with *how* to say it best, therefore avoiding that dreaded moment of "Arrgghhh, what do I say next? What am I *talking about??*" All you will have to do is look at your outline, and carry on drafting. This will make your paper stronger, and your efforts more efficient.

This highly detailed outline will also make the paper stronger by giving you a "bird's-eye view" of your research paper before it is written. Your ideas, the logical flow, and the details that you will use to support your claims will be laid out for you. You will notice early on when something is missing, or when something that no longer serves its purpose should be deleted. Doing all that work before you draft makes drafting an easier task compared to drafting from the basic outline, or, worse, from no outline at all.

In addition to helping you draft a better paper, extended outlines also help to cut down time spent on revision, since you are likely to see problems regarding ideas and organization when you create the expanded outline. And since you will draft using such details, and will not have to do the simultaneous thinking tasks of *what* and *how* to write, you will likely pay more attention to *how* to say it, so that even your editing task could become less burdensome.

After completing your outline at this level of detail, you can begin to draft. That is, turn each level of detail in your outline into the sentences and paragraphs you have planned.

Revision, Editing and Proofreading

Once the draft is complete, you must see about revising, editing and proofreading, and you must create a works cited page.

Here are some resources for those steps:

NEED GRAMMAR PRACTICE?
http://www.eslus.com/LESSONS/GRAMMAR/Gram.htm
http://www.chompchomp.com
http://owl.english.purdue.edu/exercises/

NEED INFO ON ANNOTATED BIBLIOGRAPHIES?
http://owl.english.purdue.edu/owl/resource/614/01/

NEED INFO ON CORRECT CITATIONS AND WORKS CITED PAGES?
http://owl.english.purdue.edu/owl/section/2/

You can also refer to the handbook your instructor assigned for the course for these and other writing topics.

The Research Essay: A Model

Below is an excerpt from a research paper written by a student in a freshman composition course. You should read this essay, and using the rubric in "Engaging the Gears" below, evaluate and discuss with your classmates the effectiveness of the way that this student built his or her argument.

Teen Depression: Parents, Detection, and Prevention

S. Nasrallah

When people first hear the word "depression" they often automatically think of someone who cannot get out of bed, or, someone who appears sad all the time. However, that is not always the case. Treating depression as if it were the common cold or a bruise that mends itself is dangerous. Depression is a serious mental illness, and it is an illness that is increasing in American teenagers. Kalman Heller, a psychologist who specializes in working with children and teens, reports that "about 10 to 15 percent of children and teens are depressed at any given time." While it is important to note that Heller's data does not indicate consistent depression, it does indicate that depression occurs from time to time. What is important is that the symptoms of mild depression are recognized to help prevent long-term or disabling depression in teens. Parents, teachers, and other adults who are in contact with teenagers should be informed about the major symptoms, how they should react, and how and when to seek professional help. Education and resources will prevent teens that experience periodic bouts of depression from suffering alone, hurting themselves, or committing suicide.

It is fairly easy to tell if someone is sad, but it is difficult to differentiate between sadness and depression. It is especially hard to recognize or diagnose depression in teenagers because teens are experiencing many physical and emotional changes. Teens are often stereotyped as being "rebellious" or "moody." While this may be the case for some, it is not the case for all. Rebellion and mood swings do occur in teens, but there are symptoms that are clearly recognizable and not a part of stereotypes about teenagers. Dr. Jane Framingham, also a child psychologist specialists explains the symptoms of depression in teens are much like the symptoms adults experience, but they show the symptoms in different areas of their lives. One of the symptoms is when teens drop out of a school activity that they once enjoyed. They can also isolate themselves and no longer communicate with either friends or family members. Outward anger towards others is another symptom. Parents (or other adults) may see the symptoms of decreased activity, decreased communication, isolation, and anger as teen rebellion or moodiness. It must be recognized that it is not normal for teens to isolate themselves or be openly hostile for prolonged periods of time. Once symptoms are recognized as signals of depression, recognizing and understanding the different types of depression becomes important (Framingham).

From mild to severe, there are many types of depression. It is incorrect to assume that all depressions share similar symptoms, reactions, and treatments. Professionals are trained to recognize specific types of depression, and no one should try to self-diagnose or diagnose others if they are not professionals. Teens can suffer from a variety of forms of depression and they must be properly diagnosed so they can receive the proper treatment. Parents and other adults should make sure to seek diagnosis from at least two professionals.

One of the most common forms of depression in teenagers is called Major Depressive Disorder, or MDD. According to the Teen Mental Health website (an educational mental health website authored by professionals in the field of psychology), "individuals with MDD will experience periods of time (lasting from months to years) where they experience intense depressive episodes, which are separated by periods where they experience a relatively stable mood" ("Depression"). MDD is a form of depression that can appear to happen unexpectedly. However, specialists have discovered that MDD is often triggered by a traumatic event, for example, the death of a loved one or some form of family separation. It is important for parents and adults to know that traumatic events, or sudden changes in life can trigger MDD. If a family has experienced a death or the separation from one family member, a teenager who seeks isolation or displays outward anger may be at risk.

Dysthymia is a common form of depression that is milder that MDD and usually affects children and teens. Usually, dysthymia is tracked for about seven years, but in some cases, it can last longer (Heller). Dysthymia is difficult to diagnose. Doctor Heller states that while this depression is not normally one that lasts into adulthood, it is particularly dangerous because it is "much harder to diagnose." Heller explains the six signs (or symptoms) of dysthymia, and when compared to the general list of symptoms of depression, we can see how the symptoms are different. Once again, these symptoms can appear to be "normal" for teenagers as this age group is often stereotyped as being changeable, lazy, or unfocused. Parents might see these symptoms as "normal" or something a teenager might outgrow. Teens may display poor eating habits. Perhaps they eat too little or they eat too much. The second symptom is insomnia or hypersomnia. The third symptom is low energy or bouts with fatigue. A fourth symptom is suffering from low self esteem. The fifth symptom manifests itself when teens appear to have difficulty focusing and making decisions. The sixth sign is when teens display a feeling of hopelessness. Doctors warn parents that if a teen displays two of the six symptoms, professional assistance should be sought (Heller).

It is difficult for teens to recognize or understand what may be happening to their mental health, and parents also find it difficult to accept that their child may have a mental condition that requires professional treatment. This is why the symptoms of depression, either MDD or dysthymia are often ignored. However, failure to recognize the symptoms will lead to consequences that may be hard to "fix." Teenagers spend much of their time at school where they engage with their peers, and the ways in which they engage are important to their mental well being. Parents do not go to school with their teens, but other adults, such as teachers and staff do. These adults must be vigilant and observant about how teens interact with each other. Sometimes, it is the adults at school who are the first protectors of mental health. Keeping teachers and staff educated about mental health can reduce the number of teens who suffer from long term depression.

Bullying is unfortunately a common experience for many teenagers, and the bullying often begins at school. The documentary *Bully*, shows how teens are bullied and the consequences of bullying that is ignored. This documentary shows a clear connection between bullying and teen mental health. In the documentary the Long family shares their tragic story. Mr. and Mrs. Long's son, Tyler was bullied in high school. The Long's noticed the changing behavior of their son, Tyler, but did not recognize that he was depressed, and certainly, at the time, did not know what was causing his change in behavior. Tyler committed suicide because he felt it was his only way out. A lack of communication on the part of Tyler and his parents was the primary cause. Tyler was unable to talk to his parents about what was happening in school. The Long's have been courageous and now actively work to educate other families and schools about the need to stand up against bullying and recognizing the signs of depression and getting the right professional help.

Parents and adults sometimes blame teenagers for their own depression, or they blame the bullies or others. Sometimes parents are the cause of teen depression, but fail to see how their teens are affected by decisions they make. Kevin Breel, a teen who developed a TedTalk on teen depression, appeared on The Today show in 2013. Breel is an aspiring comedian, and he uses his public image as a way to share his story. In his appearance on the Today Show, he shared his experience with his depression. Breel speaks out about how the his parents divorce triggered his depression. He explains how their divorce caused him to hate himself. He tried to distract himself by immersing himself in sports, but the depression would not go away. Breel contemplated suicide many times. Fortunately for Breel, he realized he needed to talk to someone, and that is what helped him survive. Breel knows that it is important for teens to feel they have someone to talk to whether it is a guidance counselor, principal, or teacher, and he wants to let parents and adults know that they cannot ignore the symptoms of depression and they cannot be afraid of facing the causes, whether it is a problem at school or a problem at home (Breel).

Teenagers are more likely to hurt themselves when they are depressed because they do not talk to anyone, or they are afraid to ask for help. While it is valuable to seek professional advice it is also important to listen to the narratives and stories from teens who suffered from depression. Their experiences are valid because they teach adults to look for the signs and not make assumptions about the emotional health of their teenagers.

In September of 2010, ABC News and the Good Morning America program addressed the problem of the growing number of teens struggling with depression. In a program aired on a health segment, GMA journalists interviewed several teenagers who shared their story. This media attention brought to light the need for adults (parents and others) to take notice of what is happening with teenagers. Casey, a teen on this program revealed she "didn't want to die," but that she "wanted to feel something other than what [she] was feeling, even if it was pain. Casey wanted help, but did not know how to ask for help. Instead, she began hurting herself. Another interviewee, Maggie, did not suffer from depression, but she was 12 years old when her brother committed suicide. Maggie told journalists that her brother, "was the last person I would've thought would take his life." Because of this Maggie has shared the story of her family, encouraging family members to take responsibility to avoid tragedies that can not be fixed or reversed.

While bullying and family stress can trigger depression, there are other causes of depression that are much more subtle. It is normal for teens to be occupied with thoughts of love and personal or intimate relationships. Parents and other adults must be careful to monitor how a relationship is developing when teenagers are involved.

In high school finding a partner is important. Partners share common experiences and create memories of happiness and contentment. However, this type of love can also trigger depressive symptoms and depression if left unmonitored. Teens are vulnerable to over committing themselves in a relationship. This over commitment can lead to disappointment. Parents and other adults may stereotype this type of event as being "love sick," and minimize the potential for opening the doors of depression. In a recent study on the connection between "love sickness" and teen depression, Cornell University reports that "girls, especially younger ones, are at an even higher risk for depression than boys" (Joyner qtd. in "Love Sick"). According to this article, *Love-sick Teens Risk Depression, Alcohol Use, Delinquency*, love makes teens feel happy and safe and vulnerable all at the same time. It is a roller coaster of emotions. When such relationships fail, teens may find themselves facing depression with alcohol and drugs. Often parents and adults blame alcohol and drug addiction on "bad friends" or the "wrong influence." They might not see alcohol and drug use as a consequence of a broken heart or "love sickness." While overt causes of depression such as bullying and family stress can be explained, "love sickness," like dysthymia, is harder to detect, but parents and adults must be vigilant when teens are involved in personal relationships.

Another factor of depression that most people tend to ignore is the genetic factor. Genetics play a role in depression because is someone in the family suffers from depression, like a mother or father, the children have a greater chance of having depression. In an article from the Stanford School of Medicine, researchers tackled the connection between genetics and depression. The Stanford researchers discovered that "if someone has a parent or sibling with major depression, that person has a 2 or 3 times greater risk of developing depression" (Levinson and Nichols). Most people know and accept that genetics determine hair color, or predispositions for certain physical diseases. However, genetics is often overlooked because mental illness is often looked upon as shameful, embarrassing, or a condition that should remain "unspoken" about. Parents and adults need to understand the genetic connection as valid. No one is ashamed or embarrassed is a disease like diabetes is genetic. Instead, a disease like diabetes is monitored and the family is informed so they can prepare. The same must happen with genetic depression; parents and other adult family members must acknowledge and look for the signs of depression so teens can be treated early.

Many articles on teenage depression indicate that teenage females are more likely to be susceptible to depression. The article *Clinical Characteristics of Depression among Adolescent Females: A Cross-Sectional Study* written by six experts in mental health is based on a study of teen girls in six different schools. The study allowed for research that also took into consideration socio-economic class. 602 teen females participated in this study. The study explains why females are more at risk by reporting that, "this has been attributed to genetics, increased prevalence of anxiety disorders in females, biological changes associated with puberty, cognitive predisposition and sociocultural factors" (Khalil et. al). Females are more affected because of the biological gendered changes during puberty. This is important for parents who are raising teen girls because it educates them to be sensitive to the particular needs of young women. What is also valuable is the study on socio-economic class. The economic condition of the family is also a consideration for the chance of depression Adults who work with teens must be aware that poverty can also make a teen more predisposed to depression.

Although teen girls have a much greater chance of having depression teen boys do still have chance of depression, but are less likely to get help. The article," Depressed Teens Mostly Struggle Alone," highlights specialists discussing how boys have a harder time talking to people about depression. They share that "teenage boys were consistently less likely to report depression--or to get help for it—than were girls, a pattern that continues through adulthood" (Healy). Boys are taught from a young age to be a man and being a man means asking for help is a sign of weakness. Kevin Breel and Tyler clearly represent the young men who suffer from depression. In Kevin's case, because he was able to overcome the stigma of being perceived as a "weak man" and ask for help was spared from tragedy. Unfortunately, Tyler Long could not ask for help and surrendered control of his own life by committing suicide. Parents of teen boys must be aware that while they might socialize their young men with traditional expectations, they must also teach them that emotions and feelings are real, and must be discussed in an open manner without shame.

Taking an adolescent to get professional help is a good beginning to remedy teen depression. However, parents must take a key role in this process. Parents still need to talk to their children and help them overcome the obstacles they face daily in school and at home. Teenagers are going to be a little distant and resistant at first, but with time and the parent's persistence they will start to open up about their feelings. At the end, all the hard work will pay off because the parent and the child will become closer. Depression is a serious and hard illness for adults to have. Imagine what it might be like to be 16 years old and depressed. This is why adults need to take action to assesses and help their children through this difficult journey. Families who talk to their children have a better relationship because teenagers start to trust their parents. Depression is connected to everybody and knowing more about it can help the climbing number of teens who suffer, and sometimes die, from. Everyone must take the initiative to detect, prevent, or report signs and symptoms of serious depression in teens.

Works Cited

Breen, Kevin. Interview on Today Show. *Today Show*. NBC. 8 October 2013. Web. 7 April 2014.

Bully. Dir. Lee Hirsch. The Weinstein Company, 2012. DVD.

"Depression." *Teen Mental Health*. teenmentalhealth.org. n.d. Web. 03 May 2014.

Framingham, Jane. "Teenage Depression." Psych Central.com. n.d. Web. Apr. 3, 2014.

Healy, Melissa. "Depressed Teens Mostly Struggle Alone." *Los Angeles Times*. Los Angeles Times.com. 29 Apr. 2011. Web. 3 April. 2014.

Heller, Kalman. "Depression in Teens and Children" Psych Central.com. n.d. Web. Apr. 3, 2014.

Khalil, Afaf H. and Menan A Rabie et. al."Clinical Characteristics of Depression among Adolescent Females: A Cross-sectional Study." *CAPMH*. N.p., 10 October 2010. Web. 31 Mar. 2014.

Levinson, Douglas F. and Walter E. Nichols. "Major Depression and Genetics." Stanford University School Of Medicine. depressiongenetics.stanford.edu. n.d. Web. 4 April 2014.

"Love-Sick Teens Risk Depression, Alcohol Use, Delinquency." About.com, n.d. Web. 2 Apr. 2014.

Salahi, Lara. "Teen Depression: Know the Warning Signs." *Good Morning America*. ABC News. 14 Sept. 2010. Web. 6 April 1014.

Satel, Sally. "Antidepressants: Two Countries, Two Views." *Health & Fitness*. Health & Fitness, 25 May. 2004. Web. 5 April 2014.

Engaging the Gears Activity for Practice

A Rubric for Evaluating a Research Essay

Use the following rubric to evaluate the student model research paper above, your own research paper and your peers' papers. This rubric is much like the evaluation rubric found in chapter 5, but with more detailed questions. Be sure to write thorough responses in the comment section, noting exactly what you liked, or think could use development and revision. The feedback you offer, and subsequently receive from others in return, can really help you and your fellow students focus your essays. Also, mark on the paper exactly where you see need for development, revision, editing or correction.

Area of Concern	Details of Area	Good	Fair	Needs Devel.	Additional Comments
Introduction	Does the intro effectively identify the topic?				
	Does the intro effectively establish the writer's purpose and position?				
	Does the intro draw the reader into the paper?				
Thesis	Locate and circle the thesis statement.				
	Does the thesis clarify the purpose, and focus of the essay?				
Research & Support *(Quality & Organization)*	Are claims or sub-topics offered to support the thesis in a logical manner?				
	How convincing are the examples, statistics, illustrations, and other types of support?				
	How effectively are research materials introduced and used to support the thesis & purpose of the essay?				
	How effectively are the sources integrated into the text? (E.g., quotations, paraphrases and summaries)				
Conclusion	Are you satisfied with the conclusion, or does it need additional (or deleted) info?				
	Does the conclusion leave the reader with something to "ponder" and consider?				
Title	How effectively does the title represent the paper?				
	Does the title engage the reader and draw them to the paper?				

	How appropriate is it for the rhetorical situation?			
Purpose	Does the essay inform, evaluate, argue, or solve a problem?			
	Is this purpose clear throughout the essay?			
Audience	Does the essay reveal the intended audience?			
	Does the essay clearly address the audience? Does it anticipate the readers' objections and respond to them?			
	Are there any places in the essay that are likely to surprise the reader? If so, how well has the audience been prepared for those surprises?			
Language (Diction & Sentence Clarity)	Is the language appropriate to the rhetorical situation?			
	Is the diction too formal, or too colloquial (like informal speech)?			
	Are complex terms or jargon defined clearly, and used appropriately?			
	Are the sentences clear, focused and in various sentence structures for readability?			
	Does the paper adhere to conventions of usage, mechanics, and format?			
MLA Standards	Does the essay adhere to MLA formatting for page headers, page numbers etc.?			
	Are all sources used and documented correctly and clearly?			
	Is there a complete works cited page (check to be sure all sources cited in the essay are listed on the works cited page?			

SUGGESTED READINGS, BLOGS, AND VIDEOS

(Entries with an (*) are included in this text)

Advertising, Images, and Propaganda

Rosen, Rebecca J. "Is This the Grossest Advertising Strategy of All Time?" *The Atlantic.* http://www.theatlantic.com/technology/archive/2013/10/is-this-the-grossest-advertising-strategy-of-all-time/280242/.

Piper, Tim. "Dove Evolution." https://www.youtube.com/watch?v=iYhCn0jf46U.

Piper, Tim. "Body Evolution." https://www.youtube.com/watch?v=xKQdwjGiF-s.

"What Are Some Examples of Propaganda?" http://www.wisegeek.org/what-are-some-examples-of-propaganda.htm.

Tomaselli, Fred. "Gyre." *Harper's Magazine.* http://harpers.org/blog/2014/05/gyre/.

Kayaoglu, Alex. Madonna, Extreme Makeover Photoshop. *YouTube.* https://www.youtube.com/watch?v=3FjkBr6IB7k.

Cialdini, Robert. "The Science of Persuasion." *YouTube.* https://www.youtube.com/watch?v=cFdCzN7RYbw.

Education

"Arts and Letters Daily."—A compendium of articles and essays on various topics. *The Chronicle of Higher Education.* http://www.aldaily.com/.

Rose, Mike. "I Just Wanna Be Average."

Gilbert, Daniel. "What You Don't Know Makes You Nervous." *The New York Times.* http://opinionator.blogs.nytimes.com/2009/05/20/what-you-dont-know-makes-you-nervous

Robinson, Sir Ken. "How to Escape Education's Death Valley." *TED.* http://www.ted.com/talks/ken_robinson_how_to_escape_education_s_death_valley.html.

Duckworth, Angela Lee. "The Key to Success? Grit." *TED.* http://www.ted.com/talks/angela_lee_duckworth_the_key_to_success_grit.html.

Ryan, Julia. "Are 'Tiger Moms' Better than Cool Moms?" *The Atlantic.* http://www.theatlantic.com/education/archive/2014/06/tiger-mom-vs-cool-mom/372070/.

Food, Water, and the Environment

Spurlock, Morgan (director). 2004. *Supersize Me*—documentary film.

Kenner, Robert (director). 2005. *Food Inc.*—documentary film.

Soechtig, Stephanie (director). 2014. *Fed Up*—documentary film.

*Metcalfe, John. "East Coast Cities at Risk in Future Tsunamis." *The Atlantic: Cities*. http://www.theatlanticcities.com/neighborhoods/2013/04/east-coast-cities-risk-future-tsunamis/5351/.

Pollan, Michael. "How Cooking Can Change Your Life." *RSA*. https://www.youtube.com/watch?v=TX7kwfE3cJQ.

Fox, Josh (director). *Gasland* (2010) and *Gasland 2* (2013)—two documentary films.

Maxwell-Gaines, Chris. "10 Must See Water Documentaries." *Blog*. http://www.watercache.com/blog/2011/10/must-see-water-documentaries-provide-insight-into-future-water-crisis/.

Spear, Stefanie. "Ten Best Documentaries of 2013." *Blog*. http://ecowatch.com/2013/12/29/best-documentaries-2013/.

Rosenthal, Elisabeth. "By 'Bagging It,' Ireland Rids Itself of a Plastic Nuisance." *The New York Times*. http://www.nytimes.com/2008/01/31/world/europe/31iht-bags.4.9650382.html?pagewanted=all&_r=0.

Weiss, Kenneth R. "Plague of Plastic Chokes the Seas." *Los Angeles Times*. http://www.latimes.com/news/la-me-ocean2aug02-story.html#page=1.

Narrative

Ali, Abul. "'This Is the Time for Poetry': A Conversation with Alice Walker." *The Atlantic*. http://www.theatlantic.com/entertainment/archive/2012/03/this-is-the-time-for-poetry-a-conversation-with-alice-walker/254744/.

Dillard, Annie. "Living Like Weasels."

Orwell, George. "Shooting an Elephant."

Staples, Brent. "Just Walk on By: Black Men and Public Space."

Tan, Amy. "Mother Tongue."

Lamott, Anne. "Blessed Are the Annoying." *Los Angeles Times*. http://articles.latimes.com/2006/may/07/magazine/tm-blessed19/4.

Talbot, Margaret. "About a Boy." *The New Yorker*. http://www.newyorker.com/reporting/2013/03/18/130318fa_fact_talbot.

Philosophy, Morality, and Government

Aristotle. "The Aim of Man." *Nicomachean Ethics: Book 1.* The Internet Classics Archive. http://classics.mit.edu/Aristotle/nicomachaen.1.i.html.

Jefferson, Thomas. "The Declaration of Independence."

King, Martin Luther, Jr. "Letter from Birmingham Jail."

King, Martin Luther, Jr. "I Have a Dream." *NPR.* http://www.npr.org/templates/story/story.php?storyId=122701268.

Machiavelli, Niccolo. "The Morals of the Prince."

*Thucydides. "The Funeral Oration of Pericles."

Science, Technology, and Media

Busch, Akiko. "The Surprising Benefits of Working Backward." *PBS.* http://www.nextavenue.org/blog/surprising-benefits-working-backward.

Feynman, Richard. "The Value of Science." http://www.phys.washington.edu/users/vladi/phys216/Feynman.html.

Glaser, April, and Reinish, Libby. "How to Block the NSA from Your Friends List." *Slate.* http://www.slate.com/blogs/future_tense/2013/06/17/identi_ca_diaspora_and_friendica_are_more_secure_alternatives_to_facebook.html.

Naughton, John. "The Internet: Is It Changing the Way We Think?" *The Guardian.* http://www.theguardian.com/technology/2010/aug/15/Internet-brain-neuroscience-debate.

McWhorter, John. "Txtng is killing language. JK!!!" *TED.* http://www.ted.com/talks/john_mcwhorter_txtng_is_killing_language_jk.html.

Palca, Joe. "Collaboration Beats Smarts in Group Problem Solving." *NPR.* http://www.npr.org/templates/story/story.php?storyId=130247631.

*Pinker, Steven. "Mind Over Mass Media." *New York Times.* http://www.nytimes.com/2010/06/11/opinion/11Pinker.html?_r=0.

Solove, Daniel J. "Why Privacy Matters Even if You Have 'Nothing to Hide.'" *The Chronicle of Higher Education: The Chronicle Review.* http://chronicle.com/article/Why-Privacy-Matters-Even-if/127461/.

*Ulin, David. "The Lost Art of Reading." *The Los Angeles Times.* http://www.latimes.com/entertainment/news/arts/la-ca-reading9-2009aug09,0,4905017.story.

Rugnetta, Mike. "Do You 'Choose' to Have Your Privacy Invaded by Tech?" *PBS Idea Channel: YouTube.* https://www.youtube.com/watch?v=t45BoJ_LP1U.

Gottlieb, Lori. "How Do I Love Thee?" *The Atlantic.* http://www.theatlantic.com/magazine/archive/2006/03/how-do-i-love-thee/304602/.

Turkle, Sherry. "Connected, but Alone?" *TED.* http://www.ted.com/talks/sherry_turkle_alone_together.

Social Commentary and Satire

Barry, Dave. "Road Warrior."

Brooks, David. "People Like Us." *The Atlantic.* http://www.theatlantic.com/magazine/archive/2003/09/people-like-us/302774/.

Ehrenreich, Barbara. "On (Not) Getting By in America". *Nickled and Dimed.* http://www.milkeninstitute.org/publications/review/2001_12/73-88mr.pdf.

Postrel, Virginia. "In Praise of Chain Stores". *The Atlantic.* http://www.theatlantic.com/magazine/archive/2006/12/in-praise-of-chain-stores/305400/.

*Stern, Ken. "Why the Rich Don't Give to Charity." *The Atlantic.* http://www.theatlantic.com/magazine/archive/2013/04/why-the-rich-dont-give/309254/.

Swift, Jonathan. "A Modest Proposal."

Orr, Deborah. "Richard Dawkins's Lack of Sympathy for Those Who Cling to Religion Is A Shame." *The Guardian.* http://www.theguardian.com/commentisfree/2014/jun/06/richard-dawkins-lack-of-sympathy-for-religion-shame.

Block, Laurie. "Stereotypes about People with Disabilities." *Disability History Museum.* http://www.disabilitymuseum.org/dhm/edu/essay.html?id=24.

Garber, Megan. "Saving the Lost Art of Conversation." *The Atlantic.* http://www.theatlantic.com/magazine/archive/2014/01/the-eavesdropper/355727/.

Morley, Christopher. 1920. "On Laziness." http://grammar.about.com/od/classicessays/a/onlazinessessay.htm.

Writing and Language

Iyer, Pico. "In Praise of the Humble Comma." *Time Magazine Online.* http://www.time.com/time/magazine/article/0,9171,149453,00.html.

"Words, Words, Words." Playlist of ten talks curated by *TED.* http://www.ted.com/playlists/117/words_words_words.html.

Shariatmadari, David. "8 Pronunciation Errors that Made the English Language what It Is Today." *The Guardian.* http://www.theguardian.com/commentisfree/2014/mar/11/pronunciation-errors-english-language.

"Grammar's Great Divide: The Oxford Comma" (video). *TEDEd*. http://ed.ted.com/lessons/grammar-s-great-divide-the-oxford-comma-ted-ed.

Chen, Keith. "Could Your Language Affect Your Ability to Save Money?" *TED*. http://www.ted.com/talks/keith_chen_could_your_language_affect_your_ability_to_save_money.

Gross, Jessica. "5 Examples of How the Languages We Speak can Affect the Way We Think." *TED Blog*. http://blog.ted.com/2013/02/19/5-examples-of-how-the-languages-we-speak-can-affect-the-way-we-think/.

Curzan, Anne. "What Makes a Word Real?" *TED*. http://www.ted.com/talks/anne_curzan_what_makes_a_word_real.

TRANSITIONS

Similarity/Comparison

also	analogous to
by the same token	equally
in a like manner	in like fashion
in the same way	just as
likewise	similarly

Contrast

(and) yet	although
at the same time	but
by way of contrast	contrast
conversely	despite
even so	however
if though	in contrast
in spite of	instead
irrespective	nevertheless
notwithstanding	on the contrary
on the other hand	rather
regardless	still
when in fact	whereas
while	while this may be true
yet	

Sequence/Time/Order

about	after
after a while	afterward
afterwards	again
all of a sudden	also
and then	as long as

as soon as

at the present time

at this instant

besides

during

eventually

first, second, third, finally

forthwith

further

hence

immediately

in due time

in the first place (second place)

in time

instantly

lastly

later

next

now that

once

previously

prior to

shortly

since

subsequently

the final point

till

to conclude

until

up to the present time

whenever

at first

at the same time

before

by the time

earlier

finally

formerly

from time to time

furthermore

henceforth

in a moment

in the end

in the meantime

initially

last

lately

meanwhile

now

occasionally

presently

prior

quickly

simultaneously

sooner or later

suddenly

then

to begin with

to start with

until now

when

Spatial

above	across
adjacent to	alongside
amid	among
around	before
behind	below
beneath	beside
between	beyond
down	forward
from	further
here	here and there
in front of	in the background
in the center of	in the distance
in the middle	near
nearby	next
on this side	opposite to
over	there
to the left/right	under
up	where
wherever	

Example(s)

an example	as
as an example	as an illustration
illustrated with	chiefly
especially	for example
for instance	for one thing
in detail	in fact
in general	in particular
including	like
namely	notably
particularly	specifically
such as	to clarify
to demonstrate	to emphasize
to enumerate	to explain
to illustrate	to repeat

Cause/Effect

accordingly	as / so long as
as a result	because of
consequently	due to the fact
for fear that	for the purpose of
for this reason	forthwith
granted (that)	hence
henceforth	if
in effect	in order to
in that case	in the event that
in the hope that	in view of
seeing / being that	since
so	then
therefore	thus
under the/those circumstances	unless
when	whenever
while	with this in mind
with this intention	

Introduction

as for	concerning
firstly	in the case of
initially	primarily
regarding	similarly
to begin (with)	with regard to

Emphasis

above all
essentially
frequently
most importantly
notably
significantly
surprisingly

especially
expressively
in fact
most significantly
particularly
specifically

Conclusion

as a final point
in conclusion
lastly
ultimately

finally
in the end
to conclude

Summary

accordingly
all things considered
briefly
finally
in any case
in brief
in short
in the final analysis
it follows
to sum up

after all
as a result
consequently
for this reason
in any event
in conclusion
in summary
in the long run
therefore
to summarize

SAMPLE RUBRICS

Sample Rubric for Evaluating a Reading Response (1–5 scale, 5 as highest)

	1	2	3	4	5
The reading response indicates a careful, close, and analytical reading of the assigned text. It is clear that the main point of the text has been understood.					
The reading response articulates how the text connects (or fails to connect) to the student.					
The reading response articulates how the text is important (or not) to the world in which we live.					
The reading response includes direct references and/or quotes from the assigned reading.					
The reading response offers alternative perspectives on the subject/topic of the assigned text.					
The reading response clearly indicates original thoughts and ideas responding to the text.					
The reading response is free of grammatical and mechanical errors.					
The reading response is adequate in length and feels "complete."					

Additional Suggestions or Remarks (check all that apply):

- ☐ Excessive summary of the assigned reading—focus more on analysis.
- ☐ Paragraphs need improvement. Each paragraph must present a single idea.
- ☐ Ideas are generalized. Be specific about each idea—provide examples and details.
- ☐ Analysis needs improvement—clarify the significance of ideas presented in the response.
- ☐ Excessive grammatical and mechanical errors. Difficult to read.
- ☐ Connections or examples need clarification—be precise and specific, not vague nor general.
- ☐ Avoid sarcasm/humor that detracts from analysis/response.
- ☐ Avoid bias and stereotypes.

Sample Rubric for Summary Writing (1–5 scale, 5 as highest)

This Summary:	1	2	3	4	5
Briefly outlines main ideas or key concepts.					
Avoids interpretation, evaluation, analysis, or criticism of the text.					
Limits use of direct quotes.					
Is carefully proofread.					

Sample Rubric for Evaluating an Analysis Essay (1–5 scale, 5 as highest)

	1	2	3	4	5
Begins with an engaging introduction.					
Thesis is specific and clearly articulates main argument/idea.					
The purpose/focus of the analysis is clearly presented.					
Each paragraph contains a distinct analytical point in a clear topic sentence that connects with the thesis.					
Each topic sentence is supported with logical evidence/explanation. Analysis provides necessary researched information and supporting evidence.					
Essay is logically organized; organization helps the reader to understand the thesis of the essay.					
Voice and tone is appropriate for the subject matter and audience.					
Ends with a conclusion that does not merely repeat the thesis statement. Conclusion allows the reader to understand what has been "discovered" at the conclusion of the analysis.					
Essay is indicative of a high level of effort with careful overall attention to the use of ethos, pathos, and logos.					
Research is properly integrated into essay and correctly cited.					
The essay has been carefully revised, edited and proofread.					

Sample Holistic/Non-Scaled Rubric for Academic Essay (check one that applies for each topic)

1. THE THESIS STATEMENT

- ☐ Thesis statement is clear and well articulated.
- ☐ Thesis statement is general—it is not 100% clear what the essay will establish.
- ☐ Thesis statement is weak. It is unclear what the main focus of the essay will be.

2. PARAGRAPH DEVELOPMENT

- ☐ Paragraph begins with a strong topic sentence. Discussion in the paragraph focuses on topic sentence.
- ☐ The purpose of the paragraph is understood, however some ideas need better connection to topic sentence. Review each sentence and ask, "How does this sentence contain information or explanation that is relevant to the main point of the paragraph and essay?"
- ☐ To strengthen the paragraph review topic sentences, concluding sentences, and transitions.

3.. ORGANIZATION AND STRUCTURE

- ☐ Well organized. The thesis is clearly stated and the paragraphs are arranged in such a way that the support is well connected, well articulated, and well presented. Transitions between sentences, paragraphs, and ideas are smooth.
- ☐ Organized, but there are areas that need to be reconsidered. What is the best order for the information? How can the essay be better organized and structured so as to better serve your purpose and not confuse the reader?
- ☐ Organization and structure is confusing or unhelpful. Carefully reorganize the content, thinking about ways to connect ideas logically so your readers can follow your main point(s).

4 EVIDENCE

- ☐ Evidence is well applied and well explained. It is understood how the evidence supports or is connected to the thesis statement or main point.
- ☐ Evidence is present, but needs further explanation and connection to the main point.
- ☐ Evidence is invalid or does not support the main point. Reconsider the evidence, or better explain the connection and purpose of this evidence.

Sample Holistic/Non-Scaled Rubric for Academic Essay (continued)

5. INTEGRATION OF RESEARCH

- ☐ Research is well selected, well placed, and clearly justified. All research is properly cited.
- ☐ Research is present, but requires better explanation or integration into the paper. Or needs citation correction.
- ☐ Research is absent or inadequate to support ideas. Citations may also be missing or inadequate.

6. CONSIDERING THE AUDIENCE/READER

- ☐ Writer is clearly aware of the needs and expectations of his/her reader.
- ☐ Needs more consideration of the needs of the reader. Ask: "What will the reader want here?"
- ☐ Be careful—areas are generalized or contain stereotypes (or questions) that may offend a reader.

7. RHETORICAL APPEALS

- ☐ The use of ethos, pathos and logos are evident and applied successfully.
- ☐ The use of ethos, pathos and logos are evident, but not always fully developed.
- ☐ Ethos, pathos, logos are not well applied, used incorrectly, or absent.

8. VOICE

- ☐ The voice engages the reader, is unique and appropriate to the topic and thesis presented.
- ☐ The voice does not consistently engage the reader. Consider using figurative language, and adjust sentence length, vocabulary, and tone.
- ☐ Voice is monotone and non-expressive.

9. OVERALL IMPACT

- ☐ The essay is well composed, enlightening, and well worth the time reading.
- ☐ Essay has some high points—consider working on the topic further. Explore all the possibilities of the topic presented.
- ☐ Essay needs further development.

Sample Rubric for Evaluating a Visual/Object Analysis Essay or Presentation

	1	2	3	4	5
A Grand-Slam. Gold Medal Winning Title! Yes, even presentations need a title!					
Begins with an engaging introduction that engages the reader/audience.					
Thesis is specific and clearly articulated. The main interpretation of the image/object is clearly presented to the audience.					
The image/object is broken down into "parts" and each "part" of the object or image is carefully examined and connected to the thesis statement. Each analytical point is clearly supported with logical evidence/explanation.					
Essay or presentation is logically organized and easy for reader/audience to follow.					
Voice and tone is appropriate for the object/subject matter. Humor may be appropriate, but is contained within the purpose of the essay and/or presentation.					
Ends with a strong conclusion that does not repeat the thesis statement. The conclusion allows the reader to understand what has been "discovered" at the conclusion of the analysis. The audience understands how to "use" the information provided in the interpretation of the image/object.					
The overall message is thoughtful and satisfying.					
Essay/presentation is indicative of a high level of effort.					
Research is properly cited (works cited or bibliography page).					
The essay/presentation has been carefully edited (checked for spelling, grammar, mechanics).					

Sample Rubric for Evaluating an Argument/Persuasive Essay

	1	2	3	4	5
The introduction is engaging and clearly states the argument/thesis and purpose of the paper. The argument is well defined. Your position is clearly stated.					
Each paragraph clearly supports the thesis/purpose of the essay. Each paragraph makes a claim that is well supported (with evidence, valid research and/or relevant examples) or provides information necessary to support the position. Research is smoothly integrated into the paragraphs.					
Paragraphs clearly engage in the use of ethos, pathos, or logos as a writing strategy. Ethos, pathos, and logos are used effectively in the argument.					
Arguments are sound, avoid bias and stereotypes, or are otherwise free of logical fallacies.					
Diction, tone, and voice are appropriate to the subject matter and engage the reader. Sentence variety is effective.					
Language: Grammar, mechanics, and usage are error free.					
Conclusion connects the thesis/purpose and goes beyond a summary of the essay.					

BASIC LIST OF RHETORICAL DEVICES
FOR COMPOSITION

Alliteration

A series of words that contain (or begins) with the same consonant sound.

> Tom tells tall tales.

> Consumers seek dependable, durable, and discounted products.

Allusion

An allusion is when a writer references a person, event, or story (literature) that is culturally familiar to most readers. Using an allusion can help a writer quickly make a point or illustration to a reader.

> The earthquake was a Titanic tragedy.

> Five score years ago, a great American, in whose symbolic shadow we stand today, signed the Emancipation Proclamation.
>
> > —Dr. Martin Luther King, Jr.

Amplification

When a writer uses amplification they attempt to draw attention to an important point in a sentence or a paragraph. Amplification is used to emphasize an idea by adding words or phrases to make the idea more intense.

> The activists worked tirelessly, without complaint or clamor, and with complete dedication to the cause of justice.*

*also notice the alliteration here in the repetition of the "c" or "k" sounds

> Hatred, uncontrolled hatred, is often the cause of unwarranted and tragic violence.

Analogy

An analogy highlights significant similarities between two things, concepts, or ideas.

> As cold water is to a thirsty soul, so is good news from a far country.
>
> > —King James Bible Verse 25:25

> In order to succeed, we must often struggle against what appears to be insurmountable obstacles. Like the carp that must swim upstream, against the flow of a giant river, to reach perfection and become a winged dragon, we must also find the strength to endure, persist, and triumph.

Anecdote

An anecdote is a brief story that allows writers to use narrative as a way of illustrating or emphasizing a point.

Antithesis

Contrasting ideas set against one another in usually one sentence to create a relationship between the two ideas.

> That's one small step for a man, but a giant step for mankind.
>
> —Neil Armstrong

> When the white man turns tyrant, it is his own freedom that he destroys.
>
> —"Shooting an Elephant," George Orwell

Aphorism

A brief statement that can be poetic or engage in parallel structure, and usually engages in a sentimental or melodramatic tone.

> That which does not destroy us, makes us stronger.
>
> —Friedrich Nietzsche

Epithet

This rhetorical device seeks to create an image or an emotion by adjective or adjective phrase modifying a noun by reiterating a key concept of the noun:

> Mirthful happiness; breaking dawn; life-giving water; winding road; ragged peace

Hyperbole

Hyperbole is an overstatement, or an exaggeration of a fact or idea.

> There are millions of reasons why Americans should vote in the next election.

> I am starving! Where can I get a ton of food?

Hypophora

To ask one or more question and then respond to those questions

> What does it mean to be human? Being human involves the ability to empathize, sympathize, and understand the suffering of others.

Parallelism

A sentence with repeating clauses or phrases, or, a series of sentences with repeating structure in order to emphasize similarities in the ideas, or to shows ideas as are equally important.

For the end of a theoretical science is truth, but the end of a practical science is performance.

—Aristotle

My fellow citizens: I stand here today humbled by the task before us, grateful for the trust you have bestowed, mindful of the sacrifices borne by our ancestors . . .

—President Barack Obama

Oxymoron

An oxymoron is a much like a paradox reduced to two words that appear at first to be nonsensical, yet also make sense in the context used:

> The President **clearly misunderstood** the Vice President's request for a **working vacation**.

Personification

A form of figurative language that gives human characteristics to inanimate objects or animals.

> The king of the lions roamed his territory, protecting the boundaries from invaders.

> The storm breathed its last breath at dawn, having exacted proper revenge on the townspeople.

Procatalepsis

This rhetorical strategy works much like a response to a possible counterargument, or a prebuttal, rather than a rebuttal. A writer predicts or anticipates an objection to an argumentative statement or claim and answers the objection.

> Young writers are accustomed to composing academic papers using the high speed capabilities of computer technologies, and while this may not always produce thoughtful, carefully explored thinking that the slow and methodical writing with pen and paper encourages, it does allow greater access to information, and with that information, greater ideas can emerge.

Rhetorical Question

A rhetorical question (not be be confused with the rhetorical situation or rhetoric) is a question with an obvious and premeditated, or expected response. Rhetorical questions are designed to increase reader interest, or to provoke the reader to think critically about an idea or an issue.

> Should school administrators ignore the increasingly high number of high school drop-outs?

Understatement

To purposely lessen the importance of an idea for emphasis. A statement that is subtly made for ironic purposes, or for the sake of modesty.

> I have to have this operation. It isn't very serious. I have this tiny little tumor on the brain.
>
> —Holden Caulfield, *The Catcher in the Rye*, J. D. Salinger

> "It snowed just a little bit last night." (after a winter blizzard left feet of snow on the ground)

GLOSSARY OF TERMS

A

Academic Research (*Chapter 8*)

Academic (scholarly) research is collecting information, data, tests, interviews, and surveys created and/or produced by experts in specific fields.

Ad Hominem Fallacy (*Chapter 11*)

The name-calling fallacy (ad hominem) engages in personal attacks, rather than attacks on the argument presented.

Allusion (*Chapter 6*)

An allusion is an indirect reference to a literary or historical event, person, or place.

> *His powers could only be defeated by Zeus.*

Analogy (*Chapter 9*)

Comparing a new idea in terms of another different, but more familiar idea; to compare aspects of one idea, in terms of another to promote understanding of the new idea.

> *His voice grated upon the listeners like fingernails dragged across a chalkboard.*

Analysis (*Chapter 9*)

To divide, or break up the subject into its parts for interpretation or explanation.

Anecdote (*Chapter 9*)

A brief story or narrative used as illustration of an idea or event.

Argument (*Chapter 8*)

To take a position on a controversial issue and attempt to persuade others of its validity.

Article (*Chapter 9*)

A piece of writing about a particular subject or topic, often found in journals, newspapers, and magazines.

Assumption (*Chapter 4*)

A an unquestioned belief. An unproven idea held as true to support an argument.

Aural Image (*Chapter 10*)

We use this term when we need to differentiate from other image types. Imagery, as literary term, refers to any words, pictures or ideas that appeal to our senses, creating a mental image of that appeal: sight (visual image), hearing (aural image), touch (tactile image), smell (olfactory image), taste (gustatory image).

B

Bandwagon Fallacy (*Chapter 11*)

Bandwagon appeals are emotional appeals to your sense of belonging. Everyone else does it, so why shouldn't I? *Or, no one does anything so why should I? Here your loyalty to the group is at play, rather than the morality of the action/inaction itself.*

Begging the Question (*Chapter 11*)

This kind of faulty reasoning runs in circles because it asks you to see the argument as also the fact that supports it. In its most obvious forms, we can see it here:

I lost my keys because they were hard to find.
Loud parties are annoying because they make so much noise.
Speeding is dangerous because vehicles are going too fast.

Bias (*Chapter 8*)

Bias occurs when an expert or a source in a specific subject area may be motivated to report or make discoveries that support a personal goal or aim, or a specific position or belief.

C

Call To Action (*Chapter 1*)

When you write to call to action, you are persuading people to both think differently and behave differently.

Cause and Effect (*Chapter 9*)

To determine how one event causes a secondary event. Or to understand, or claim that a particular event was caused by a prior event.

Circular Logic (*Chapter 11*)

See Begging the Question.

Classification (*Chapter 9*)

To sort information or ideas into groups to facilitate understanding and analysis.

Compare/Contrast (*Chapter 9*)

To highlight similarities and/or differences.

Complex Sentence (*Chapter 6*)

A complex sentence has an independent clause joined by one or more dependent clauses.

For example: John and Sarah went to the party after they finished writing their essays.

Compound Complex Sentence (*Chapter 6*)

A sentence with two (or more) independent clauses and one or more dependent clauses.

> *Today, we must study hard and engage in active learning so that tomorrow we will be prepared to solve the problems and conflicts that may arise in our complex world.*

Compound Sentence (*Chapter 6*)

A compound sentence contains two independent clauses joined by a coordinator.

> *Mom was watching football so Dad went to the grocery store.*

Concession (*Chapter 12*)

While debate appears to be about arguing (or persuading), it is also important to understand that no position is 100 percent fail-proof. It is important to concede, or to acknowledge the merits of an opposing perspective.

Connotative Meaning (*Chapter 6*)

Connotative meaning is the attitude or feelings we associate with the meaning.

Counterargument (*Chapter 12*)

Counterargument works to argue against a main claim. It is an argument posed in opposition to another argument. They are supported logically and with coherent explanation and details. Opposing a perspective is much like making a claim—both must be clearly and fully thought out.

Criteria (*Chapter 4*)

Rules or parameters for evaluating, judging, or determining the quality of something, or to identify or define it.

Critical Thinking (*Chapter 2*)

Critical thinking is focused control over the paths our thoughts take, the information that will be included, and how that information will or should relate. In other words, it is attentive, focused and goal oriented. It is purposeful inquiry, analysis and evaluation.

Criticism (*Chapter 4*)

To critique, or to engage in (or receive) criticism is to evaluate a text using specific criteria, and critical thought.

Critique (*Chapter 4*)

See **Criticism**.

D

Deductive Reasoning (*Chapter 11*)

Deductive reasoning is reasoning that takes a general principle, and reasons the details from it. That general principle is often a conclusion drawn from earlier reasoning.

Definition (*Chapter 9*)

To draw a line or boundary around the meaning you want your readers to understand; to pronounce the scope of your meaning.

Denotative Meaning (*Chapter 6*)

Denotative meaning is the literal and practical meaning of a word, often found in the dictionary definition.

Description (*Chapter 9*)

A written or oral representation of an object, person, place or idea. In composition, it is used to help audiences "see" the idea, etc., that you are working with.

Dialogue (*Chapter 4*)

Is an activity in which you engage with others about ideas, to discuss ideas in order to refine and improve their quality.

Diction (*Chapter 6*)

Diction is word choice. Your audience and genre will help you make this choice, but even within those helpful guides you have a wide range of language choice at your disposal.

E

Editing (*Chapter 6*)

When we edit, we look specifically at the language that expresses our ideas in order to simplify and clarify the sentences in terms of diction, style and syntax.

Educate (*Chapter 1*)

When you write to educate, you are combining knowledge (writing to inform) with a set of critical criteria used to help process that information in a particular context.

Either-Or Fallacy (*Chapter 11*)

An either-or logical fallacy sets up a false argument that limits choice to only two options, when other options are likely available.

You are either with us or against us.

Entertain (*Chapter 1*)

When you write to entertain, you write with the expectations of the audience foremost in your mind, as what entertains each audience may differ.

Enthymeme (*Chapter 11*)

The enthymeme will be more familiar to you if think of it as a thesis, or a thesis statement, or the main idea in an argument, without its premises revealed. We call what is absent the underlying assumption *because it is a hidden, or underlying, idea on which the argument rests.*

Ethos (*Chapter 1*)

One of the elements of rhetoric, ethos refers to the writer's ability to demonstrate the qualities of credibility, transparency, and trustworthiness.

Evaluation (*Chapter 3, 9*)

To evaluate is to critique for value using a set of specific criteria; to determine the value. When evaluate a text, we compare the text, or some aspect of the text to the values we already hold either about structure, content or topic.

xplanation (*Chapter 9*)

To explain is to clarify an idea, process, action or object; to expose the details of something.

xpository (*Chapter 9*)

The expository essay (or expository writing) is a genre that seeks to explain and inform a reader about a particular topic.

G

Generalizations (*Chapter 4*)

Generalizations are formed by taking specific examples, or experiences, and applying that to a general class. These are common ways of organizing information, but are often vulnerable to logical fallacy (see **Hasty Generalization***).*

Genre (*Chapter 1*)

Genre is the category or type of writing you might choose in response to your rhetorical situation.

Grounds (*Chapter 13)*

See **Premise***.*

H

Hasty Generalization (*Chapter 11*)

A hasty generalization is a fallacy that concludes an outcome, or creates or assigns a category based on insufficient evidence. One type of hasty or faulty generalization comes in the form of stereotype.

Hypothetical Scenario (*Chapter 9*)

An invented situation to assist in modeling or explaining an idea.

I

Imaginative Thinking (*Chapter 2*)

Imaginative thinking is a kind of investigation of potential, a "poke your head up" kind of thinking that allows you to think out your ideas without placing limits or boundaries, and without rules.

Inductive Reasoning (*Chapter 11*)

Inductive reasoning moves from the specific details to a broader inference, *and when the connections themselves can be tested and repeated, as in the scientific method,* conclusions *can be drawn.*

Inference (*Chapter 3*)

Inference is a conclusion we make about what is not known by examining what is known, or what is factual.

Inform (*Chapter 1*)

When you write to inform, you are providing the audience with only the information *about a topic.*

Interview (*Chapter 8*)

Interviews are strategically designed questions about a specific topic and for a specific person, or a group of people, with common traits or experiences.

L

Literary Critiques (*Chapter 9*)

Literary critiques evaluate the importance of a piece of literature through theoretical perspectives, or by examining structure and form as a literary concern.

Literary Texts (*Chapter 9*)

Literary texts are a particular genre of writing, and generally are defined as fiction, creative writing, drama, poetry, and certain types of non-fiction that employ literary elements.

Logical Fallacy (*Chapter 11*)

Generally defined, logical fallacies are breaks in logical thinking, misrepresentations of facts, or sometimes a combination of these errors. These errors can and often do exist whether or not the conclusion proves true.

Logos (*Chapter 1*)

Logos comes from the Greek word for logic. Appeals to logos are appeals to the intellect.

M

Metacognate (*Chapter 2*)

To think about HOW we think; to think about the processes we use to think, and which information we choose, and why; to think about the purpose of a thought, or evaluate the quality of a thought.

N

Narrative (*Chapter 9*)

The narrative genre allows writers to use the conventions of storytelling to deliver a main idea.

Non Sequitur Fallacy (*Chapter 11*)

A non sequitur is an error in the logical connection of two events or ideas. It means "it does not follow."

O

Observation (*Chapter 9*)

An observation (or to observe) is to witness or share experiences from a first-person point of view.

P

Parameters (*Chapter 12*)

Parameters are measurable conditions that clearly define what is considered the boundary, or the limits on how we "look" at a text, or an object, or idea. In a formal debate, parameters exist to keep the participants on topic, and focused on the question raised.

Paraphrasing (*Chapter 13*)

To paraphrase is to take another's ideas or words, and restate them (while still citing the author) in concise language to support your thesis.

Pathos (*Chapter 1*)

Pathos refers to language or ideas that appeal to emotion.

Persuade (*Chapter 1*)

To cause action or to change an opinion, usually through reasoning of ideas and evidence.

Philosophy (*Chapter 11*)

An academic field which examines knowledge, and the different modes of logic, and moral reasoning.

Post Hoc Ergo Propter Hoc Fallacies (*Chapter 11*)

Post hoc fallacies assume a cause-and-effect relationship in reverse or false order. It claims that because of B, A must occur. When in fact, it is simply a coincidence, or unrelated entirely.

Premise *(Chapter 11)*

A premise is an idea that informs, or proves a conclusion. It is the basis for a conclusion, or the reasons for a conclusion.

Process or Procedure Writing(*Chapter 9*)

Writing that explains how something occurs, it documents the steps that lead to a goal, product, solution, etc.

Proofread (*Chapter 6*)

To look at a text to be sure that words, grammar, and mechanics are used correctly. We also proofread for formatting consistency, such as margins, font size, and other types of formatting according to genre and audience expectations.

R

Rationalization Fallacy (*Chapter 11*)

Rationalization occurs when a writer creates an excuse for action (or inaction).

> *I didn't get into that school, but I didn't want to go anyway.*

Rebuttal *(Chapter 12)*

A rebuttal is a denial, contradiction, or invalidation of the counterargument. It refutes the claim made in the counterargument.

Redundancy (*Chapter 6*)

Redundancy occurs when you repeat the ideas using different words to say essentially the same thing. Or it occurs when you use different words to say the same thing.

> *This **new and novel** design is appealing.*

Research Paper (*Chapter 9*)

The research paper is a paper that asks students to investigate and analyze, and often claim a position on a particular subject area, using appeals to logic and presenting data and facts and in a logical manner.

Research Strategy (*Chapter 9*)

An investigation of your topic and purpose to plan what to research and how to develop your ideas in the most effective way possible.

Rhetoric (*Chapter 1*)

Rhetoric is the language we use to effectively please our audience, or persuade them—and it is also the study of the techniques and rules for using language effectively to persuade.

Rhetorical Situation (*Chapter 1*)

Is the situation for which you write. Specifically, it includes your purpose for writing, your topic, your audience's assumptions and expectations, and your own assumptions and expectations.

S

Scope (*Chapter 12*)

Scope is setting the rhetorical situation, or the purpose of the debate. Remember, arguments and debates rarely move toward a goal of complete victory. They work toward reasonable understanding among differing perspectives in order to find workable solutions to complex problems.

Slippery Slope Fallacy (*Chapter 11*)

A slippery-slope fallacy claims that one action will cause something else, and usually worse, to happen.

> *If you give an inch, they will take a mile.*

Social Technologies (*Chapter 9*)

Social technologies like Twitter, Facebook, and Instagram (to name a few) are primarily used to communicate with a select group of individuals. However, social technology spaces can be very public too. These spaces are usually informal spaces where people share a wide variety of information.

Straw Man Fallacy (*Chapter 11*)

A straw man fallacy ignores the opposition's actual position, then claims they hold a position that they don't actually hold, and then attacks that position. Essentially, when this fallacy is used, it misrepresents an opponent's argument to make it easier to attack.

Summary (*Chapter 3*)

Summary is a condensed statement of the main ideas presented by a writer.

Surveys (*Chapter 8*)

Surveys evoke responses to questions in order to collect data.

Syllogism (*Chapter 11*)

*Syllogisms are formal logical structures that take two premises to conclude a third idea. The general principle is called the **M**ajor **P**remise (MP), and the specific example is called the **m**inor **p**remise (mp), and the conclusion is **C**. The formal structure of syllogism allows you to think through a claim and test it for soundness and reasonableness.*

MP:	All people are mortal.
mp:	Alex is a person.
C:	Alex is mortal.

Synthesis (*Chapter 3*)

Synthesis is the combining of ideas to form new ideas, usually through a thorough analysis of each text/idea(s) separately, finding similarity or dissimilarity, and examining the underlying assumptions that each idea relies on. Then, when you, the writer, apply synthesis, you combine that information/data to form a new, related idea.

T

Thesis (*Chapter 4*)

A thesis is the main critical idea, and the thesis statement is that idea expressed in language to serve a purpose, usually to persuade or analyze, but can also be used to inform, or educate.

Tone (*Chapter 6*)

Tone refers to the words that convey an attitude, or feelings about an idea; is the mood or attitude you present in your writing or speech with words that rely on connotation.

Visual Rhetoric (*Chapter 10*)

Images and objects that use appeals to the rhetorical elements of ethos, pathos, and logos.

V

Voice (*Chapter 6*)

Writers create a voice that is all their own, and this sometimes occurs naturally and often without thinking. But, most writers develop their style by crafting together their own authentic sense of language with the expectations of an audience, or the conventions of genre. They can adopt different "voices" in writing to satisfy those expectations.